The Edge of Time

The Edge of Time

**Peter & Patti
Lalonde**

HARVEST HOUSE PUBLISHERS
Eugene, Oregon 97402

All Scripture quotations in this book are taken from the King James Version of the Bible.

Cover design by Koechel Peterson & Associates, Minneapolis, Minnesota

THE EDGE OF TIME

Copyright ©1997 by Ontario #1006094 and Ontario #1006095

Published by Harvest House Publishers
Eugene, Oregon 97402

Library of Congress Cataloging-in-Publication Data

Lalonde, Peter.
    The edge of time / Peter and Patti Lalonde.
        p. cm.
    Includes biographical references.
    ISBN 1-56507-537-4
        1. Biblical—prophecies.   I. Lalonde, Patti, 1959– .   II. Title
BS647.2.L345 1997
220.1'5—dc20   96-41547
                                                                                                          CIP

97   98   99   00   01   02   / BF /   10   9   8   7   6   5   4   3   2   1

Contents

Introduction

We are standing at the edge of a dramatic moment in history, watching life-changing events take place in the world around us every day. Indeed, the scenes on the world stage are changing with each passing moment. The new backdrops that have appeared in the Middle East, Europe, and the area that once made up the Soviet Union make this unfolding drama fact, not fiction. Some say the plot that is unfolding is leading us into a new world order and a new age of peace and prosperity. Others claim the changes are leading us toward a precipice in history, the edge of time. Yet others say it's all just hype leading up to the new millennium. Nonetheless, it is commonly agreed that we are living in a truly exciting time.

What is even more exciting is the fact that these dramatic changes we see taking place were foretold thousands of years ago in the Bible! Indeed, students of Bible prophecy are standing in awe of current events. Skeptics are giving them a second look. Even the casual observer is starting to shake his head in wonder at them. Whether viewed by a Bible believer or a skeptic, the evidence is clear: Something unique is occurring in history.

We are living in a time filled with great expectancy and anticipation. The question is, "What are we living in anticipation of?" For some it is the anticipation of an age of peace and prosperity. For Bible-believing Christians, however, it is the anticipation of watching, from front-row seats, a drama unfold that will culminate in the return of Jesus Christ to this planet to establish His millennial kingdom on earth.

Unfortunately, by believing that Bible prophecy is nothing more than a confusing mix of figurative heads, horns, and beasts, many Christians have been missing out on some of the most fascinating, faith-building parts of the Bible. By knowing very little about the characters and events in the prophetic play today, they have failed to comprehensively piece the acts and scenes together, putting the whole drama into clearer focus. As a result, these same Christians have no idea how unbelievably accurate the Bible is in describing the very days in which we are living.

On the other hand, Christians who do comprehensively study Bible prophecy are seeing with clarity some of the most exciting world events in history unfold in its fulfillment. In response to the unfolding drama, they have been compelled to live holy lives and win souls for the kingdom of God in anticipation of the soon return of their Savior.

By reading this book, we hope that you too will come to see how accurate the prophecies in the Bible are. We pray that you will walk away with an understanding of what lies ahead, of who the major actors in this final drama in history are, and of what to watch for as events build to the climax that only God Himself could have foreseen. But most of all, we hope that in coming to an understanding of Bible prophecy, you will walk away with an even greater faith in your Lord and Savior.

A Way That Seems Right

Why Study Bible Prophecy?

*B*ible prophecy is extremely fascinating. We should study it and seek to come to an understanding of God's plan for the ages. Some people have neglected prophecy, claiming it is too "negative." Some have even argued, "If it's all going to happen anyway, and there's nothing we can do to stop it, why worry about it?" A Canadian alliance of twenty-six evangelical denominations even went so far as to declare that the expectant waiting for the imminent return of Jesus Christ is actually a "bogus theology" which is "paralyzing" the efforts of *Christians who want to reform this world*.[1] Others have argued that we should go on with life as usual, and if the Lord comes, He comes. If He doesn't, He doesn't. And if He doesn't, well then, we didn't waste a whole lot of time "foolishly gazing into the heavens."[2]

But to gaze into the heavens is exactly what Jesus told us to do. If Jesus did not want us to watch for His coming, He would not have taken so much time to clearly describe the signs that would precede His coming. Nor would He have promised a special blessing to those who make the effort to read and understand the prophecies of the Bible.[3]

Furthermore, when the disciples asked Jesus, "What shall be the sign of thy coming, and of the end of the world?" He did not tell them it would be a waste of valuable time to be watching for these things. Instead, from both the detailed answer He gave and the tremendous amount of space given to these signs in the Scriptures, it would seem that Jesus thought it was important for believers to keep a close watch on these signs.

Why does the Lord want us to study prophecy? Well, imagine it is a lazy summer day. A Christian man is floating in his boat along a peaceful river. He is relaxed, enjoying the warm sunshine. Then he hears the Lord say to him, "My son, I need to warn you that there are troubles waiting for you up river. When you come around a bend in this river, you are going to notice there are some treacherous rocks sticking out of the water. It is going to get turbulent, and waves are going to crash over the bow of your boat. I want you to look around because there are going to be some very specific markers along the shoreline that are going to help you determine where you are on this river. Your boat will begin to take on water and slowly start to sink. Then you will notice a waterfall up ahead; a waterfall more frightening than Niagara Falls. And your boat is going to reach the very brink of the fall."

This is when our friend in the boat interrupts, and with a trembling voice asks the Lord why He is telling him all this "negative" stuff. But the Lord encourages him by saying, "I want you to know that before your boat goes over that waterfall, you are to look up, because I am going to reach down from heaven at that moment, and in the twinkling of an eye I am going to pull you up out of that boat, so that where I am, you may be also! I want you to remember, my son, your hope is not in that boat. It is in *Me*!"

A More Sure Word

The Bible is a message to mankind that promises hope for those who place their faith and trust in God's Son, Jesus Christ. The prophetic portions of the Scriptures are to console us, to instruct us, and to build our faith in God as we face present and future turmoil. Indeed, many of the signs of the times are truly troubling. But by telling us in advance what is going to take place in the world around us, God is giving us the assurance that He is in control. No turn of events will take Him by surprise. Likewise, it need not take us by surprise either. Everything that takes place in the world is already known by God. He allows events to happen to fulfill His own purpose. While the events may be troubling to our fleshly man, our spiritual man should see them as signs of the Lord's imminent return, first to catch away all who trust in Him, and later to save Israel and reign from Jerusalem for one thousand years.

Now that we know Bible prophecy should encourage us to believe that God is in control of the situation, what should our response be? First, if our trust is in our Savior Jesus Christ, we have no cause to be filled with fear. Surely this is the most beautiful message we can receive from the prophetic Word. While the rest of the world is trembling with fear at "those things which are coming on the earth,"[4] we as believers can rest in great hope and assurance. This is why Jesus told us that in the last days we would "hear of wars and rumours of wars: see that ye be not troubled, for all these things must come to pass."[5]

Second, Bible prophecy serves as a reminder to the believer that true hope cannot be found in this world. Like the man in the boat, we know that we are not to focus on the seaworthiness of our vessel. God has already told us it is headed for destruction. Bible prophecy should wake

us up, shake us up, and cause us to examine whether we
are living our lives in holiness and righteousness. As the
Apostle Peter put it:

> The day of the Lord will come as a thief in the
> night; in which the heavens shall pass away with
> a great noise, and the elements shall melt with fer-
> vent heat, the earth also and the works that are
> therein shall be burned up. Seeing then that all
> these things shall be dissolved, what manner of
> persons ought ye to be in all holy conversation
> and godliness, looking for and hasting unto the
> coming of the day of God, wherein the heavens
> being on fire shall be dissolved and the elements
> shall melt with fervent heat? Nevertheless we, ac-
> cording to his promise, look for new heavens and
> a new earth, wherein dwelleth righteousness.[6]

The point behind Peter's words is very clear. If we accept the truth of the prophetic Word of God, then our focus
should not be on the problems of, or the good times in,
this world. Our focus should instead be on the coming of
the Lord. Our concerns, if we take the prophetic Word seriously, should be shifted from the cares of daily living to
concern for the spiritually lost and dying.

Contrary to what some evangelicals have claimed, directly related to this call to take our eyes off the world is
the call to set our eyes on the skies. Luke 21:28 states very
plainly what we are to do when we see Bible prophecy
being fulfilled: "When these things begin to come to pass,
then look up and lift up your heads; for your redemption
draweth nigh."

The predominant message for the believer is not the
bad news, but the *good news it foreshadows*. And the good
news is the imminent return of our Lord and Savior Jesus
Christ.

I Didn't Hear That!

Let's embellish our boat-on-the-river story a bit more. Imagine for a moment that this boat of life we're floating in has another passenger. This passenger, however, is not a believer in Jesus Christ. So, even though he's in the same boat as the Christian, he didn't listen to God's warning. When this boat hits turbulent waters, with the waterfall in plain view up ahead, this other passenger doesn't believe there is a promise of hope before the boat goes over the brink because he rejected God's promise. Of his own free will, he chose to ignore the markers along the shoreline as signs of a soon-coming rescue by Jesus Christ.

Now, these two passengers in the boat are seeing the same events, but their reactions to the events will be different. The Christian sees the markers, or signs, that God has told him to watch out for and reacts with peaceful and joyous anticipation of salvation. The unbeliever, on the other hand, while having no assurance of his future and no hope of a rescue, places his faith in his own efforts to preserve his life. If we understand this critical point, we can move toward a fuller understanding of the times we are living in.

The Great Fear

Today, many in the world fear that we may be facing some sort of climactic ending to life on this planet unless some changes are made quickly. Again, the world is right in believing that something dramatic and tragic is going to occur, but there is no understanding of what the response to it should be.

Take the fear of war as an example. For decades the world lived in fear of a war of apocalyptic proportions between the Communist Soviet Union and the Capitalist United States. Then in 1989 the Berlin Wall came down, symbolizing the end of the Cold War. People breathed a sigh of relief. The Cold War was finally over and we could begin constructing an age of peace and prosperity.

The relief was short-lived, however. Just a couple of short years later, the "sword of Damocles" hung over us once again as word came that Iraq had invaded Kuwait. Saddam Hussein's brazen defiance ignited an international retaliation against the nation that is descended from the ancient Babylonian Empire; a nation that is one day destined for complete destruction according to Bible prophecy. The message behind the eruption of the Gulf War was clear. It was not just the student of Bible prophecy who recognized that the possibility of an Armageddon still loomed over us. The realization hit the entire world. All it would take is one pariah nation, or one crazed despot, to send a seemingly peaceful world into a tailspin.

Several years after the Gulf War was over, it was revealed just how much potential there was for Saddam Hussein to unleash catastrophic chemical and germ warfare. Events such as the bombing of the World Trade Center in New York City and the deliberate emission of a deadly nerve gas in Tokyo's subway system by doomsday cultists demonstrated that even peaceful soil is at risk of urban terrorism. The number of countries possessing, or who are suspected of possessing, nuclear, chemical, and biological weapons is increasing daily. There are also grave warnings being heard that such weapons may have found their way into the hands of terrorist groups.

Authorities agree that as long as common sense prevails, we need not worry too much about the outbreak of mass, destructive warfare. But can we be sure that common sense will continue to prevail, in light of the fact that terrorists now seem more willing than ever to inflict greater material damage and cause more casualties to achieve their goals?

Since the Berlin Wall came down in 1989, global conflicts have doubled, according to the National Defense Council Foundation. This lobbying and research group, based in Washington, D.C., counted seventy-one conflicts in 1995, as opposed to thirty-five in 1989.[7]

Indeed, even with the Cold War over, we are living in a time of great fear of war and terrorism. As Christians, however, we have no need to fear such threats of conflict. Jesus already forewarned us that one of the signs preceding His second coming would be "wars and rumors of wars."[8] We know that this rise in conflicts and threats of terrorism around the world are part of the markers we have been told to watch for along the shoreline as we travel in this boat of life.

In addition to the outbreak of war, the world is also contending with environmental degradation as a result of man's industrial and technological progress. Global warming, which many blame on man-made gases that are trapping the sun's heat, threatens to make droughts, storms, and floods more severe in the coming days. Global warming, as well as disasters like oil spills, threatens to wipe out wildlife. It is even feared that environmental degradation could wipe out entire ecosystems if something is not done to turn the mess around. Many fear it may already be too late to turn back the pages of history.

There is no question that countless men, women, and children the world over are aware of these signs of impending warfare and environmental doom, just as the Christian watching for them is. Where they differ from the Christian is in their understanding of these signs. It naturally follows, therefore, that their response to them is different. As the child of God sees these signs, he or she should be filled with peace and hope. Those who do not trust in God's assurances, however, will be overcome with distress, their hearts "failing them for fear."[9]

The humanist, the atheist, the agnostic, the secular scientist, or politician—all who have not accepted Jesus as the Christ or the Messiah—cannot take their eyes off the world around them. They are not waiting for the return of Jesus to save them. To them, their only remaining hope is to personally attempt to save this world from destruction. They believe it is only through their own strength that they can turn the boat around and paddle away from the waterfall ahead. They believe it is within their power to row this boat into peaceful waters. They are not looking for the new heaven and new earth that are promised in the Bible. They are looking to build a new heaven and a new earth in the here and now.

It is this earth-based hope that has essentially become the foundation stone of the New Age movement. The heart of this movement is not the crystals, trance channelers, holistic healers, or reincarnationists, although they are definitely a part of it. Nor is the heart of the movement "human potential," or the belief that we are gods. These are only the nuts and bolts that piece the New Age movement together. The heart of the movement is its *rejection of hope in Jesus Christ* in the face of impending doom and planetary crises. The determination to solve man's problems without God is its foundation. Indeed, far from being an odd-ball assortment of former hippies and eccentrics, the New Age movement has essentially become a collection of all those trying to create global peace without the Prince of Peace, Jesus Christ. Our Christian friend in the boat was told to watch for the progression along the shoreline toward such an era.

We're in This Boat Together

In the late 1980's and early 1990's, we witnessed the emergence of terms like "global village," "spaceship Earth," "interdependence," and "one world." These phrases, which were once uttered only by hard-core globalists and New Agers, have now reached the mainstream. They are common ideas, resulting from a successful conscious-ness-raising campaign to convince us that planetary crises can only be solved through action on a global level. Whereas Christians preach individual salvation, messengers of the New Age have been preaching that there will be planetary salvation. John Randolph Price, for instance, the organizer of World Peace Day, wrote:

> [I see] images of a new heaven and a new earth. . . . This world will be saved. The planet will be healed and harmonized. We can let the kingdom come . . . which means that this world can be transformed into a heaven right now. . . . This is no fantasy. This is not scientific or religious fiction. This is the main event of our individual lives.[10]

The biblical message of individual salvation is at odds with such a concept of planetary salvation. Indeed, the New Age movement's rejection of God's promise of a "blessed hope" has become very clear. In the late 1980's, a new gospel was beginning to be preached the world over. Comments from New Age organizations, like the following from the group Planetary Citizens, were in abundance: "Someone is always trying to summon us back to a dead allegiance: Back to God, the simple-minded religion of an earlier day . . . Back to simple-minded patriotism. . . . [We must] take the future into our own hands."[11]

Psychiatrist and best-selling author M. Scott Peck echoed a similar sentiment: "The most extraordinary result of nuclear technology is that it has brought the human race as a whole to the point at which physical and spiritual salvation are no longer separable."[12]

Even former Soviet president Mikhail Gorbachev was preaching that man must take his destiny in his own hands, claiming that old religious ideas of salvation were a waste of time. Writing in *Perestroika*, Gorbachev warned:

> For all the contradictions of the present-day world,
> for all the diversity of social and political systems
> in it, and for all the different choices made by the
> nations in different times, this world is neverthe-
> less one whole. We are all passengers aboard one
> ship, the Earth, and we must not allow it to be
> wrecked. There will be no second Noah's Ark.[13]

The New Age rejection of God's plan for individual salvation is clear from the new gospel being preached today. It has also become clear that man will make an attempt at his own plan of salvation—on a planetary scale.

Peace and Safety and the New World Order

Shortly after introducing *glasnost* and *perestroika* to his own nation, Mikhail Gorbachev began to preach to the world the concept of global cooperation. Having gained great popularity everywhere in the world, except in his homeland, he became one of the first modern-day politicians to openly and boldly proclaim the time for a new world order was ripe.

Speaking to an audience at Stanford University in 1990, Gorbachev noted:

> It is appropriate now to ponder the destinies of the
> world since it was here in San Francisco that the United
> Nations was founded 45 years ago. I think it is very

symbolic that it is this sunny city that was selected as the place to proclaim the foundation, the establishment of this organization, whose efficiency we need very much.

Let us look at the conclusions drawn at that time right after a horrible war. The United Nations was set up to, I quote, "maintain peace and security and remove the political, economic and social causes of war; to settle disputes in conformity with the principles of justice and international law; to promote relations among nations based on the principle of equal rights and self-determination of peoples; a respect for human rights and for fundamental freedoms without distinction as to race, sex or religion." Marvelous words, a marvelous appeal, but, alas, it is only now that we have come closer to addressing the tasks in practical terms.

It is only now that the international politics is really starting to adjust itself to these ideas and principles. And all of us have felt how much we need the United Nations if we really are to move toward a new world, and new kinds of relationships in the world in the interest of all countries. . . .

Let us think about the future. Our two countries have more than enough reasons to be partners in building it, in shaping new security structures in Europe and in the Asian Pacific region. And also in the making of a truly global economy, indeed, and the creation of a new civilization.[14]

Working through the Gorbachev Foundation, USA, he continues to promote the concept of a new world order and the creation of a new civilization with as much zeal today:

The whole world is at the threshold of dramatic changes. Moreover, this will not be just one more transition from one stage to another, of which

there have been so many in history. Many signs
indicate that it will be a watershed of historic
scope and significance, with a new civilization
coming to replace the existing one. . .[15]

Gorbachev is not alone, however, in his belief that a
new world order is on the threshold. Indeed, the idea of a
new world order resounds through the corridors of many
political institutions today. It was the Iraqi invasion of
Kuwait in 1990 that seemed to provide an ideal opportunity to demonstrate how the nations of the world could
unite to ensure the peace and safety of a new civilization.
Former U.S. President George Bush seized the moment by
approaching the United Nations with a request to lead a
cooperative international force against Saddam Hussein.
Gaining consensus from the world community, Bush
boldly proclaimed:

A new partnership of nations has begun. And we
stand today at a unique and extraordinary moment. The crisis in the Persian Gulf, as grave as it
is, also offers a rare opportunity to move toward
an historic period of cooperation. Out of these
troubled times, our fifth objective, a new world
order, can emerge: a new era, freer from the threat
of terror, stronger in the pursuit of justice, and
more secure in the quest for peace. An era in which
the nations of the world, east and west, north and
south, can prosper and live in harmony.

A hundred generations have searched for this
elusive path to peace, while a thousand wars
have raged across the span of human endeavor.
And today that new world is struggling to be
born. A world quite different from the one we've
known. A world where the rule of law supplants
the rule of the jungle. A world in which the

nations recognize and share responsibility for freedom and justice. A world where the strong respect the rights of the weak. . . . This crisis is the first assault on the new world that we seek.[16]

While it was the united effort of the international community that was responsible for thwarting the efforts of Saddam Hussein, the bloody Bosnian war, which dragged on for several years, demonstrated that the new world order still lacks unity on many issues. This has not disheartened the movers and shakers, however. Their vision of a new civilization for mankind remains strong.

The Gospel of This Earth

Talk of a new world order does not echo solely throughout the corridors of political institutions. The call for a new civilization can be heard ringing through the halls of many ecclesiastical buildings as well. Indeed, it is no secret that many of the conflicts in the world today arise because of religious beliefs. Recognizing that religious conflict the world over plays a great role in hindering world peace, many leaders from churches claiming to represent Christianity began to call for unity among the Christian denominations. Hence, the World Council of Churches was born in 1948. Rev. W. Franklyn Richardson of the Central Committee of the World Council of Churches (WCC), when asked about the Council's role in the future, responded:

> The WCC tries to get the churches to come together on various things collectively. . . . I guess it's similar to the United Nations of the Church. . . . I think that the future for the world is that we are becoming more of a village, that this is a "global village" and that everything that happens in the

world is related. . . . We are in one world, one community, and we're going to have to learn how to
live together in it, or else we're going to destroy
each other. And that is going to be the hardest
lesson. The church is going to have to aid the
world in understanding that.[17]

The time for unity among the world's religions, not
just Christian denominations, is ripe as well. The Evangelical Press reported:

More than 200 representatives of world faiths gathered
in Khartoum, Sudan, Oct. 8-10 [1994] to discuss a need
for a world council of religions.

The proposal, which had strong support from Muslim
participants, followed the U.N. Conference on Population and Development, held in Cairo in September, where
Muslim and other religious groups stood against the possibility of legalizing abortion worldwide. Muslim groups
expressed a desire at the conference to foster cooperation between religions, but at the same time affirm religious liberty and pluralism.

The proposed council of religions would enable the major
religions—particularly Christianity and Islam—to join
together to offer an alternative vision to what is considered to be a materialist, secularist world view that dominates society. One observer said that the *meeting called
for a new political world order* [emphasis added].

Among participants at the conference were religious officials from 30 countries, including high-ranking Islamic
political and religious representatives from Egypt, Libya,
Pakistan, Yemen, Palestine, and Jordan. One of the
world's leading Muslims, Hassan al Turabi, head of the
National Islamic Front of Sudan, was a prominent
speaker. The Middle East Council of Churches and the
Anglican Church were represented, and Cardinal Arinze,

president of the Pontifical Council for Inter-Religious Dialogue, represented the Vatican.

"An increasing number of Muslims are putting inter-religious dialogue on their agenda," Tarke Mitri, representative of the World Council of Churches, told Ecumenical News International. "There were in Khartoum people who have not been inclined to inter-religious dialogue in the past. Here we have something that may bear fruit."[18]

The new gospel of a new heaven and a new earth in the here and now, as well as of planetary salvation, is gaining momentum. It is a gospel that is at odds with the Christian gospel, however. The global cause seems so noble. The arguments in favor of a new world order seem so persuasive. Born-again Christians who do not possess the same earth-based world view have a difficult time justifying their opposition to it. As Christians set their focus on eternal matters rather than on the temporal dangers the world is facing, they seem narrow-minded. Even some evangelical leaders have derided such thinking as irresponsible and escapist. It is becoming obvious. The world is growing increasingly intolerant of such thinking. Any view that is not earth-based, we are told, has no place in the new world order.

A Way That Seems Right

In essence, what is being preached today by a broad spectrum of groups and peoples is the need for a global system consisting of a world government, a world economy, and a world religion. It is with this understanding that we can begin to discern one of the most important messages of Bible prophecy. God warned that man, because he does not comprehend what the signs of the times mean, and because of his rejection of Christ, will try to build a man-centered kingdom of peace on earth.

Interestingly, in a report on the popularity of the Communist Party prior to the June 1996 Russian presidential elections, *Time* magazine quoted General Albert Makashov, who was sitting on one of the seats held by the Communist Party in parliament at the time, as saying, "What is our maximum program? The Kingdom of God on earth—or communism, as we call it—before the third millennium."[19] Essentially, this is exactly what mankind is attempting to do today, but on a global scale. Man is trying to build the kingdom of God on earth, without God.

In Revelation, chapter 13, we are given a very clear picture of a last-days world system. Incredibly, this picture looks like the new world order that is being called for today. The Bible warns that mankind is going to be deceived into allowing the greatest villain in all history to put the finishing touches on this final world system. Even worse, mankind is then going to allow this villain to rule over it. Who is this villain? The prophesied Antichrist.

The Word of God points out three central pillars of this kingdom over which the Antichrist will be given control in the last days:

1. World government: "Power was given him [the Antichrist] over all kindreds, and tongues, and nations" (Revelation 13:7; cf. Daniel 7:23).

2. World economy: "He [the false prophet] causeth all, both small and great, rich and poor, free and bond, to receive a mark in their right hand, or in their foreheads: and that no man might buy or sell, save he that had the mark, or the name of the beast, or the number of his name" (Revelation 13:16-17).

3. World religion: "All the world wondered after the beast. And they worshipped the dragon which gave power unto the beast: and they worshipped the beast, saying, Who is like unto the beast? who is able to make war with him? . . . And all that dwell upon the earth shall worship him, whose names are not written in the book of life of the Lamb slain from the foundation of the world" (Revelation 13:3,4,8).

It is breathtaking to realize that the construction of the new world order we are witnessing today may very well be the fulfillment of this last-days empire described in Revelation 13! With the world's rejection of the Prince of Peace, and in its rush to build its own earthly kingdom, the Antichrist's kingdom is being prefabricated for him. And just as the "Anti"-Christ is a false Christ, or false Messiah, this "anti"-kingdom will be a cheap, albeit very convincing, imitation of Christ's coming millennial kingdom on earth.

When the Bible speaks of the final world empire that will encompass the globe, it is intertwined with references to this new emperor who will one day rule it. Since the Bible indicates that the emergence of this prophesied empire seems to be simultaneous to the reign of the Antichrist, we should take a closer look at this coming world ruler and his entrance onto the world stage. Once we understand more about him, we should also be able to understand the nature of the false kingdom of peace that is being constructed today. But to do this, we must first understand the role Israel plays in Bible prophecy. Indeed, Israel has a key part in the prophecies of the Antichrist and his manmade kingdom on earth.

The Promised Land and the Holy City

The Temple Mount in Jerusalem is a tiny piece of property, yet it is perhaps the most controversial and sought-after piece of real estate in the world. It is claimed to be the third most holy site for the Muslim faith, which now holds sole rights to it. Religious Jews declare it should be theirs because it is their *most* holy site. It was on this spot, Mount Moriah, that their father Abraham was to sacrifice Isaac for God (who then provided a lamb to be sacrificed in Isaac's stead). And it was on this holy site that the first two Jewish temples resided. Even the Christian faith holds an interest in the Temple Mount. It is on the Temple Mount that history has, over the centuries, been witness to construction, destruction, rebuilding, and yet more destruction. Some of its history is peaceful. Some of it is bloody.

In late 1990, in the midst of the Persian Gulf War, the world's attention was riveted to the Temple Mount and its Western Wall in Jerusalem. A number of Arab protesters began hurling rocks from the Temple Mount down at Jewish worshippers lined up at the Western Wall for prayer. This Western Wall is the last existing part of the wall that surrounded the second Jewish temple. Denied access to the Temple Mount, Jews are relegated to worshipping at this remaining piece of rampart. This is the closest they can come to the site of their former sacred temple.

The Arabs were protesting the actions of a group known as the Temple Mount Faithful, whose goal is to see the construction of a third Temple on the Mount. Rumor had it that members of the group were heading towards the Mount with the foundation stone for the Third Temple, and it was this incident that momentarily drew the world's attention away from what appeared to be a conflict of global proportions.

In the fall of 1996, in the midst of the U.S. presidential elections and turmoil in Russia because of President Yeltsin's failing health, the world's attention was again turned to the Temple Mount. Several days of violence between Palestinians and Jews had erupted. The riots began when Jews started to lengthen the rabbinical tunnels situated along the Western Wall.

It wasn't the nature of the attacks from the Temple Mount that managed to turn the eyes of the world towards it, however. Instead, it was the fact that God had prophesied that in the last days Israel and Jerusalem would be at the center of His plan for the end times.

The Promised Land

If there is one thing that is paramount to understanding Bible prophecy, it is the central role that Israel plays in the last days. The fact that the Jewish people are back in their land, after having been scattered to every corner of the earth for two and half millennia, is truly a miracle. But it is much more than that. Israel's return to her homeland in 1948 is one of the most significant prophetic fulfillments in all of history. The rebirth of the state of Israel confirmed the truth of God's Word in two dramatic ways. It completed God's prophecy that He would scatter and then regather His chosen people.

> *The Lord shall scatter thee among all people, from one*
> *end of the earth even unto the other.*[1]

Although the Jews were driven from their land because of sin and unbelief, God promised them He would ultimately regather them in the land in the end times. The Hebrew prophet Ezekiel recorded this promise:

> *I will take you from among the heathen, and gather you*
> *out of all countries, and will bring you into your own*
> *land.*[2]

Ezekiel was even specific enough to record that Israel would at first return to the promised land in unbelief. Such is the case today. Many Jews in modern-day Israel are secular, rather than religious Jews. God said, however, He would begin to spiritually revive them in the end times (Ezekiel 37).

In their present state of unbelief, however, many Jews in modern-day Israel are willing to trade portions of this promised land for peace. Others believe that the Jews were disobedient to God, therefore they have no claim to the land any longer. However, take a look at Genesis 15, where God promised the land to Abraham: "In the same day the Lord made a covenant with Abram, saying, Unto thy seed have I given this land, from the river of Egypt unto the great river, the river Euphrates."[3]

Let's take a closer look at this covenant that God made with Abraham:

> And he [Abraham] said, Lord God, whereby shall I know that I shall inherit it?
>
> And he said unto him, Take me an heifer of three years old, and a shegoat of three years old, and a ram of three years old, and a turtledove, and a young pigeon.

> And he took unto him all these, and divided them in the midst, and laid each piece one against another: but the birds divided he not.
>
> And when the fowls came down upon the carcasses, Abram drove them away.
>
> And when the sun was going down, a deep sleep fell upon Abram; and, lo, an horror of great darkness fell upon him. . . .
>
> And it came to pass, that, when the sun went down, and it was dark, behold a smoking furnace, and a burning lamp that passed between those pieces.
>
> In that same day the LORD made a covenant with Abram.[4]

During the time of Abraham, it was customary for men to divide an animal carcass in two parts and then pass between the parts to ratify their covenant. However, the covenant in Genesis 15 was a covenant between a man and God. But what kind of covenant was this? Abraham fell asleep before God even showed up! Since Abraham had fallen asleep, he did not pass between the divided animals. It was God alone who passed between the animal parts (verse 17). Thus Abraham could not break his end of the bargain. The only party who could break the covenant is God, which is, of course, impossible. So, even though the Jews have a history of rebelliousness and disobedience towards God, they can't break the covenant. The land is theirs unconditionally!

God's Word also foretold that the final regathering to this promised land would take place only after it had lain waste for centuries. In 1867, American writer Mark Twain visited the land of Palestine. He recorded his observations of the desolate wasteland he came in contact with on each step of his journey in a book titled *Innocents Abroad*. Of the Jezreel Valley, he wrote:

"There is not a solitary village throughout its
whole extent . . . There are two or three small clus-
ters of Bedouin tents, but not a single permanent
habitation."

He described the area of the Galilee as a land of "un-
peopled deserts" and "rusty mounds of barrenness."

"A desolation is here," he continued, "that not even
imagination can grace with the pomp of life and action . . .
We reached [Mount] Tabor safely . . . We never saw a
human being on the whole route." Jericho was described
as a "moldering ruin" and Bethlehem was "untenanted
by any living creature." The area surrounding Jerusalem
he described as "rocky and bare, repulsive and dreary."
And of the holy city of Jerusalem he observed:

" Renowned Jerusalem itself, the stateliest name
in history, has lost all its ancient grandeur, and become a pauper village."

Twain's summation of the entire land of Palestine
painted a bleak picture:

"Palestine sits in sackcloth and ashes. Over it
broods the spell of a curse that has withered its
fields and fettered its energies . . . Palestine is desolate and unlovely . . . It is a hopeless, dreary, heart
broken land."[5]

Indeed, Twain's record of the land of Israel during his
visit confirmed that God's prophetic word had truly been
fulfilled.

In addition to this prophecy, God's Word also foretold
us that before the Jews were regathered in the promised
land, they would be persecuted and afflicted in every
nation of the world where they dwelt: *"Among these nations shalt thou find no ease, neither shall the sole of thy foot
have rest: but the Lord shall give thee there a trembling heart,*

*and failing of eyes, and sorrow of mind: And thy life shall hang
in doubt before thee; and thou shalt fear day and night, and shalt
have none assurance of thy life.*"[6]

One need only think of the Inquisition, the Russian
pogroms, or Nazi Germany and the Holocaust to realize
that this prophecy has been fulfilled to the letter. Indeed,
we know from history that *all* of these events happened
to the Jews and their land just as prophesied. However,
these prophecies were only the beginning.

Jerusalem, a Burdensome Stone

The prophet Zechariah foretold that in the last days
Jerusalem would become for the world a "cup of trembling" and a "burdensome stone."[7] This prophecy is being
fulfilled today, right before our very eyes. According to
the United Nations' partition of Palestine in 1948, the
Palestinians were designated land that would have con-
stituted the state of Palestine. The Jews were also given
land, which was to be the state of Israel. It was only a small
part of the land they had held deed to in biblical times.
Having just barely survived the Nazi Holocaust, however,
the Jews readily accepted this small part of their heritage
offered to them by the world community. The holy city of
Jerusalem was to be an international city, according to the
U.N., belonging to neither the Palestinians nor the Jews.
Events turned out far differently than planned, however.

Before the Jews even had a chance to unpack their bags
and settle into their new tiny nation in May of 1948, their
surrounding Arab enemies moved in for an attack. As far
as the Arabs were concerned, there would be no welcome
mat laid out for a Jewish state in the Middle East. Mirac-
ulously, being outnumbered in tanks, troops and planes,
the Jews managed to hold onto the land that had been partitioned to them. But even more miraculous was the fact

that they conquered the western half of Jerusalem as their own. For close to two decades they held onto West Jerusalem, while Jordan controlled the eastern half of the holy city, as well as land that had been partitioned by the U.N. to the Palestinians.

Between 1948 and 1967, Jordanian occupation of the territories prevented Jews living in the remainder of Israel from reaching out and touching their Jewish history. Benjamin Netanyahu recorded in *A Place Among Nations* the Jewish sentiment over their divided land and divided holy city at that time:

> Most of all, Israelis remembered the Western Wall, the hallowed rampart of the Jewish Temple that was buried inside the Arab-controlled section of divided Jerusalem. The holiest place of Judaism was barred to them as Jews—even though it was only a few hundred yards away across a no-man's land.

> The eerie feeling of imprisonment, of being so close and yet so very far away from the cradle of Jewish history, was hauntingly captured a few weeks before the outbreak of the Six Day War by the publication of Naomi Shemer's "Jerusalem of Gold," a song that deeply moved the entire country.[8]

When the Six Day War did break out, the Jews conquered East Jerusalem, thus fulfilling yet another of the prophecies found in Zechariah:

> *"Jerusalem shall be inhabited again in her own place, even in Jerusalem."*[9]

The uniting of Jerusalem was a highly emotional moment for Israeli Jews. Again, Netanyahu recorded how deep the feelings ran:

> "Thousands of Israelis streamed through the Old City to the Wall—following the steps of the

soldiers to the place where, just hours earlier, secular, battle-weary paratroops had wept to a man over the privilege granted to them of sewing back together the broken heart of the Jewish people. Like the soldiers, the citizens of Israel stood before the ancient Wall, touching the massive stones in wondrous awe.[10]

It was with the fulfillment of this part of Zechariah's prophecy that the other part of his prophecy was able to commence: the controversy over Jerusalem in the last days. Following the Jewish victory in the Six Day War, Israeli Defense Minister Moshe Dayan, in what could perhaps be called the first "land for peace" deal, gave the Temple Mount back to the Arabs. This diplomatic move was not enough to appease the Arabs, or the world, however, as long as the city of Jerusalem remained in Jewish hands. Immediately following the announcement that Jerusalem was to be the undivided capital of the State of Israel, virtually all the nations of the world refused to recognize it as such. Even today foreign embassies are situated in Tel Aviv, symbolizing the world's rejection of the Jewish claim to Jerusalem as the capital.

The 3000th anniversary of this claim, dating from King David's capture of the city of Jerusalem, was in 1996. Anniversary celebrations were planned to span over fifteen months with operas, ballets, symphonies, and other cultural performances. Most of the international community, however, boycotted the Jewish celebrations, again symbolizing the world's rejection of Jerusalem as the capital of Israel.

But it wasn't just the 3000th anniversary of Jerusalem that concerned the international community in 1996. It was the fact that May, 1996, had been scheduled as the commencement date for talks between Israeli Jews and

Palestinians over the status of East Jerusalem as the possible capital of a future Palestinian state. As part of the
peace agreement signed in September, 1993, by Israel and
the Palestine Liberation Organization, the ruling Labor
Party, under Prime Minister Yitzhak Rabin, promised that
in addition to discussions on the creation of a Palestinian
state, talks on the status of Jerusalem would be held as
well, no later than May of 1996.

It was the signing of this Declaration of Principles that
appears to be the demarcation point of major controversy
over the holy city in these last days. Immediately, Israeli
Jews, whether opposed to or in favor of the Mid-East peace
process, emphasized that Jerusalem would never be divided again. Dror Zeigerman, the Israeli Consul General
to Canada at the time, noted: "When we finally come to
the table to sign a comprehensive peace agreement, [the
Palestinians] will also have to grant concessions. They
must understand that for Israel itself there are some things
we cannot give up. For example, Jerusalem. United
Jerusalem, and all the area around Jerusalem, is part of
the State of Israel. Jerusalem will never be the capital of
an Arab state, or the capital of the Palestinians."[11]

Even peacemaker Shimon Peres, the leader of the
Labor Party, while serving as Foreign Minister and later as
Prime Minister following the assassination of Yitzhak
Rabin, swore that Jerusalem would not be divided. Many,
however, did not believe his sincerity on the matter.
Indeed, intelligence reports had suggested he was waiting
until after the 1996 elections to seriously discuss giving the
Palestinians autonomy over East Jerusalem if re-elected:

> Speaking on the morning of 19 March to a gathering of
> 50 mayors from around the world, Peres reiterated for
> the umpteenth time: "All the reports of plans to divide

Jerusalem are false. There is no intention to divide the city."

But our own sources in Jerusalem are convinced that the Labour government is being economical with the truth. It is trying desperately to hold the line on Jerusalem until re-elected on 29 May. It will then negotiate a division of the city with the Palestinians.[12]

Peres, of course, did not win the 1996 Israeli election for Prime Minister. Benjamin Netanyahu of the Likud Party became the new Prime Minister of Israel in the spring of that year. During his campaign he promised the Jewish population in Israel that Jerusalem would forever remain the undivided capital:

> Jerusalem has been the capital of the Jewish people for the last three thousand years. It is going to remain that way, undivided, united, with freedom of access to all faiths. In terms of sovereignty, it will remain the capital of Israel, the capital of the Jewish people.[13]

Even if Prime Minister Netanyahu is pressured into softening on any of his campaign promises, especially those regarding the future status of Jerusalem, he will have to contend with many of the Likud Party's hardliners, including Ariel Sharon, Israel's former defense minister. In a May 10, 1996, article that appeared in Israel's daily newspaper *Yediot Aharanot*, Sharon was quoted as saying: "Jerusalem will be united for ever, and the capital of Israel only. The PLO and Palestinian Authority offices will be moved from there. The Palestinian security forces in East Jerusalem and on the Temple Mount, who are in control there illegally, will be expelled from the city. U.N. forces or observers will not be posted in the area. The grave mistake of stationing them in Hebron was enough."[14]

Such hardline policy could, of course, put the Mid-East peace process in grave jeopardy. And there will, no doubt, be tough international pressure placed on the Likud government to soften its policy and cave in to Palestinian demands. Indeed, one thing is certain: The issue of Jerusalem will be a tough issue to solve. After all, the Palestinians have warned that the peace process will never be successful until this issue is resolved in their favor. The Palestinians have been adamant that the peace process will not continue on a peaceful path if the Jews continue to deny them East Jerusalem. PLO leader Yasser Arafat, chairman of the Palestinian Authority, warned:

> What is more important than all of this is the subject of Jerusalem, as Israel is insisting on the attempt to overlook the subject, and I am saying to them: Jerusalem is to us Palestinians, Arabs, Muslims, and Christians the starting point in all the negotiating process.... God willing we will pray in Jerusalem whether Israel likes it or not.[15]

Likewise, Hanan Ashrawi, the former spokeswoman for the Palestinian negotiating team, had warned:

> Jerusalem is an indivisible part of the occupied territories and it is a fundamental issue. It is the heart of occupied Palestine. It is the heart of the Arab world. It is the heart of the Islamic world, and no person, group or Palestinian leadership can relinquish it. Because without Jerusalem we would have given up the source of strength and self-momentum of the Palestinian cause.... We also see Jerusalem as the capital of the Palestinian state and reject any attempts at defining its future in advance.... Arab Jerusalem remains the Jerusalem of the Arabs, the Jerusalem of Palestine, and the essence and beating heart of Palestine.[16]

Not wanting to be left out of the picture, the Vatican, which it claims represents the Christian faith in Jerusalem, announced that it would like to see more of an "international umbrella" over the holy city. This comment was made by Monsignor Claudio Mario Celli after signing an historic agreement between Israel and the Vatican on January 6, 1996. The purpose of the fundamental agreement was to open diplomatic ties between the two states, which have been cold since the founding of Israel in 1948. Indeed, the Catholic church has been cold towards the Jews since long before the nation of Israel was born. The purpose of the agreement was to ensure that all the religious faiths that claim to have an interest in Jerusalem would be guaranteed access to their holy sites located there.

According to the *Jerusalem Post:*

> Uri Mor, head of the department of Christian communities of the Religious Affairs Ministry, says that during the negotiations his ministry took special care in wording the final agreement so that it would not infringe on the other churches. In fact, he says, the document enshrines in international agreement what until now has been only custom.

> Until now, Mor explains, Israel was not legally committed to respect the status quo agreement on the holy places, although it has done so in practice. In the fundamental agreement to be signed last week, Israel made such a commitment, he says.[17]

It seems that in these last days just about everyone holds some kind of interest in Israel and Jerusalem. And, as the 1996 riot amongst Arabs and the Temple Mount Faithful at the Western Wall foreshadowed, the Temple Mount itself will be the central focus of the world's attention. Indeed, it will be the center stage for much of the prophetic drama that lies ahead.

The Third Temple

One of the most dramatic prophecies concerning Israel, which is still to be fulfilled, concerns the building of the Third Temple. Religious Jews are certain there will be a Third Temple and are even now preparing for it. Temple treasures are being fashioned, based on instructions taken from the Bible. A model of the Third Temple has been constructed and sits on exhibit in Old Jerusalem. Even a computerized list of candidates who fulfill the requirements of a Temple priest has been drawn up, and rabbinical students have been training for ancient Jewish temple rites and sacrifice. So why haven't the Jews started building the Third Temple? What is keeping it from being constructed?

For one, millions of Arabs are standing in the way of its construction. Religious Jews will accept no other site than the Temple Mount for the Third Temple. However, as mentioned in the last chapter, the Temple Mount today is under the control of Muslim Arabs. Furthermore, the Temple Mount houses the Muslim Dome of the Rock, which is built over a spot on a rock that had supposedly been left by the prophet Muhammad during a night vision as he journeyed from Mecca to Jerusalem. The other structure that is of significance to the Muslims on the Temple Mount is the Al Aqsa mosque. But how holy are the Temple Mount and these symbols of Islam? Thomas Ice and Randall Price, the authors of best-selling books on Bible prophecy, suggest they are not truly that important to the Muslim faith:

> In the beginning the Rock itself had no religious meaning to Islam. It was only after some time, and most likely in order to attract visitors to Jerusalem, that the stories of Jerusalem being the place of final resurrection and of Mohammed's night journey were invented. In fact, the name of Jerusalem is not mentioned even once in all of the *Qur'an* (or *Koran*, the holy scripture of Islam).
>
> Some Muslim authorities have argued the 'Night Journey of Muhammad' refers to Jerusalem when it says that he went to al Aqsa, the name of the mosque which today is built south of the Dome of the Rock. However, the word *al Aqsa* simply means "far corner," and it is supposed that it was originally located in the east corner of Mecca, not in Jerusalem. . . .
>
> Muslim prayer, even today, is in the direction of Mecca, not Jerusalem. According to an early account, when Ka'b al-Ahbar proposed to the Caliph 'Umar that the place of prayer in Jerusalem should be fixed north of the Dome, so that Muslims would turn during their prayers toward the Rock at the same time they turned toward Mecca (which lies to the south of Jerusalem), the caliph rejected his advice because he considered it a Jewish scheme to coerce Muslims to prostrate themselves toward an object of Jewish worship, the Holy of Holies in the Temple. He is said to have retorted to Ka'b: 'By Allah, O Ka'b, in your heart you are still a Jew, for I have seen how you took off your shoes [before entering the Temple Mount], but we Muslims were not ordered to sanctify this Rock,

we were only ordered to turn [in our prayers] towards the Ka'ba [in Mecca].'[1] There are records of early caliphs who deliberately avoided the site of the Rock, or who prayed with their backs to it to show their religious indifference. . . .

In the same vein, a Muslim cemetery was placed in front of the Golden Gate, considered the original eastern entrance to the Temple. This was intended to keep the Jewish (and Christian) Messiah from entering through it, since passage through an unwalled cemetery incurs defilement. If the Jews could not enter the gate, they could not rebuild the Temple on the Temple Mount as prophesied.

The point we want to make by showing how Jerusalem became sacred to Islam and why Muslims felt it necessary to build on the Temple Mount is that there is no historically justifiable claim for Jerusalem or the Temple Mount as a holy place in Islam. It was not until AD 1187, when the Crusaders were finally dislodged by the Muslim leader Salan-ad-Din (Saladin), that Jerusalem was confirmed as the third holiest place in Islam (after Mecca and Medina). As we have noted, nothing in the *Qur'an* supports this reverence. In fact, the *Qur'an* actually supports the historic claim of the Israelis to the land. In Sura V, v. 21, citing the words of Moses in the story of the spies, it is written: "Oh my people, enter the Holy Land that has been promised to you."[2]

Nonetheless, the Arabs would never allow the Jews at this point in history to rebuild the Third Temple on the Temple Mount. Nor would the international community for that matter. There is a completely different, but related, issue over building plans in Jerusalem.

Jerusalem's Housing Plans Under Fire

In early May of 1995 it seemed, once again, that the Middle East peace process might be doomed to failure. This time the controversy was over the Israeli government's building and housing plans for East Jerusalem, which required the expropriation of Arab-held land. Jerusalem's deputy mayor at the time, Uri Lupoliansky, noted: "The Arabs simply must understand that there are more Jews living in this city, and they need places to live."[3]

This infuriated the Palestinian Authority, which immediately called on the Arab League, the U.S., Russia, and the U.N. Security Council to pressure the Israeli government to dispense with the plan. The Security Council, siding with the Palestinians, proposed a resolution condemning Israel's plan, but the U.S. vetoed it.

Still coming under international pressure, the Israeli government announced that it would not expropriate *all* of the intended land in East Jerusalem, but it would still require 53 hectares for new housing and a police station. Then several days later, apparently having caved in completely to international pressure, the Israeli government announced that it was backing off of its land seizure plan altogether. According to media reports, "It was the first time in Israel's 47-year existence that the government had reversed a decision to expropriate land in Jerusalem—historically the world's most fought-over city."[4]

What other city in the world receives so much international attention over a mere housing plan? If the international community would stand in the way of Jews building houses on Arab-held land in East Jerusalem, it would definitely stand in the way of religious Jews building a Third Temple on the Temple Mount, which would surely ignite a holy war.

Whatever the sentiments of the Arabs and the world are today, however, we can be certain that the construction cranes will head to the Temple Mount one day for the building of the Third Temple. How do we know this? From God's prophetic Word. Daniel 9:27 tells us that the Antichrist is going to sign a covenant with Israel, which is to last for seven years. In the midst of that contractual period the Antichrist is going to break the covenant. Furthermore, the prophet Daniel tells us the Antichrist is going to "cause the sacrifice and the oblation to cease." From this Scripture, therefore, we know that during that time Jews will have already reinstated temple worship. Also, in II Thessalonians 2:4 we are told that the Antichrist is going to sit "in the temple of God, shewing himself that he is God." Clearly, the temple will exist at that time.

Far from being an isolated prophecy, however, the building of the Jewish temple seems to be inter-related to the rise of the Antichrist, who will promise to bring peace and a new world order. It is not too much to say, in fact, that one of the central pillars of the peace covenant between the Antichrist and Israel could be the building of the Third Temple on the Temple Mount. To understand how all of these events are interconnected in the future, we need to review some of Israel's historical past.

Seventy Weeks

In 70 AD, Israel's Second Temple was destroyed, Jerusalem was burned, and the Jews were scattered by the Romans. God allowed this to happen to His chosen people because they had rejected Jesus Christ, their Messiah. Just as He had promised them, God sent the Messiah to Israel. However, because they were looking for a conquering hero to subdue their enemies, to bring them peace and to sit on

David's throne, the Jews did not recognize Christ, who fulfilled the role of the suffering Servant (Isaiah 43). They could not see that it was prophesied that He would come *twice*.

Hundreds of years before Jesus was born, the prophet Daniel was given an overview of God's plan for His chosen people. Daniel and the Israelites were being held in captivity by the Babylonians, who destroyed the first Jewish temple. Daniel was praying for God's mercy upon the children of Israel, and as he prayed, the angel Gabriel appeared before him. The angel told Daniel that God had heard his prayer and wanted to give him an understanding of what would happen to Israel in the future. What followed in that dramatic chapter of the Bible is a prophetic overview of what lay ahead for the descendants of Abraham, Isaac, and Jacob. It is this overview that will help us understand the role of Israel, the Temple Mount, and the coming false messiah in the last days.

In what is known as "the prophecy of the seventy weeks" (Daniel 9), the prophet Daniel was told that at the end of these seventy weeks, Israel would be purged of her sins and saved by her Messiah. Numerous well-respected Bible commentators such as Sir Robert Anderson and Robert Duncan Culver agree that each "week" actually represents seven years. Hence, the seventy weeks equal a 490-year period.

The prophecy of the seventy weeks given in Daniel 9 is broken down into different segments of time. The first 483 years, Daniel was told, were to be measured from the time of "the going forth of the commandment to restore and to build Jerusalem"[5] until the coming of the Messiah.

Sir Robert Anderson (1841–1918) was widely recognized as a popular lay-preacher, an author of bestselling books on the Bible, and the one-time Chief of the Criminal

Investigation Department of Scotland Yard. He used his scientific investigative skills and his knowledge of the Bible to prove, with pinpoint accuracy, the date of the decree to rebuild Jerusalem (Nehemiah 2:4-8). Anderson wrote of his findings:

> The edict in question was the decree issued by Artaxerxes Longimanus in the twentieth year of his reign, authorising Nehemiah to rebuild the fortifications of Jerusalem.
>
> The date of Artaxerxes's reign can be definitely ascertained—not from elaborate disquisitions by biblical commentators and prophetic writers, but by the united voice of secular historians and chronologers.

Anderson calculated that 483 years following this edict, the Passover during which Christ was betrayed and crucified took place:

> The statement of St. Luke is explicit and un-equivocal, that our Lord's public ministry began in the fifteenth year of Tiberius Caesar. It is equally clear that it began shortly before the Passover. The date of it can thus be fixed as between August AD 28 and April AD 32, when Christ was betrayed on the night of the Paschal Supper, and put to death on the day of the Paschal Feast.

Anderson concluded, therefore, that:

> The seventy weeks are therefore to be computed from the 1st of Nisan 445 B.C. [March 14].[6]

To simplify, Sir Robert Anderson calculated that it was exactly 483 years to the day from the time that Nehemiah was given the decree to rebuild Jerusalem until the day we know as Palm Sunday! It was on Palm Sunday, of course, that Jesus was presented to Israel as the long-awaited

Messiah and King. In fulfillment of a prophecy given in
Zechariah 9:9, Jesus sent two of His disciples to get a foal
of an ass upon which He would ride into Jerusalem:

> All this was done, that it might be fulfilled which
> was written by the prophet, saying, Tell ye the
> daughter of Sion, Behold, thy King cometh unto
> thee, meek, and sitting upon an ass, and a colt the
> foal of an ass.[7]

The Scriptures tell us that the multitude cast their gar-
ments and palm leaves on the path as He rode down the
Mount of Olives towards Jerusalem.

> They that went before, and they that followed,
> cried, saying, Hosanna; Blessed is he that cometh
> in the name of the Lord: blessed be the kingdom
> of our father David, that cometh in the name of
> the Lord: Hosanna in the highest.[8]

Despite the fact that Jesus fulfilled all of the Old Testament prophecies that had been given to Israel concerning
His coming, we know that ultimately He was not received
as her Messiah. Indeed, as Jesus had forewarned, the Jews
declared, "We will not have this man to reign over us"
(Luke 19:14). He wept over the slowness of their hearts:

> If thou hadst known, even thou, at least in this thy
> day, the things which belong unto thy peace! But
> now are they hid from thine eyes. For the days
> shall come upon thee, that thine enemies shall cast
> a trench about thee . . . because thou knewest not
> the time of thy visitation.[9]

Exactly 483 years after the day when the commandment to rebuild Jerusalem had been given, Israel failed to
recognize her day of visitation and rejected her Messiah.
At that moment, the prophetic clock of God's dealing with

Israel stopped. Israel spurned her Messiah because He did not come as a conquering King in her eyes.

The Jewish people as a whole failed to recognize that the prophecy of the seventy weeks in Daniel had foretold that the Messiah would be "cut off, but not for himself."[10] What a beautiful picture of God's plan of salvation! The Jewish Messiah was indeed cut off, or killed, but not for Himself. It was for us. As we know, God gave His only Son to die for the sins of all who would simply believe in Him.

When the Messiah was cut off, God's attention was no longer focused solely upon Israel. There was a new entity to consider—the church, that group of people from all the nations of the world would accept Jesus Christ as their Savior. Does this mean that Israel has been forgotten by God forever? Of course not. If you will remember, it had been revealed to Daniel that Israel would be purged of her sins and saved at the end of a 490-year period. Only 483 years had passed, however, from the decree to rebuild Jerusalem until the Messiah. There is still a seven-year period left in this prophecy dealing with Israel. The prophetic time clock for Israel has simply been interrupted by the church age.

The Bible does not give a time frame for how long the church age will last. How is Israel to know when the final seven years in Daniel's prophecy of the "seventy weeks" begins? For one, it makes sense that if the prophetic time clock for Israel stopped with the birth of the church, it will start again when the church is gone. Such an idea fits with the biblical teaching of the rapture. More specifically, such an idea fits snugly with the belief in a pre-tribulation rapture. Remember, the tribulation lasts for seven years. Furthermore, it is the final of the seventy weeks that was determined upon Israel, and Israel alone.[11]

While the word *rapture* is not found in the Bible, biblical scholars agree that such a promise has been given to all believers in Christ in the last days. God's Word says there will be a generation of Christians who will never know death. These Christians will suddenly be "caught up" to meet the Lord in the clouds. This blessed event is known as the rapture:

> The Lord himself shall descend from heaven with a shout . . . and the dead in Christ shall rise first. Then we which are alive and remain shall be caught up together with them in the clouds, to meet the Lord in the air: and so shall we ever be with the Lord.[12]

After the church is gone, the final week that has been determined upon Israel can begin.

Another sign by which Israel will know that the final week has commenced is the covenant described in Daniel 9:27: the same covenant confirmed by the Antichrist, the false messiah.

The False Messiah

When the Jewish people rejected Jesus as their long-awaited Messiah, He uttered an incredible pronouncement upon them. Of the blindness of their hearts He said, "I am come in my Father's name and ye receive me not: if another shall come in his own name, him ye will receive."[13]

He was forewarning them that the day would come when they were going to accept an impostor as their messiah—the Antichrist. As we mentioned earlier, it is this false messiah who will likely play a key role in the construction of the Third Temple on the Temple Mount.

Interestingly, there are Jewish religious sects today that believe the construction of the Third Temple coincides with the revelation of the Messiah.

In 1967, when Defense Minister Moshe Dayan handed the Temple Mount back to the Wakf, the Islamic authority, religious Jews took it as a slap in the face. Not only were they disappointed at losing their most holy site, but also their hopes that the messianic age was about to be ushered in had been dashed. They felt betrayed by their secular brothers. Indeed, today the Temple Mount is not only an issue of contention between Arabs and Jews; it is an issue of contention *amongst* Jews: religious and secular.

As things stand in the world today, the construction of a Third Temple on the Temple Mount seems impossible. The Wakf does not even allow people from other religious faiths to pray on the Temple Mount, let alone build a house of worship there. Anyone from a faith other than Islam is considered an infidel. It is difficult to know exactly how events will come about in the future. We can ponder and speculate, but our ideas may prove to be wrong when the actual biblical fulfillment takes place. But this we do know for certain from the prophetic Word: There will be a Third Temple.

While Muslims reject the idea of a Jewish presence on the Temple Mount, religious Jews claim that when the Third Temple is constructed, there can be no Muslim presence on the Mount. Furthermore, many religious Jews today believe the existing Dome of the Rock will have to be moved in order to accommodate the Third Temple. Gershon Salomon, founder and head of The Temple Mount Faithful, for instance, told us: "I believe this is the will of God. It [the Dome of the Rock] must be moved. We must, you know, take it from the place. And today we have all the instruments to do it, stone by stone, very carefully, and then to put it in a package and mail it back to Mecca, the place from where it was brought."[14]

Many students of Bible prophecy, however, believe that the Jews may somehow be convinced to accept a Gentile presence on the Temple Mount. We cannot know this for certain, but we do know that a description given of the Third Temple in the book of Revelation omits the outer court because it will be given to the Gentiles:

> There was given me a reed like unto a rod: and the angel stood, saying, Rise, and measure the temple of God, and the altar, and them that worship therein.
>
> But the court which is without the temple leave out, and measure it not; for it is given unto the Gentiles: and the holy city shall they tread under foot forty and two months.[15]

Perhaps the Antichrist will convince Jews and Muslims to accept each others' presence on the holy site in the days ahead. Perhaps he will even convince them to accept a "Christian" presence there as well. After all, the Antichrist is coming as a false savior for the entire world. He will promise something for everyone. Jews, Muslims, and "Christians" will all look to him for leadership and as the fulfillment of prophecy.

How will he convince Israel and the world to follow him? In order to understand this impostor, we need to understand exactly who and what he will be impersonating. To do this, let us jump ahead to the end of the seventy weeks: the end of the seven-year tribulation period, when the real Messiah, Jesus Christ, returns to the world for His second coming.

The Great Pretender

There is a popular saying that in a group of three Jews, there will be four opinions. When it comes to ideas about what the coming of the Messiah will be like, this certainly seems to hold true. However, there seems to be a predominant theme about the Messiah's appearance when you ask the average Jew about His coming.

Several years ago, while we were visiting Jerusalem, we set up a video camera and a microphone on Ben Yahuda Street one Saturday evening after Sabbath had ended. Ben Yahuda Street is a popular gathering spot for both young and old, especially following the Sabbath. Husbands and wives sit at outdoor cafes drinking espresso and nibbling on pastries or Israel's popular snack food, the *falafel*. Young couples walk arm in arm, browsing over the wares of outdoor artisans and vendors. Friends gather to watch the performances of jugglers, mimes, or musicians. Indeed, it seems like a setting that could be in many North American or European cities on a warm Saturday evening, except for the fact that most of the young men walking arm in arm with their girlfriends are wearing military uniforms, carrying an Uzi over their shoulders. It serves as a constant reminder that in the midst of seeming normalcy, Israeli Jews constantly live in fear of a terrorist attack or the outbreak of war.

We asked many of these Israelis to stop and tell us on camera about their views of the coming of the Messiah. While some of the views varied, one constant theme that kept cropping up about the coming of the Messiah was that He would bring peace to Israel and to the world.

The idea that the Messiah will bring peace when He comes is taken from passages in the book of Zechariah. In vivid detail, the prophet describes a scene in which the entire world is gathered against Israel to push her into the sea. Just as Israel and the holy city of Jerusalem are at the edge of destruction, the Messiah Himself will return to defend her.

> Then shall the Lord go forth, and fight against those nations, as when he fought in the day of battle.
>
> And his feet shall stand in that day upon the mount of Olives, which is before Jerusalem on the east, and the mount of Olives shall cleave in the midst thereof toward the east and toward the west, and there shall be a very great valley; and half of the mountain shall remove toward the north, and half of it toward the south.... And the Lord shall be king over all the earth.... It shall come to pass in that day, that I will seek to destroy all the nations that come against Jerusalem.
>
> And I will pour upon the house of David, and upon the inhabitants of Jerusalem, the spirit of grace and of supplications: and they shall look upon me whom they have pierced, and they shall mourn for him, as one mourneth for his only son, and shall be in bitterness for him, as one that is in bitterness for his firstborn.[1]

At that moment Israel will mourn as they look upon "Him whom they have pierced," and will recognize Him as her Messiah. He will finally bring true peace to Israel and establish His millennial reign from the throne of David.

Close to two thousand years ago, the Jewish people rejected Jesus as He came down the Mount of Olives. The next time Christ stands on the Mount of Olives, however, Israel will receive Him. He will not be coming again as the suffering Messiah to bear the sins of the world. He is coming again in power and glory to set up His millennial kingdom on earth. It is then that there will be a time of judgment. Sin and transgression will come to an end. Only those who have placed their faith in Christ will be allowed to enter His millennial kingdom. Finally, the 490-year period that had been determined upon Israel will have come to an end.

With this understanding of the second coming of the true Messiah, and of the fact that He is coming to set up His kingdom of peace and righteousness on earth, we can now turn the clock back seven years to the arrival of the impostor.

Waiting In the Wings

Knowing Zechariah prophesied that Christ will be coming to the Mount of Olives to rescue Israel from her enemies and to establish His millennial kingdom on earth, the possibility exists that there may be some kind of uprising in the Middle East for which the nations of the world are present when the false messiah makes his entrance on the world stage. In fact, the entire world may fear it is at the brink of a war of apocalyptic proportions. At that moment the Antichrist could dramatically arise with "all power and signs and lying wonders."[2] It is indeed likely that he will rise in the midst of chaos to deceive the world. After all, it seems that it is only in the midst of chaos that the world would accept an idea that would never before have been accepted. Globalist Dietrich Fischer pointed out when speaking on U.N. reform:

> To reach agreement on reforms to be taken is not easy. It has usually taken a major catastrophe to shake up the international community sufficiently to attempt to create a new world order.[3]

Whatever the scenario is that will make Israel and the world take notice of the Antichrist, the most important thing, it seems, is that he will bring peace. We do know that today many Israeli Jews are longing to live in peace with their neighbors. We also know that many Jews are expecting the coming of the Messiah to bring them this peace. Randall Price, a popular author of bestselling books on Bible prophecy, observed:

> In a paper entitled "Waiting in the Wings," which was distributed all over Israel, the appeal was made to give Messiah the signal to come. The article, in part read: "We must show him we want him with all our heart. He is ready. He is just waiting for the signal from us. Moshiach is waiting in the wings. He is ready. When he comes the curtain will rise on the most magnificent stage set we could imagine—world peace and disarmament, glory and honor for the Jews, the end of strife and jealousy. We must show him through our good deeds, through our tangible anticipation, through our longing for him, that we are ready."[4]

Sadly, the description given of the Messiah by many Jews today fits the description of the Antichrist, not Jesus Christ. It appears from their descriptions of him that they are awaiting a mortal man. Again, Price observes:

The Lubavitcher promotion of a coming messiah who will be a strictly human, non-miracle-working Jewish leader has opened the field for many such messianic candidates. The Lubavitchers are preparing the Jewish world to accept as messiah whoever is instrumental in bringing about the erection of the Third Temple. . . .

Rabbi Manis Friedman, interviewed by University of Maryland professor Susan Handelman in the Hasidic journal *Wellsprings*, reveals the Lubavitcher opinion:

"If he goes on to build the Temple and gather all Jews back to Israel, then we will know for sure that he is the Moshiach. Moshiach comes through his accomplishments and not through his pedigree. Maimonides says that once he builds the Temple and gathers the Jews back to Israel, then we will know for sure that he is Moshiach. He doesn't have to say anything. He will accept the role, but we will give it to him. He won't take it to himself. And his coming, the moment of his coming, in the literal sense, would mean the moment when the whole world recognizes him as Moshiach . . . that both Jew and non-Jew recognize that he is responsible for all the wonderful improvements in the world: an end to war, an end to hunger, an end to suffering, a change in attitude."

This new Jewish concept of the messiah, then, is that of a mortal man and a leader with sufficient charisma to capture and command the admiration of the world—if not its devotion. He will be recognized not by his lineage (as the biblical Messiah—a descendant of the Davidic dynasty), but by his acts of global significance.[5]

Does this description not fit the great pretender, rather than the true Prince of Peace?

A Covenant is Made

In Genesis, chapter 15, a covenant was made by God, promising His servant Abraham that his seed would be

unable to be counted, just like the stars in the heavens.
And God promised Abraham that, although his seed
would be slaves in the land of Egypt for four hundred
years, after that his descendants would inherit the land
"from the river of Egypt unto the great river, the river Euphrates."[6] Abraham's descendants, of course, became the
nation of Israel.

In Hebrews, chapter 8, Israel is promised that an even
better, everlasting covenant is going to be made with
Christ as the mediator:

> Behold, the days come, saith the Lord, when I will
> make a new covenant with the house of Israel and
> with the house of Judah:
>
> Not according to the covenant that I made with
> their fathers in the day when I took them by the
> hand to lead them out of the land of Egypt; be-
> cause they continued not in my covenant, and I
> regarded them not, saith the Lord.
>
> For this is the covenant that I will make with the
> house of Israel after those days, saith the Lord; I
> will put my laws into their mind, and write them
> in their hearts: and I will be to them a God, and
> they shall be to me a people:
>
> And they shall not teach every man his neighbour,
> and every man his brother, saying, Know the Lord:
> for all shall know me, from the least to the greatest.
>
> For I will be merciful to their unrighteousness,
> and their sins and their iniquities will I remember
> no more.[7]

The Antichrist is going to attempt to impersonate the
real Messiah. The prefix "anti" is often thought to mean
"against." However, it has another meaning as well: "in
place of." The Antichrist will try to take the place of Christ.

It only seems fitting, therefore, that he will also try to come up with a covenant of his own. Daniel 9:27 tells us this is exactly what he is going to do. Indeed, many Bible commentators such as Sir Robert Anderson believe it is this covenant which will be the signal that the last of the seventy weeks in Daniel's prophecy has begun. Indeed, verse 27 tells us that the covenant is to last for seven years.

Daniel 9 does not give much detail about the Antichrist's covenant. However, there are some likely conclusions we can draw about its contents. For one, verse 27 says that in the midst of the contractual period, the Antichrist is going to "cause the sacrifice and the oblation to cease." It seems likely, therefore, that the covenant could include a clause giving Israel the right to build the Third Temple and to once again practice the ancient ritual of sacrifice.

The contract may also include some "land for peace" deals. After all, "land for peace" is very much at the heart of the Middle East peace negotiations taking place today. Furthermore, Daniel 11:39 tells us the Antichrist is going to "divide the land for gain." In Scripture, "the land" always refers to Israel.

It is very likely that the covenant will somehow guarantee peace for Israel, something that Israel is struggling for today. In October of 1991, the Madrid Peace Conference was born out of secret talks in Oslo, Norway, between Israel and the Palestine Liberation Organization. It took the world by surprise to learn that these two long-time enemies had agreed to sit down with mediators from the world community and begin negotiations for peace.

The result of two years of heated debate was the signing of the Declaration of Principles between Israel and the PLO on September 13, 1993. That same month, an initiative for peace had commenced between Israel and

Jordan. This led to the signing of a full peace treaty between the two nations on July 25, 1994. Not since 1979, when Israel and Egypt signed the Camp David Accords, had such great strides been made for peace in the Middle East.

The road, however, remained rocky, even in the midst of negotiations, and it is far from completed. But peacemakers were determined that there would be peace in the region. In December, 1993, then Israeli Deputy Minister of Foreign Affairs, Dr. Yossi Beilin, promised:

> In the new world order that has arisen since the Gulf conflict and the dismantling of the Iron Curtain, most of the nations of the Middle East and their leaders have come to understand that national security interests are best promoted by a shift away from exclusive dependence on military force.

> This enlightened comprehension is the foundation of our vision. Peace is just ahead of us on the horizon. We can make it a concrete reality, one step at a time.[8]

At the time of writing this book, Benjamin Netanyahu had just been elected as the Prime Minister of Israel. His victory worried would-be peacemakers. During his campaign, Netanyahu promised his supporters there would be no Palestinian state because that would place the state of Israel in jeopardy. He promised that East Jerusalem would not be given over to the Palestinians. He promised that Jewish settlements in the West Bank would be cultivated and strengthened. And as for giving Syria the Golan Heights, he commented: "No sane Israeli government should give away the Golan Heights because it will be left with a piece of paper but without peace."[9]

It is too early to tell what direction the peace process will take under Benjamin Netanyahu. But one thing is certain: Somewhere down the not-too-distant road, it will be the Antichrist who will appear to finally make peace in the region, and in the world. But God's Word forewarns those who follow the Antichrist that he shall "by peace destroy many."[10] Nonetheless, the world will honor him, believing he has established a kingdom of peace on the planet. The kingdom of the Antichrist, however, is nothing but a cheap imitation of Christ's millennial kingdom on earth.

Rising from the Ashes of History

The Bible does not identify who the Antichrist is, nor does it appear that his identity will be revealed while the church remains on earth (II Thessalonians 2). But God's Word tells us where he will come from. Daniel 9:26 reveals, "The people of the prince that shall come [the Antichrist] shall destroy the city and the sanctuary." Daniel was in the captivity of the Babylonians, who had already destroyed the First Temple, when this prophecy was revealed to him. Therefore, this verse is referring to the destruction of the Second Temple and Jerusalem. The Second Temple and the city of Jerusalem were completely destroyed by the Roman Empire in A.D. 70.

How can the Antichrist rise out of the Roman Empire? Even those with only a vague knowledge of history know that the Roman Empire has long since turned to dust and ashes. However, a case for a Revived Roman Empire can be made today.

In the second chapter of the Book of Daniel, we find the startling account of the dream of Nebuchadnezzar, king of Babylon. The dream had been very troubling to

Nebuchadnezzar, but he could not remember what the dream was about. He gathered his sorcerers and sooth-sayers before him, asking them to tell him what the dream was and to reveal its meaning. When they could not, Nebuchadnezzar ordered that all the wise men of Babylon be sentenced to death. This decree condemned the prophet Daniel and his companions as well. However, Daniel managed to convince Nebuchadnezzar to give him some time to pray to God, and He would reveal the interpretation of Nebuchadnezzar's dream. God revealed the dream and its meaning to Daniel in a night vision (verse 19).

What the king had seen, Daniel explained, was a great image that resembled a man (Daniel 2:31-45). This "man" had a head of gold. His chest and arms were made of silver. His belly and thighs were made of brass. His legs were made of iron and his feet were part iron and part clay. Since the king couldn't figure out what this meant, he was greatly pleased when Daniel was able to interpret the dream for him. Imagine his surprise when the Hebrew prophet told the king that what he had seen was an outline of the future, from Nebuchadnezzar's day until the end of history!

The image was made of various metals, representing four different kingdoms in history that would rule over the earth, Daniel revealed. The first of these was Nebuchadnezzar's Babylon. Daniel simply said, "You are this head of gold." This was the perfect symbol for the empire, since Babylon was known as the Golden City.

However, the king then learned that "after you will arise another kingdom inferior to you." This kingdom was represented by the silver chest and arms, the two arms representing a two-part kingdom. In 539 B.C., just as prophesied, the Medo-Persian armies conquered Babylon and became the new superpower of the day (Daniel 5:30-31). Never as powerful as Babylon, the Medo-Persian empire was silver compared to the Babylonian golden age.

After that, the prophet spoke of "another third kingdom of brass, which shall bear rule over all the earth."[11] History tells us that the Greek Empire, under the leadership of Alexander the Great, defeated Persia in 331 B.C. His kingdom extended from India to Egypt and Europe—the entire known world. Alexander even decreed that he be called "King of the World." That empire was symbolized by the abdomen and thighs made of brass (cf. Daniel 8:20-21).

Finally, Daniel spoke of a fourth kingdom that would be as strong as iron. The two iron legs of the statue represented the power that succeeded Greece—the Roman Empire, whose armies were called the "iron legions." In 63 B.C., the Romans conquered all the lands surrounding the Mediterranean and ruled for over 500 years with an iron fist. However, that is where the historical record matching Nebuchadnezzar's dream came to an end for many centuries. There has been no superpower in history after the Roman Empire that has corresponded to the description of the feet made partly of iron and partly of clay.

Many students of Bible prophecy, however, believe that this empire, which is merely an extension of the fourth, the Roman Empire, can be identified today.

The Case for a Revived Roman Empire

Can we actually see anything in existence today that could be considered at least an embryo of the Revived Roman Empire? Yes. Go back to 1951, when what was known as the European Coal and Steel Community [ECSC] came into being. This was the seed from which prophecy buffs believe the Revived Roman Empire began to grow. In 1957, with the signing of the Treaty of Rome, the ECSC sprouted to become the European Economic Community. Then, as time went by, the EEC extended its powers beyond the economic sphere. It therefore became known as the European Community. Again, by the mid-1990's, the powers of the EC had continued to grow. Being described as a community no longer seemed appropriate, so it became the European Union (EU). It is the modern-day EU that many students of Bible prophecy believe fits the description of the final world empire revealed in Nebuchadnezzar's dream. After all, it's no secret that the modern-day EU is made up of territory that once belonged to the ancient Roman Empire.

Some students of Bible prophecy believe that what we should be watching for is the emergence of a kingdom with the exact same boundaries as the original Roman Empire. This teaching, however, overlooks the fact that the prophecy tells us the final world empire is an outgrowth from and an evolution of the fourth empire, not just a duplicate of it. The ten toes on the image in Nebuchadnezzar's dream (or ten horns, as they are identified in Daniel 7) represent an entirely new phase of the Roman Empire. J. Dwight Pentecost notes:

> This beast is seen to be the successor to the three preceding empires. This may suggest not only the idea of power, but also geographical extent, so that this final form of Gentile power may encompass all the territory held by all the predecessors.[12]

Some students of Bible prophecy also believe that the Revived Roman Empire will only consist of ten nations. At the time of writing, the European Union has fifteen member nations with more expected to join in the future.

However, some still hold to the ten-nation concept, claiming that the EU is just temporarily oversized and some nations will drop out. Others believe there will be ten core nations forming the Revived Roman Empire. This idea centers on the belief that the ten toes (or ten horns) represent ten nations. The problem with this theory is that it overlooks the clear wording of Scripture:

> I considered the [ten] horns, and behold, there came up among them [that is, from among the ten horns] another little horn, before whom there were three of the *first* [ten] horns plucked up by the roots.[13]

> The ten horns out of this kingdom are ten kings that shall arise: and another shall arise after them [after the ten]; and he shall be diverse from the first [ten], and he shall subdue three kings.[14]

First of all, from a biblical point of view, we must note that the ten horns are identified clearly as ten "kings" in the last days. Nowhere are these ten horns identified as "nations." So it appears that the Revived Roman Empire could very well extend beyond the boundaries of ten nations.

Second, this would fit with what we see taking place in real time today. As we mentioned earlier, at the time of writing, the European Union has fifteen member nations. Furthermore, many nations from Eastern Europe, now that they are free from the clutches of the former Soviet Union, are lined up at the door waiting for entry, and it appears they will be welcome inside. Indeed, it seems that since the Cold War ended, just about everyone is scrambling to be accepted in some way into the European Union.

There is no question that one of the greatest symbols of a changing world and a changing Europe was the dismantling of the Berlin Wall. Europe had been ravaged by tribal and national wars for centuries. Following the atrocities of World War II, the Berlin Wall divided the continent into east and west; the east being robbed of its historical and cultural identity by the military force of the Soviet Union. The west came under the influence and protection of the world's other superpower: the U.S. When the Berlin Wall finally came down, it seemed that the continent long divided by the Cold War could finally be united in peace. The world recognized that a united Europe was about to rise to prominence in the world. After all, the west had already become an economic and military force to be reckoned with in the world.

Even Russia, once driven by the need to conquer the world for communism, has not been ignorant of Europe's place as a significant emerging world power. On January 25, 1996, the Council of Europe voted 164-35 to allow Russia to join its 38-member body. The move was a step towards fulfilling former Soviet President Mikhail Gorbachev's desire that his nation be part of the new Europe. It was at the Council of Europe's headquarters in Strasbourg that Gorbachev made his speech about Russia becoming part of a "common European house."

Canadian politicians also began to make it clear that they did not want to be left standing outside of this European house. Former Canadian External Affairs Minster Joe Clark explained:

> You have almost a renaissance in Europe, in its sense of its role in the world. . . . If there was a time when Europe may have felt it was secondary to the United States or Japan, that time has passed. There's a sense that they are where the action is.[15]

Even former U.S. Secretary of State James Baker began to speak of "the New Europe and the New Atlanticism."[16]

The euphoria over this "New Atlanticism" never waned in the years that followed. Indeed, it only grew stronger. In September of 1994, *Intelligence Digest* observed:

> We have noted an increase in the number of calls for a Transatlantic Treaty to replace NATO as the main interface between Europe and America. . . .

> In April 1993, the outgoing U.S. ambassador to the European Union, James Dobbins, called for "institutional innovation on the order of the Atlantic Alliance and the European Community" in order to reconstruct relations between America and Europe in the post-Cold War world.

> In Europe, the pressure for a Transatlantic Treaty comes most from Germany. In November 1992 Chancellor Kohl specifically expressed his hope that the two existing Transatlantic declarations between the EC and the U.S./Canada would be translated into a comprehensive treaty between Europe and North America in due course.

> The intention of those who advocate a Transatlantic Treaty is fourfold. First, by agreeing to a treaty between the European Union and North America rather than between 12 or more individual states, this will bring non-NATO members such as Ireland and Austria into the institutional structure; second, unlike NATO the new treaty will cover economic relations; third, the very action of negotiating such a treaty will have the effect of solidifying the European Union's common foreign and security policy; and fourth, at least in the economic sphere, the negotiation of the treaty will have the same effect on NAFTA (the North American Free Trade Agreement, which links the U.S. with Canada and Mexico in a trade bloc).[17]

Great strides have been made towards this transatlantic alliance since. In early 1996, the U.S. and the EU:

... reached agreement on an ambitious action-plan for deepening political and economic relations in the post cold war era.

The blueprint was signed in December in Madrid at a meeting attended by President Bill Clinton, Prime Minister Felipe Gonzalez of Spain, and President Jacques Santer of the European Commission.

The action-plan covers 150 points, from faster trade liberalization in telecoms and maritime shipping to joint action to tackle organized crime and killer viruses. Beyond the declaration's immediate promise of a "transatlantic marketplace" is the hope of a future free trade area.[18]

Indeed, it appears that the powers and influence of the Revived Roman Empire will expand well beyond the borders of its ancient predecessor. As Harlan Cleveland, an insider in numerous global think tanks, including the Aspen Institute, noted:

The European Community will be at the center of things...

Europe's destiny is no longer in Europe. It is now so bound up with the future of the globe—with world security, the world economy, world development, the global environment—that there is no such thing as a "European" solution to the questions that matter. ... The puzzle is whether Europe's economic integration will gradually produce also a new kind of world power, a collective projection of European civilization.[19]

More significantly, the idea of the Revived Roman Empire's influence expanding over the globe is fully in keeping with Bible prophecy concerning the scope of the Antichrist's reign:

> Power was given him over all kindreds, and tongues, and nations.[20]

The Democratic Kingdom of the Antichrist

Another element of the Revived Roman Empire that is distinct from its predecessor is the addition of "clay" to the mix. As the prophet Daniel explained to Nebuchadnezzar:

> Whereas thou sawest the feet and toes, part of potters' clay, and part of iron, the kingdom shall be divided; but there shall be in it the strength of the iron, forasmuch as thou sawest the iron mixed with miry clay. And as the toes of the feet were part of iron, and part of clay, so the kingdom shall be partly strong, and partly broken.[21]

Just what do the iron and the clay most likely represent? This is important because these are the two defining characteristics of this last-days form of the Roman Empire. J. Dwight Pentecost notes:

> The final form of the Gentile power is marked by a federation of that which is weak and that which is strong, autocracy and democracy, the iron and the clay.[22]

So the clay represents the addition of democracy. While liberal democracy is a product of the twentieth century, it has taken much of its inspiration from the ancient Romans. Indeed, the U.S. even adopted some of Rome's structure and symbols—the Senate, for example, and the Roman eagle, which was selected as the American icon.

The emperors of the Roman Empire managed to establish a peaceful political system with the introduction of some democratic processes. *Pax Romana* had really been pieced together and enforced through military conquest and strength. In his classic book *The Decline and Fall of the Roman Empire*, Edward Gibbon wrote:

> In the second century of the Christian era, the Empire of Rome comprehended the fairest part of the earth, and the most civilised portion of mankind. The frontiers of that extensive monarchy were guarded by ancient renown and disciplined valour. The gentle but powerful influence of laws and manners had gradually cemented the union of the provinces. Their peaceful inhabitants enjoyed and abused the advantages of wealth and luxury. The image of a free constitution was preserved with decent reverence: the Roman senate appeared to possess the sovereign authority, and devolved on the emperors all the executive powers of government.[23]

The Roman Empire, however, could not really be described as a democratic power system Gibbon added:

> The terror of the Roman arms added weight and dignity to the moderation of the emperors. They preserved peace by a constant preparation for war; and while justice regulated their conduct, they announced to the nations on their confines that they were as little disposed to endure as to offer an injury.[24]

Since the decline and fall of the Roman Empire in A.D. 476, Charlemagne, Napoleon, Hitler, and others have tried to reunite Europe by force. It has never worked. Yet now, exactly as the Bible has prophesied, Europe is coming together, not through military conquest and iron force, but through democracy: the clay of the kingdom in its final form.

Indeed, democracy has become widely respected across the globe, and is sweeping the nations of the world. Who would have thought before the Berlin Wall came down in 1989 that democracy would be allowed to begin to expand freely without Communist interference? Nonetheless, democracy has prevailed, and it appears that it will only grow in strength and popularity. Harlan Cleveland observed:

> The main trading economies are, by no coincidence, the world's leading democracies. It's in their mutual interest to enhance the economic environment for expanding political democracy worldwide. . . .
>
> An open-ended club of democracies is already in formation as the best kind of living monument to the democracy movements of recent years.[25]

Indeed, the leading nations in the world today are trying to establish universal peace by spreading the concept of democratic cooperation, rather than through military conquest. While it is true that some military strength may be used to hold the empire together in the future, the world, beginning with the European Union, has managed to start piecing together a modern-day form of *Pax Romana* through the democratic process. This is what makes the Revived Roman Empire different from its predecessor.

However, it may not only be the fact that the Revived Roman Empire will combine autocracy with democracy—the iron and the clay—that makes it different from any other world power that has existed in the past. It is very possible that the *type* of democracy that dominates the

Revived Roman Empire will be unlike any that has existed as well. It could well be a democratic system that is unique to the Revived Roman Empire, rather than one that already exists in the democracies of the world today. Such an idea fits with calls we are beginning to hear today for the establishment of a "new democracy."

New Democracy in the Revived Roman Empire

We hear much talk today of a *new* world order. If, however, Bible prophecy is true concerning the Revived Roman Empire being an extension of the former Roman Empire, we should also expect to see some elements from the *old* order being revived as well. Take the current trend of removing sovereignty from the nation-state as an example. The nation-state never existed in the Roman Empire, nor in the Holy Roman Empire, which dominated Europe from the fourteenth to the nineteenth century. It is very likely, therefore, that it will not exist in its revived form either. During the rule of the Holy Roman Empire, attempts were made to unite Europe, but the semblance of unity was only established by force and frequent brutality. As Protestantism began to expand, European princes found new opportunities to rebel against the Holy Roman Empire during the Reformation. The façade of unity began to fall apart. Out of the midst of the ensuing chaos, the nation-state was born in the seventeenth century, the brain-child of Cardinal de Richelieu of France. Richelieu was very much a French nationalist. His concerns focused more on the affairs and strength of France, which would be placed in jeopardy by a united Europe under the reign of the Holy

Roman Empire. Richelieu, noted Henry Kissinger, "feared a unified Central Europe and prevented it from coming about. In all likelihood, he delayed German unification by some two centuries. . . . Richelieu thwarted the Habsburgs and the Holy Roman Empire was divided among more than 300 sovereigns, each free to conduct an independent foreign policy."[1]

As we return to Roman influence, however, we should be hearing calls for the dismantling of the nation-state system. We should be hearing calls for a united world order resembling the unity and universal peace that had been experienced under Roman rule. We should be hearing calls for the removal of authority from the individual nation-state to be placed in the hands of a global government reminiscent of Roman authority. Are we hearing such calls today? Indeed we are. In a special report, Intelligence International Ltd. observed:

> There have long been advocates of world government in the U.S. and elsewhere. A statement of their aims will set the scene. On 17 February 1950, for instance, a leading member of the Council on Foreign Relations, James P. Warburg, told a U.S. Senate Committee: "We shall have world government whether we like it or not . . . by consent or by conquest."

> In 1976, Professor Saul Mendlovitz, director of the World Order Models Project, said there is "no longer a question of whether or not there will be a world government by the year 2000."

> One prominent advocate of global government is Zbigniew Brzezinski, who served as national security adviser to President Carter. Over 20 years ago he declared in his book *Between Two Ages* that "national sovereignty is no longer a viable concept." He suggested a piecemeal "movement toward a larger community of developed

nations . . . through a variety of indirect ties and already-developing limitations on national sovereignty."[2]

While globalists were at one time more openly vocal about the need for a world government, the intelligence report added that:

> More recently, the advocates of world government have toned down their rhetoric, not wanting to frighten the audience. For instance, Senator Alan Cranston (D-Calif.), a former president of United World Federalists, told *Transition*, a publication of the Institute for World Order, that: "The more talk about world government, the less chance of achieving it, because it frightens people who would accept the concept of world laws." He added: "I believe deeply in the need for world law . . . I believe in the concept of federalism on the world scale."[3]

Indeed, people have had to be persuaded through media campaigns to accept the concept of global institutions and world laws gradually, in a piecemeal fashion just as Brzezinski had suggested. Furthermore, fears of global nuclear devastation during the Cold War were widely publicized, and so was the solution: placing the problem in the hands of a global overseer such as the United Nations. People the world over began to unite in protest, believing that only some global institution could keep nations possessing nuclear weapons in line. Then when the Cold War ended, a new problem of global proportions surfaced: environmental degradation. Again, being gently persuaded by media campaigns such as "Our Common Future," which was based on a U.N. Commission report, the peoples of the world united in protest. They were being convinced that only a global institution could ensure that individual nation-states would follow guidelines for turning the world around. The peoples of the world have been told that only an international court can bring justice for crimes such as the war crimes that recently took place in Bosnia under the banner of "ethnic cleansing." They have been told that only global economic institutions can ensure world trade is conducted fairly, and that only they can oversee the fair distribution of the world's resources to poorer nations. After years of consciousness-raising through the media, piece by piece the world is beginning to accept the increasing authority of global institutions such as the United Nations and the World Trade Organization. Global elitists have successfully convinced people there is no other way.

Indeed, the nation-state is seen as a hindrance to solving problems that affect the entire world. How can a national politician focus on solving global environmental problems, for instance, when he or she has to solve problems of unemployment at home? Four years is just not enough time to be concerned about the world's problems, especially if the politician wants to be re-elected for another term in his own nation-state. World government, say globalists, would get rid of such selfish concerns, allowing the rulers of the world to focus on bigger issues.

The Economic Solution

Another hindrance to a new world order, we are told, is the gap between the economic prosperity of some nations and the poverty of others. Mikhail Gorbachev, for instance, noted that one of the problems facing the international community is:

> The growing gap in the level and quality of socioeconomic development between rich and poor

countries.... Through television, those in poverty can see the material well-being of the wealthy. Hence the unprecedented passions and brutality and even fanaticism of mass protests. Here, too, is the breeding ground for the spread of terrorism and the emergence and persistence of dictatorial regimes with their unpredictable behavior in relations among states.[4]

If there was a fair distribution of the wealth, globalists tell us, one of the main causes for conflict will have been diminished. This is exactly what the United Nations had in mind when it held its "World Summit for Social Development" in Copenhagen, Denmark in March 1995. Prior to the summit, the U.N. was distributing a fact sheet titled "The World Summit for Social Development" to explain the goals of and purpose behind the gathering of heads of states. According to the fact sheet:

> The Summit furthers the commitment, made in the Charter of the United Nations, to promote higher standards of living, full employment, and conditions of economic and social progress and development with a view to the creation of conditions of stability and well-being.[5]

By wiping out poverty, which leads to social disorder, which then leads to war, there will be world peace, or so the theory goes. The U.N. literature went on to explain:

> The struggle against poverty has been part and parcel of the intellectual and political evolution of the notion of social progress in world culture since the end of the eighteenth century.[6]

> "The world can never be at peace unless people have security in their daily lives," say the authors of *Human Development Report 1994*, a study

commissioned by the United Nations Development Programme. Future conflicts may often be within nations rather than between them—with their origins buried deep in growing socio-economic deprivation and disparities. The search for security in such a milieu lies in development, not arms.[7]

Man's solution to these problems then is global socialism:

The interdependence of economic and financial decisions, often via multi-national corporations, has helped fuel a rapid expansion of markets. But the benefits are not being apportioned equally, as in the case of developing countries that have not been able to share in globalized foreign investments. New forms of international cooperation must be devised that will make it possible for all to share in the positive aspects of economic globalization.[8]

God's Word, however, tells us that wars come from our own lusts and greed:

From whence come wars and fightings among you? come they not hence, even of your lusts that war in your members?

Ye lust, and have not: ye kill, and desire to have, and cannot obtain: ye fight and war, yet ye have not, because ye ask not.

Ye ask, and receive not, because ye ask amiss, that ye may consume it upon your lusts.[9]

Man has decided, however, to ignore God's warnings to and solutions for mankind. Man has decided to try and build a kingdom of peace on earth without Him.

Unfortunately, many politicians in the world today are now treating the Middle East conflict as an economic problem as well. Even God's chosen people are trying to, once again, establish peace in the Middle East without the Prince of Peace. For example, failing to recognize that the Middle East conflict between Arabs and Jews actually has spiritual roots going back to Isaac and Ishmael, and Jacob and Esau, Shimon Peres believes that resolving the issue of poverty in the Middle East will ultimately bring peace to the region. While serving as Israeli Foreign Minister, Peres wrote:

> The world has changed. And the process of change compels us to replace our outdated concepts with an approach tailored to the new reality . . .

> Thus, the key to maintaining an equable and safe regional system is in politics and in economics . . .

> The scale has tipped in the direction of economics rather than military might.[10]

Interestingly, Mr. Peres also noted in the midst of this quote:

> There is, however, an alternative approach [to national military might]: bilateral and multilateral pacts, extending beyond the borders of the countries involved and covering the entire expanse within reach of the deadly missiles—that is, treaties that cover whole regions.[11]

The development towards regional pacts is exactly what we are already seeing take place today.

Regionalism

Just as globalists have planned, the borders of individual nation-states will slowly begin to disappear. In the meantime, individual nations are beginning to merge together through regional pacts and treaties. We have seen such regions come together under economic agreements such as the EFTA (European Free Trade Association), NAFTA (North American Free Trade Agreement), ASEAN (Association of South East Asian Nations), APEC (Asia-Pacific Economic Cooperation Forum), and, of course, the European Union. Indeed, it appears that regional pacts could be one of the key catalysts for dismantling the nation-state and for a unified world order. As Kenichi Ohmae, author and director of McKinsey and Company, Inc., stated:

> What we are seeing now is the disappearance of these national borders, as evidenced in Europe. The emergence of regional states is quite clear . . .
>
> The same borderless phenomenon is taking place in North America [i.e., with NAFTA]. . . .
>
> [A]s the national borders disappear between Canada and the U.S., regions emerge and the regions around the five Great Lakes will become very important. . . .
>
> Countries like Canada with very long national borders—horizontally very long—will be very difficult to govern as one nation. For example, Vancouver has much more to do with Japan and China, particularly with Hong Kong, than with Toronto and Quebec.
>
> One of the attractive features of Orange County is that it has this region state formation with northern Mexico.[12]

Interestingly, it appears then that it is through the economic sphere that the concept of regionalism has really come into its own. Take the European Union as an example. Intelligence International Ltd. explained:

> Part of the subterfuge, in the attempt to move towards supranational government without anyone noticing it much, has been to concentrate on the economic and trade spheres. . . .

> The European Union (EU) is the best and most-developed example of this. When the British were faced with the question of whether or not to join this organization in 1972, it was a Common Market they were joining. It progressed to become the European Economic Community, then the European Community, and finally the European Union.

> This progression in nomenclature has been matched by a progression in the accumulation of supranational powers. . . .

> In other words, regional trade blocs lead inevitably to regional government, with supra-national authority . . . until there is little or nothing left for national governments to control . . . [13]

Indeed, globalists would like to see the EU model applied to the entire world, divided into regions rather than nation-states. And who would govern these regions? Perhaps the United Nations. The U.N. Charter was designed with regional government in mind. On the U.N.'s 50th birthday, U.N. Secretary General Boutros Boutros-Ghali explained:

> It was a major advance for world affairs when in 1945 regionalism was enshrined in Article Eight of the United Nations Charter as an essential component of international cooperation.

Chapter Eight of the Charter deliberately refrains from defining very precisely what it means by "regional arrangements and agencies." But it clearly sees regionalism and internationalism working not at odds, but together.

This vision motivated the U.N. in its earliest years to create regional economic commissions. During the Cold War period the United Nations Economic Commission for Europe (ECE) was one of the few effective bodies whose membership spanned both eastern and western Europe. . . .

In the political and security fields, however, for more than four decades little use was made of Chapter Eight of the United Nations Charter. Regional bodies were often under suspicion as being possible instruments of the superpowers.

Boutros-Ghali added that in the post-Cold War years this is beginning to change, noting:

Regional associations are essential to international democratisation. . . . They facilitate the process of democratisation of the international system.[14]

Democratizing the U.N.

Today, many are suggesting that as the world becomes more interdependent, the democratic systems practiced in individual nation-states may no longer suffice. Perhaps it is time, they suggest, that we look at revamping democracy as we know it. As David Held, Professor of Politics and Sociology at the Open University, noted:

More and more nations and groups are championing the idea of "the rule of the people"; but they are doing so at just that moment when the very efficacy of *democracy as a national form of political organization* appears open to question [emphasis added].

Held concluded that:

> As substantial areas of human activity are progressively organized on a global level, the fate of democracy, and of the independent democratic nation-state in particular, is fraught with difficulty. In this context, the meaning and place of democratic politics, and of the contending models of democracy, have to be rethought in relation to overlapping local, national, regional, and global structures and processes.[15]

There are many, including Mr. Held, who believe that the United Nations should be at the center of a new global democracy. Take the following comments by Hanna Newcombe, editor of *Peace Research Abstracts Journal*, and co-founder of the Canadian Peace Research and Education Association, as an example. When speaking on the concept of a new world order that had begun with the Persian Gulf War, Newcombe noted that it appeared to be a world order dominated by the U.S. She suggested:

> Instead of *Pax Americana*, we should aim at *Pax Democratica*. It would be a multilaterally structured world system without a ruling hegemon, under the regime of a universal world organization, a revamped United Nations—what we have called the Third Generation System [the first being the League of Nations, and the second being the U.N. in its present form]. *Democratica* in this sense means both democratically structured as between nations, and composed of states which are democratically structured internally.[16]

Former Soviet president Mikhail Gorbachev has been heard calling for new democracy as well. Speaking to an audience of 3,500 leading businessmen and financiers in Tulsa, Oklahoma, Gorbachev noted, "Democratic systems need to be reinvented.... Two important ways to do this are through more citizen involvement and decentralization."[17]

Notice that Gorbachev claimed one way to reinvent democracy is "through more citizen involvement." Indeed, this is an idea that is becoming more prevalent in the new world order that is being born. Speaking on U.N. reform, Hanna Newcombe explained the idea of citizen involvement in a new democratized world:

> To democratize the United Nations further, we should consider adding a House of Peoples or a People's Assembly to present "House Nations" (the General Assembly).[18]

Newcombe suggested this could be done by allowing Non-Governmental Organizations (NGOs) to get involved, or through elected parliamentarians from nation-states. She added:

> One might argue that a People's Assembly based on parliamentarians is more representative democratically, since parliamentarians are directly elected in their own countries, at least in those that are democracies internally. However, a People's Assembly based on NGOs would present, though in a somewhat hap-hazard self-selected manner, the informed or politically involved sector of each nation's public opinion, skipping the apathetic or uninformed population sector. The ultimate ideal, of course, is direct elections, but the above two are suggestions for intermediate states.[19]

Indeed, it appears essentially that the end goal is for the U.N. to become the federal government of the world, with officials directly elected by the nations of the world. But as Newcombe pointed out, NGOs may better represent the People's Assembly. In other words, it appears that when you delve deeper into the thoughts of globalists, the concept of "citizen involvement" on a national level may just be a lot of rhetoric. The ultimate goal is simply to bypass the nation-state so that a global government headed by the U.N. would be representing the peoples of the world directly. Nation-states, it seems, would simply place their sovereignty in the hands of a global government headed by the U.N., and would then eventually disappear. As Michael Oliver, National President of the United Nations Association in Canada, commented:

> One pathway to change that is enjoying increasing support is the democratization of the U.N. The famous "We the Peoples . . . " phrase that opens the preamble to the U.N. Charter invites us to look forward to a time when states and their governments no longer monopolize the exercise of power within the U.N., a time when decisions are reached by a more participatory process. *No one expects the sovereign state to fade quickly away, but perhaps it can begin to share power* [emphasis added].[20]

Again, however, the idea of the citizens being actively involved in the decision-making process is highly unlikely. It would seem unlikely that the global architects would leave it in the hands of the general population around the world—most of whom would be apathetic or uninformed, as Newcombe pointed out—to make critical decisions, the effects of which would be felt across the globe. Ultimately, what it seems that globalists have in mind is for the real thinking to be left up to a group of select persons.

A Global Brain Trust

Bible prophecy tells us that at some point in the tribulation period, ten kings are going to rule with the Antichrist for a brief time:

> The ten horns which thou sawest are ten kings, which have received no kingdom as yet; but receive power as kings one hour with the beast. These have one mind, and shall give their power and strength unto the beast.[21]

It is impossible to say exactly who these ten kings are or what will be their role in the last days. Perhaps they will be ten kings from royal bloodlines, or ten of the world's most brilliant thinkers who will work with the Antichrist to bring about peace, unity, and prosperity to the earth. The concept of these ten kings being some of the world's most brilliant thinkers would tie in with another trend we have seen develop in recent years, that of a council of select persons.

Back in 1990, Ramses Nassif, press spokesman for former U.N. Secretary General U Thant, had noted:

> How then could the United Nations be reformed and modernized? I think a group or a commission of eminent persons is needed.... Jimmy Carter ... could make an able chairman for such a commission.[22]

Likewise, the United Nations Association, UNA, has called for a "Global Watch Committee" of prestigious leaders to lead the international community.

Reacting to the 1987 stock market crash known as Black Monday, Paul Streeten of Oxford University had suggested "a surrender of some national sovereignty and the transfer of sufficient power to the decision makers who could manage the system . . . a Council of Wise Persons."[23]

Even Mikhail Gorbachev has promoted such an idea in the past several years. More recently, he called the concept a "global brain trust" at the State of the World Forum held in San Francisco from September 27 to October 1, 1995. More than 500 heads of state, spiritual leaders, corporate heads, scientists, and intellectuals gathered for the prestigious event. In his opening address, Gorbachev told his elite audience:

> The most that we can hope to achieve is to try to understand the main tendencies that are shaping the world today and caution the decision makers against imprudent actions and errors of judgment. To do this, we shall need to think together, and more than one such discussion will be required.
>
> So from the outset, I would like to suggest that we consider the establishment of a kind of global brain trust to focus on the present and the future of our civilization.[24]

Futurist author John Naisbitt supported Gorbachev's concept of a global brain trust:

> It is time to start a "State of the World Network," a network of the global brain trust that you speak of, a network that will link all of us and expand our number for continuous dialogue on the creation of the first global civilization.[25]

Of course, globalists are vague about such a would-be power. Would they be elected officials? Or would they be self-appointed? The most detail given by Gorbachev was:

> This idea of a brain trust can only succeed if en-
> dorsed and actively pursued by people who are
> widely respected as world leaders and global cit-
> izens.[26]

Of course, we are not saying that any of the participants in such a possible future global brain trust are necessarily going to be among the eventual ten kings that will
rule briefly with the Antichrist. All we are saying is that
the prophesied pattern is definitely beginning to emerge.

A Global Head of State

Before we go further, let's briefly sum up the new
world order based on the new democracy that seems to
be developing today. First, global visionaries anticipate
nation-states slowly sharing power with a global institution such as the U.N. Eventually they would like to see
nation-states hand over all of their sovereign rights to this
global institution and merge together with other nations
to form regional governments. In essence, this global institution would play the role of the White House in the
U.S., or the Canadian Parliament, but on a global scale.

Next, global visionaries would like the people of the
world to elect officials to this new global government.
They would perhaps prefer that they be represented by
NGO's at this global level. Allowing the people to play
some kind of participating role in the U.N., for example,
would give the global institution the semblance of being
democratic. However, the real thinking would be left up
to a group of global advisors, such as Gorbachev's global
brain trust.

All that seems to be missing in this democratic new world order is a supreme leader. Interestingly, part and parcel of the calls for U.N. reform have been calls to reform the office of the Secretary General. Geoffrey Grenville-Wood, the former National President of UNA/Canada noted:

> One major area that clearly needs reform is the office of the Secretary-General itself. It would seem that not enough attention has been paid to the role the Secretary-General is expected to play on the world scene. In the public's mind, he is seen as the world's foremost international civil servant. The office is the embodiment of the hopes of mankind for a peaceful and prosperous world. Unfortunately, the reality is that the office has no real independent authority and is severely circumscribed by budgetary and political considerations. In the new era this reality will have to change.[2]

Grenville-Wood suggested that the place to start may be in the way a U.N. Secretary-General is selected. He went on to mention a 1990 report on U.N. leadership that had been put together by Erskine Childers and Brian Urquhart. Interestingly, the report recommended that the office of the Secretary General "be limited to a seven-year single term." Is this a foreshadow of the seven-year tribulation period prophesied by Scripture?

Indeed, it appears that the elements of the Antichrist's democratic kingdom on earth, right down to a possible seven-year term, are even now in the development stage.

6

Spirituality in the Revived Roman Empire

A few years ago we visited the city of Rome. One of the first things that drew our attention was the fact that there were so many remains from temples dedicated to gods and goddesses in the city, mixed with churches claiming to represent all of Christendom. What was left standing of the Roman Forum—which was the center of political, legal, administrative, and religious life in Rome—housed the remains of such structures as the Temple of Vespasian, the Temple of Saturn, the shrine and fountain of Juturna, and the Temple of Venus and Rome.

We purchased a book from one of the many street vendors displaying their wares for the vast number of tourists who visit Rome each year. Under the section "Religion and the Temples" we read:

> The Roman religion, just as it had welcomed from the beginning the Etruscan triad, so during the course of the centuries generously adopted the divinities of all the people who became part of the civilisation of Rome; indeed, the Greek divinities, which were already famous in literature and art, were assimilated with the old Italic divinities, which had a completely different character. Thus Hera became Juno, Athene was turned into Minerva, Ares

into Mars, Aphrodite into Venus, and so on; only Apollo remained as he had been in Greek mythology. Thus the Greek Olympus became the Roman Olympus, which was further enriched by many other foreign divinities, such as the Magna Mater (Cybele) who had her temple on the Palatine, Isis who had a large sanctuary built in the Egyptian style in the Campus Martius, the oriental divinities whose sanctuary has been discovered on the Janculum, and finally Mithras, the Persian God of the Sun, whose worship, which included initiations, mysteries and symbolic ceremonies, spread more than any other cult. . . .

New divinities, which we might call political, also became part of this Olympus: the Goddess Rome, Concordia, *the deified Augustus and the other emperors who had proved themselves deserving of deification. . . .*

At the highest point in civilisation of the Empire, Hadrian, the emperor who was architect, poet and philosopher, decided to reunite, almost symbolically, the forms of Greek architecture and Roman architecture in the Pantheon, *dedicated to all the gods.* This was Rome's greatest temple; is also the only one to have come down to us intact and the only one in which Christianity was grafted directly onto pagan worship [emphasis added].[1]

Indeed, the fact that the Roman Empire had embraced all religions, all gods and goddesses, was certainly in evidence from the ruins left standing in the center of its history. But a description of the history of the Roman Empire would not be complete without mentioning the influence Christendom had on it. Of this influence Edward Gibbon wrote:

A candid but rational inquiry into the progress and establishment of Christianity may be considered as a very essential part of the history of the Roman empire. While that great body was invaded by open violence, or undermined by slow decay, a pure and humble religion gently insinuated itself into the minds of men, grew up in silence and obscurity, derived new vigour from opposition, and finally erected the triumphant banner of the Cross on the ruins of the Capitol. Nor was the influence of Christianity confined to the period or to the limits of the Roman empire. After a revolution of thirteen or fourteen centuries, that religion is still professed by the nations of Europe.[2]

As the Revived Roman Empire rises from the dust on the pages of history, we should expect to see Christendom, and other faiths from the nations of the world—including those deemed pagan—having an influence on the new civilization that is waiting to be born. We believe that we are indeed seeing this trend today.

Christendom Under the Holy Roman Empire

The political system that dominated Europe between the eighth and fourteenth centuries was known as feudalism. There was no centralized power in this system, or anywhere in the Holy Roman Empire—only a fragmented web of urban centers, rural areas, monarchies, and duchies. Claimants to power over these localized areas were constantly in conflict. The result was frequent war and tension. There was, however, one apparent unifying element during that period. That unifying factor was "Christendom" under the authority of the Roman Catholic church. David Held explains:

> The Holy Roman Empire existed in some form from the eighth until the early nineteenth century. At its height, it represented an attempt, under the patronage of the Catholic Church, to unite and

centralize the fragmented power centres of
Western Christendom into a politically unified
Christian empire.

In medieval Europe there was no alternative "political theory" to the theocratic positions of pope
and the Holy Roman emperor.[3]

The supposed unity of the Holy Roman empire broke
down when "Christendom" and the authority of the papacy came under scrutiny during the Reformation.
Seeking to escape papal authority, the peoples of the Holy
Roman Empire strove to develop political systems apart
from the Roman Catholic Church.

In essence, therefore, the nation-state was born out of
a challenge to the authority of the papacy over politics.
Zbigniew Brzezinski noted:

The French Revolution was also critical in injecting
into the emerging European national consciousness strong doses of idealism, of faith in the un-
limited scope of reason, and of a secular bias
against established religion. . . .

To the extent that the church had buttressed the
traditional order, its power had to be broken. Its
precepts were to be replaced by the elevation of
the notion of loyalty to the nation-state as the
highest moral imperative. Moreover, the confident
belief that "rationality"—rather than religiously
defined morality—could guide political behavior
generated a propensity to engage in social engi-
neering for the sake of idealistic goals.[4]

As the Roman Empire begins to appear on the world
stage in its revived form, we should expect to see a re-
versal of the nation-state as a divider between church and
state. We should expect to hear more calls for the inter-

twining of religion and Christendom with politics once again. God's prophetic Word is clear that religion will indeed be an influential factor during the tribulation period. Following the rapture of the true church at the beginning of the seven-year tribulation period, there will be a false church that comes into existence. And since Christendom had such an influence over the Roman Empire, it is likely to be a characteristic element of the Revived Roman Empire, as well as the faiths of the world that join this new Roman civilization.

The Religious Whore

The apostle John on the isle of Patmos was given a vision of this false church, which he saw as a whore riding upon a beast:

> There came one of the seven angels which had the seven vials, and talked with me, saying unto me, Come hither; I will shew unto thee the judgment of the great whore that sitteth upon many waters: With whom the kings of the earth have committed fornication, and the inhabitants of the earth have been made drunk with the wine of her fornication.

> So he carried me away in the spirit into the wilderness: and I saw a woman sit upon a scarlet coloured beast, full of names of blasphemy, having seven heads and ten horns.

> And the woman was arrayed in purple and scarlet colour, and decked with gold and precious stones and pearls, having a golden cup in her hand full of abominations and filthiness of her fornication:

> And upon her forehead was a name written, MYSTERY BABYLON THE GREAT, THE MOTHER OF HARLOTS AND ABOMINATIONS OF THE EARTH.

> And I saw the woman drunken with the blood of the saints, and with the blood of the martyrs of Jesus: and when I saw her, I wondered with great admiration.
>
> And the angel said unto me, Wherefore didst thou marvel? I will tell thee the mystery of the woman, and of the beast that carrieth her, which hath the seven heads and ten horns.
>
> The beast that thou sawest was, and is not; and shall ascend out of the bottomless pit, and go into perdition: and they that dwell on the earth shall wonder, whose names were not written in the book of life from the foundation of the world, when they behold the beast that was, and is not, and yet is.
>
> And here is the mind which hath wisdom. The seven heads are seven mountains, on which the woman sitteth.[5]

While to some these verses of Scripture may sound like a confusing mix of heads, horns, and beasts, it is more than possible to understand these biblical passages. After all, at the very beginning of the book of Revelation we are promised: "The Revelation of Jesus Christ, which God gave unto him, to shew unto his servants things which must shortly come to pass; and he sent and signified it by his angel unto his servant John: who bare record of the word of God, and of the testimony of Jesus Christ, and all things that he saw. *Blessed is he that readeth,* and they that hear the words of this prophecy, and keep those things which are written therein: for the time is at hand" (emphasis added).[6]

Clearly, when Jesus sent an angel to give this revelation to John on the isle of Patmos, He expected that believers in the last days would understand what had been recorded. So now that we know we can understand these prophetic passages, what is it that we can determine from them?

While the prophet Daniel told us that the Revived Roman Empire would be an alliance of democracies, the apostle John revealed the other central defining characteristic of this last-days empire. John, seeing a panorama of events still far into the future, saw the same political beast that Daniel had seen. Revelation 17 even refers to the same "ten horns" and "ten kings" that Daniel did. However, John also saw something that Daniel did not see: He saw a whore riding on top of this political beast.

John was even given a number of clues regarding the identity of this whore, who is called "Mystery Babylon the Great, the Mother of Harlots and Abominations of the Earth." We know that the whore symbolizes a false church. As Dr. John Walvoord pointed out:

> The picture of the woman as utterly evil signifies spiritual adultery, portraying those who outwardly and religiously seem to be joined to the true God but who are untrue to this relationship. The symbolism of spiritual adultery is not ordinarily used of heathen nations who know not God, but always of people who outwardly carry the name of God while actually worshipping and serving other gods.... In the New Testament the church is viewed as a virgin destined to be joined to her husband in the future, but she is warned about spiritual adultery.[7]

Furthermore, many respected Bible scholars and students of Bible prophecy agree that this religious whore will be characterized by Roman influence. For one, Revelation 17:9 says that she sits on seven heads which are "seven mountains." Even today Rome is known as the city of the seven hills. The whore is said to be "drunken with the blood of the saints, and with the blood of the martyrs of Jesus" (verse 6). It is a well-known historical fact that the Roman Coliseum was used for the persecution of Christians. And during the Reformation, Protestants and other "heretics" were persecuted by the authorities of the Holy Roman Empire. Note that this religious whore is said to have "committed fornication" with the kings of the earth. Again, it is historical fact that the Roman church during that period known as the Holy Roman Empire was in bed with the monarchies and rulers of Europe. There seems little doubt that the apostate church of the tribulation period revealed to John will be an extension of the spirituality of the Roman Empire.

Christendom in the Revived Roman Empire

It is when the true church of Jesus Christ has been removed from the earth at the rapture that the religious whore will be free to rule with the political beast in the tribulation period, thus fulfilling the Revelation 17 prophecy. Nonetheless, just as the democratic kingdom of the Antichrist is struggling to be born today, so too is this false church of the tribulation period. Today, calls can be heard suggesting that the movers and shakers behind the revival of the Roman Empire not forget their religious roots. For instance, as far back as 1985, before the collapse of communism, Pope John Paul II urged that Eastern Europe be allowed to return to its Christian faith. According to an *Associated Press* report:

> Pope John Paul II has called for the people of Communist Eastern Europe to be allowed to practice Christianity unhindered.

> In the fourth encyclical of his six-and-a-half year papacy, the Polish-born Pontiff yesterday

envisioned a civil and cultural union of Europe based on Christian faith.

He said he sees no other way "of overcoming tensions and repairing the divisions and antagonisms . . . which threaten to cause a frightful destruction of lives and values."[8]

Four years later, communism collapsed. And with the collapse of communism, we were told the way was paved for a "united Christian Europe" to emerge in its wake. When Communist leader Mikhail Gorbachev visited the Pope of Rome, it marked the first time in history that a supreme leader of the Soviet Union had visited the Vatican. A *Washington Post* article described the euphoria over the historic meeting:

> The Romans, it is sometimes said, have been indifferent to politicians for 2,000 years. Emperors, popes, kings, presidents, dictators, despots, fools—all have come and gone here.
>
> Then Mikhail Gorbachev arrived. . . .
>
> "Gorbachev, king of Rome," read the front-page banner headline of La Repubblica newspaper. . . .
>
> "He's a planetary figure, surreal, almost evangelical," gushed one man. . . .
>
> Gorbachev showed his customary flair for symbolism and skillful public relations. Tonight, for instance, the Soviet leader presented his vision of a "common European home" in the same room where the Treaty of Rome, which created the European Community, was signed 42 years ago.[9]

Gorbachev's visit symbolized a new era; an era in which Europe could finally be "Christianized." With communism finally out of the way, the Catholic Church, said the *World Press Review*, could now focus on "grander ambitions":

> The ambition that John Paul has unveiled is much broader. "A united Europe is no longer only a dream," he said in Prague. "It is an actual process that cannot be purely political or economic. It has a profound cultural, spiritual, and moral dimension. Christianity is at the very roots of European culture."[10]

The time for a re-mingling of politics and religion seemed ripe. Even Jacques Delors, who headed the European Commission for a decade, supported a new Christian influence for political Europe. *The New Day Magazine* described Delors as "a complex mixture. Timid, yet pugnacious, pessimistic yet determined, this Latin, a practicing Catholic and a convinced socialist, has succeeded in imposing his views on a European Community dominated by Conservative Anglo-Saxons. . . .

"In fact, his religion influences his whole life."[11]

Boris Johnson, who was the EEC Correspondent in Brussels, wrote:

> We knew that Jacques Delors was religious. We knew he was a Christian Socialist. We knew he prayed before each Wednesday's meeting of the 17 EEC Commissioners, prompting inevitable quips on the lines of "Delors is my shepherd."

> Few, though, imagined there could be any connection between the Commission president's enthusiasm for religion and his Euro-federalism.

> Few, that is, apart from a handful of his closest advisers, including a Belgian ex-priest, who believe there is now a spiritual void in Britain and other EEC countries; and

that Mr. Delors should fill that void by subtly turning European federalism into a semi-religious crusade.[12]

There seems to be little room for doubt: The trend toward the prophesied political beast with the prophesied religious whore riding upon it is emerging in these last days. However, remember that Rome was not exclusionary. The divinities of all who wished to become part of Roman civilization were embraced. Enter the ecumenical movement.

Ecumenism and a New Morality for Man

We cannot discover European unity without reappropriating Europe's Christian roots.

In the past Christian faith gave unity and coherence to culture and society....

Christian disunity has also largely contributed to the disunity of Europe and the wider world. In my own country I long for Anglicans and Roman Catholics, together with other Christians, to work together much more closely....

But for the universal Church I renew the plea I made at the Lambeth Conference: Could not all Christians come to reconsider the kind of Primacy the bishop of Rome exercised within the early Church, a "presiding in love" for the sake of the unity of the Churches in the diversity of their mission? In Assisi, without compromise of faith, we saw that the Bishop of Rome could gather the Christian Churches together. We could pray together, speak together and act together for the peace and well-being of humankind, and the stewardship of our precious earth. At that initiative of prayer for world peace I felt I was in the presence of the God who said "Behold I am doing a new thing."[1]

This comment was made by Robert Runcie during one of his many ecumenical speeches while he served as Great

Britain's Archbishop of Canterbury for the Anglican Church. Since Runcie's speech, the ecumenical movement has taken great strides in uniting for the sake of "the peace and well-being of humankind, and the stewardship of our precious earth." Many evangelical Protestant and Catholic leaders ratified their commitment to this unity in 1994 by signing a document known simply as *Evangelicals and Catholics Together* (ECT). Those who signed the document promised one another that they would together "work to deepen, build upon, and expand this pattern of convergence and cooperation."

This trend towards ecumenism in the last days seems very fitting with the prophecies of Revelation. As under Roman rule, all religions will be equally embraced in the Revived Roman Empire.

Birth of the Ecumenical Movement

Perhaps the birth of the ecumenical movement can be chalked up to a series of religious and philosophical congresses that took place at the Chicago World's Fair in 1893. The gathering was known as the first World Parliament of Religions. In his opening address, organizer Charles C. Bonney noted:

> We meet on the mountain height of absolute respect for the religious convictions of each other; and an earnest desire for a better knowledge of the consolidation which other forms of faith than our own offer to their devotees. The very basis of our convocation is the idea that the representatives of each religion sincerely believe that it is the truest and the best of all; and that they will, therefore, hear with perfect candor and without fear the convictions of other sincere souls on the great questions of life.[2]

One of the ten objectives of the first World Parliament of Religions was to "bring the nations of the earth into a more friendly fellowship, in the hope of securing permanent international peace."[3] One hundred years later, the goal was the same.

On August 28 to September 5, 1993 the second World Parliament of Religions was held in Chicago, Illinois. About 6,000 delegates representing 150 world religions and quasi-religions gathered for the centennial celebration. There were representatives from the Buddhist; Orthodox; Roman Catholic; Anglican and other Protestant denominations; Hindu; Jewish; Confucian; Native American; Jain; various Muslim groups; Taoist; Wiccan; Unitarian Universalists; the Fellowship of Isis; the Covenant of the Goddess; The Center for Women, the Earth, and the Divine; the Temple of Understanding; the Theosophical Society; the Earth-Spirit Community; and many, many more faiths.

The opening plenary included an invocation and address by Native American elders. The Dalai Lama of Tibet was a featured speaker at the closing session. Equal voice and footing was given to each of the religions represented. And together these representatives put together a document titled *Towards a Global Ethic (An Initial Declaration)*.

A New Morality for a New Civilization

The *Global Ethic* document is essentially a set of rules for living on this planet; a set of rules that supposedly all the religions of the world can agree upon. It replaces intolerant and exclusionary teachings, such as those of biblical Christianity, with ethical principles found in each of the world's religions, even secular humanism. It is, so to speak, a social contract for a new world order. While the causes and goals listed in the document are noble, the purpose behind them is to provide an earth-based salvation for humanity, rather than the spiritual salvation offered through Jesus Christ, man's only true hope. This document highlights, once again, man's attempt to build a millennial-type kingdom on earth without the Prince of Peace. Following are some excerpts from the *Global Ethic Initial Declaration*:

We condemn the abuses of the Earth's ecosystem.

We condemn the poverty that stifles life's potential; the hunger that weakens the human body; the economic disparities that threaten so many families with ruin.

We condemn the social disarray of the nations; the disregard for justice which pushes citizens to the margin; the anarchy overtaking our communities; and the insane death of children from violence. In particular we condemn aggression and hatred in the name of religion.

But this Agony Need Not Be.

It need not be because the basis for an ethic already exists. This ethic offers the possibility of a better individual and global order, and leads individuals away from despair and societies away from chaos.

We are women and men who have embraced the precepts and practices of the world's religions:

We affirm that a common set of core values is found in the teachings of the religions, and that these form the basis of a global ethic.

We affirm that this truth is already known, but yet to be lived in heart and action.

We affirm that there is an irrevocable unconditional norm for all areas of life, for families and communities, for races, nations, and religions. There already exist ancient guidelines for human behavior which are found in the teachings of religions of the world and which are the condition for a sustainable world order . . .

No New Global Order Without a New Global Ethic!

We women and men of various religions and regions of Earth therefore address all people, religious and non-religious. We wish to express the following convictions which we hold in common:

- We all have a responsibility for a better global order.

- Our involvement for the sake of human rights, freedom, justice, peace, and the preservation of Earth is absolutely necessary.

- Our different religious and cultural traditions must not prevent our common involvement in opposing all forms of inhumanity and working for greater humaneness.

- The principles expressed in this Global Ethic can be affirmed by all persons with ethical convictions, whether religiously grounded or not.

- As religious and spiritual persons we base our lives on an Ultimate Reality, and draw spiritual power and hope therefrom, in trust, in prayer or meditation, in word or silence. We have a special responsibility for the welfare of all humanity and for the planet Earth. We do not consider ourselves better than other women and men, but we trust that the ancient wisdom of our religions can point the way for the future.[4]

Likewise Mikhail Gorbachev has been calling for a new set of values for mankind: a new morality for a new civilization. He stated:

The recognition of the world as an integral whole
calls for a change in our value system, or to put it
more precisely, for actualizing the initial values
that are inherent in the nature of the human being
as a social and spiritual entity. . . .

We need to find a paradigm that will integrate all the
achievements of the human mind and human action,
irrespective of which ideology or political movement
can be credited with them. This paradigm can only
be based on the common values that humankind
has developed over many centuries.[5]

Mr. Gorbachev apparently believes there is inherent
good within the nature of man, and that this inherent good
is reflected in each of the world's religions, just as the
signers of the *Global Ethic* document proclaimed. God's
Word, however, tells us that the last days will be like the
days of Noah.[6] Going back to the first book of the Bible
we read: "And God saw that the wickedness of man was
great in the earth, and that every imagination of the
thoughts of his heart was only evil continually."[7]

The Greening of Religion

Interestingly, the *Global Ethic* document produced at
the World Parliament of Religions condemned "the abuses
of the Earth's ecosystem," stating that the world's religions and peoples of the earth must share "responsibility
for the care of Earth." Gorbachev's values for a new civilization suggested the same:

It is my view that the individual's attitude toward
nature must become one of the principal criteria
for ensuring the maintenance of morality. Today
it is not enough to say, "Thou shalt not kill." Ecological education implies, above all, respect and

love for every living being. It is here that ecological culture interfaces with religion. . . .

Honoring diversity and honoring the earth creates the basis for genuine unity.[8]

Indeed, one of the central pillars for the new spirituality for mankind is worship of the earth. In our years of
research we have watched the environmental movement
grow from a small embryo into one of the largest movements to have ever swept across the globe. We have seen
it expand from a mere political entity into one that em-
bodies the spiritual as well as the physical. In essence, we
have watched the environmental movement become a religion in and of itself.

In June of 1992 the United Nations Conference on Environment and Development (UNCED), simply known as
the Earth Summit, took place in Rio de Janeiro, Brazil.
Donald B. Conroy, President of the North American Coalition on Religion and Ecology (NACRE) had said: "In 1992
the largest conference in U.N. history, and potentially the
most important meeting ever held on the environment
will be convened. . . . All heads of state from around the
world are invited to this unparalleled meeting to deal with
the twin crises of ecological devastation and human development."[9]

There was, of course, much fanfare and hoopla leading
up to the conference, not only with the general population, but within the church as well. Already many churches
had become involved in environmental issues. Many pas-
tors and church leaders had already been encouraging
Christians to "embrace a broader sense of salvation:
'salvation of humankind and redemptive creation.' This
is what Richard Land, executive director of the Southern

Baptist Convention's Christian Life Commission, told ministers gathered in Nashville to promote Earth Day 1990."[10]

Others were blaming Christianity and biblical teachings for the environmental degradation facing mankind. This comment was found in the *St. Petersburg Times*:

> It's going to take a rethinking of Western society's interpretation of those Bible passages, particularly the one that gives humans dominion over all living things. "Be fruitful and multiply," God said; "fill the Earth and subdue it."

> Another contributing factor to the Earth's demise is the salvation-oriented view that many Christian groups maintain. Why bother with taking care of this world when a much better one is waiting just around the corner?[11]

So perhaps out of guilt, or in an attempt to show the world that Christians would do their share of the work in paddling this boat-of-life, many within the Christian community decided to join that group, wanting to become good stewards of the earth. Unfortunately, many were at the same time being swept up in a worldview contrary to the Word of God. We're not talking about the environmental movement's encouragement to recycle, or to use biodegradable household cleansers. There's nothing wrong with these teachings. What we're talking about is the spiritual element that was surfacing within the environmental movement.

In its consciousness-raising campaign, the movement was telling us that the "Earth"—Mother Earth, Gaia, the Earth Goddess—is sacred. Children were the prime targets for this message. Cartoons like Captain Planet were featuring the earth goddess Gaia, as was the Teenage Mutant Ninja Turtles comic strip. The environmental movement was truly becoming a religion. This is why many followers of pagan religions and goddess worshippers who honor the sacredness of the earth were attracted to the environmental movement like bees to honey.

Even Vice President Al Gore, a practicing Southern Baptist, suggested that perhaps the time had come to consider some of the wisdom of ancient religions based on respect for the planet. In his book *Earth in the Balance* he wrote:

> The emergence of a civilization in which knowledge moves freely and almost instantaneously throughout the world has led to an intense new interest in the different perspectives on life in other cultures and has spurred a renewed investigation of the wisdom distilled by all faiths. This panreligious perspective may prove especially important where our global civilization's responsibility for the earth is concerned.
>
> Native American religions, for instance, offer a rich tapestry of ideas about our relationship to the earth.[12]

He then went on to quote a prayer given by Chief Seattle in 1885 in which the chief noted, "Every part of the earth is sacred to my people....Remember that the air is precious to us, that the air shares its spirit with all life it supports." Gore also quoted an Onondaga tribal prayer that "offers another beautiful expression of our essential connection to the earth": "O Great Spirit, whose breath gives life to the world...."

Gore also claimed that through archaeological and anthropological studies, it has been discovered that the prevailing ideology of pre-historic Europe was "based on the worship of a single earth goddess." He pointed out that teachings in the Muslim *Qu'ran*, and the Hindu prayer, the *Atharvaveda*, all emphasize an interconnectedness between man and nature. In these last days the earth and nature have been given a spirit. It is only fitting, therefore, that respect for the earth be included in the code of ethics for a new civilization, forming a key tenet for the new spirituality of the Revived Roman Empire.

Human Rights

Another predominant movement in our time has developed around the issue of human rights. The issue has become so prevalent, Mikhail Gorbachev feels it should also be included in a new code of ethics for mankind. Included in the "1996 Action Plan of the State of the World Forum" was the Core Initiative to draft a "Charter of Human Responsibilities." The Action Plan noted:

> In partnership with the International Consultancy on Religion, Education and Culture (ICOREC) and the Alliance on Religion and Conservation (ARC), the Forum has launched a major international effort to craft and seek broad agreement on a new Charter of Human Responsibilities. The aim of the charter is to provide a broader ethical context of the principles inherent within the Universal Declaration of Human Rights [a U.N. document]. As existing definitions of human rights delineate the contradistinctions of specific individual rights to those of the greater community, the Charter of Responsibilities would accentuate those positive obligations each individual should assume in the service of humanity and the rest of creation.[13]

When putting this book together, we struggled over whether to include the issue of human rights within the sphere of the political beast or the religious whore. It does indeed seem to fit in with both. It is a political issue in that it is one of the main reasons given for U.N. reform. How can the U.N. assure human rights on a global scale and live up to the preamble to the U.N. Charter—"We the Peoples . . . "—if it cannot interfere with the sovereignty of individual nation-states? Indeed, we believe the issue of human rights addressed in treaties such as the U.N.'s Universal Declaration of Human Rights (1948) and the U.N.'s Covenant on Rights (1966) may be catalysts for undermining the authority of the individual nation-state down the road. As was the case with developing regional governments, the Europeans seem to be leading the way in building a model which the rest of the world can follow to make this happen. David Held observed:

> Of all the international declarations of rights which were made in the post-war years, the European Convention for the Protection of Human Rights and Fundamental Freedoms (1950) is especially noteworthy.

What the initiative does, Held explains, is to allow citizens in European nations

> to petition directly to the European Commission on Human Rights, which can take cases to the Committee of Ministers of the Council of Europe and then (given a two-thirds majority on the Council) to the European Court of Human Rights.

Held noted that,

> it has been claimed that, alongside the other legal changes introduced by the European Community, it no longer leaves the state "free to treat its own citizens as it thinks fit" (Capotorti, 1983, p. 977; cf. Coote, 1992). It is interesting, in addition, to note that the Treaty of European Union (the Maastricht

Treaty) makes provision, in principle, for the establishment of a European Union citizenship and
an ombudsman to whom citizens may directly appeal.

Held concluded:

Human rights have also been promoted in other
regions of the world, partly in response to United
Nations encouragement that such rights should
be entrenched in institutions at regional levels ...

Respect for the autonomy of the subject, and for
an extensive range of human rights, creates a new
set of ordering principles in political affairs which,
where effectively entrenched, can delimit and cur-
tail the principle of state sovereignty itself.[14]

So then, the issue of human rights will be central, it
seems, to the political beast. However, in the end, we
decided to place the issue of human rights under the
sphere of the religious whore. In a sense, representatives
from 150 of the world's religions saw fit to place it there.
The signers of the *Towards a Global Ethic (An Initial Declaration)* document included human rights under a new code
of conduct at the World Parliament of Religions. Under
the heading "A Fundamental Demand: Every Human
Being Must Be Treated Humanely," the signers agreed:

We are all fallible, imperfect men and women with limitations and defects. We know the reality of evil. Precisely
because of this, we feel compelled for the sake of global
welfare to express what the fundamental elements of a
global ethic should be—for individuals as well as for
communities and organizations, for states as well as for
the religions themselves. We trust that our often mil-
lennia-old religious and ethical traditions provide an

ethic which is convincing and practicable for all women and men of good will, religious and non-religious. . . .

The spiritual powers of the religions can offer a fundamental sense of trust, a ground of meaning, ultimate standards, and a spiritual home. Of course religions are credible only when they eliminate those conflicts which spring from the religions themselves, dismantling mutual arrogance, mistrust, prejudice, and even hostile images, and thus demonstrate respect for the traditions, holy places, feasts, and rituals of people who believe differently.

Now as before, women and men are treated inhumanely all over the world. They are robbed of their opportunities and their freedom; their human rights are trampled underfoot; their dignity is disregarded. But might does not make right! In the face of all inhumanity our religious and ethical convictions demand that *every human being must be treated humanely!*

This means that every human being without distinction of age, sex, race, skin color, physical or mental ability, language, religion, political view, or national or social origin possesses an inalienable and untouchable dignity. And everyone, the individual as well as the state, is therefore obliged to honor this dignity and protect it. Humans must always be the subject of rights, must be ends, never mere means, never objects of commercialization and industrialization in economics, politics and media, in research institutes, and industrial corporations. No one stands "above good and evil"—no human being, no social class, no influential interest group, no cartel, no police apparatus, no army, and no state. On the contrary: Possessed of reason and conscience, every human is obliged to behave in a genuinely human fashion, to do good and avoid evil![15]

While the efforts of the declaration are noble, God's Word tells us that it is only through Jesus Christ that we can become a new spiritual being, living according to a code of ethics based on biblical principles. But just as man is trying to build a kingdom of peace without the Prince of Peace, so is he trying to establish a kingdom of righteousness without Him as well. It is only by being washed in the blood of the Lamb that we become righteous. Rebellious man, however, believes he does not need salvation through the washing of the blood of the Lamb to establish morality on earth.

Interestingly, the final church mentioned in the Book of Revelation is the Laodicean church, which is described as being prosperous, believing it has need of nothing (3:14). Jesus, however, tells the church of Laodicea that it is spiritually blind and naked. The name *Laodicea* means "people's rights" or "justice of the peoples."

As Christians, however, we have given up human rights. We are dead in Christ. When we were buried in baptism, we were buried in the likeness of Christ's death: "I am crucified with Christ; nevertheless I live, yet not I, but Christ liveth in me; and the life which I now live in the flesh I live by faith of the son of God, who loved me, and gave himself for me."[16] This is how we can truly become a new creation, a new spiritual man.

Fraud and Deceit

U nder the rule of the Roman Empire, there was a semblance of universality. But this appearance of universal peace had been achieved only through military conquest and military rule. As strong as the Roman Empire was, it eventually collapsed under the duress of slow social decay and violence.

Hundreds of years later, what was known as the Holy Roman Empire tried to take the place of the ancient Roman Empire. It attempted to add a sense of moral religious authority through the Roman Catholic Church. The Holy Roman Empire likewise tried to achieve a sense of universality, but it too failed.

It appears that the shortcomings of both the ancient Roman Empire and the Holy Roman Empire will be overcome in the Revived Roman Empire. Again, universality in the Roman Empire was achieved only by military force, thereby giving it an appearance of true universality. In the Revived Roman Empire, however, the sense of universality will be achieved on a global scale willingly, through a democratic process.

As for the Holy Roman Empire, political universality never existed because of the fragmentary nature of the

117

feudal system. Its appearance of universality was achieved only through the strong authority of the papacy. The secular emperor had no strong authority. Henry Kissinger noted:

> For most of the medieval period, however, the Holy Roman Emperor never achieved that degree of central control. . . . The most important reason was that the Holy Roman Empire had separated control of the church from control of the government. Unlike a pharaoh or a caesar, the Holy Roman Emperor was not deemed to possess divine attributes.[1]

Unlike the emperor of the Holy Roman Empire, however, the Antichrist will experience control and authority. Indeed, the False Prophet, who could very well be the head of the future "universal church," will ensure that the new emperor has divine attributes ascribed to him and is worshiped by the world: *"He [the False Prophet] exerciseth all the power of the first beast [the Antichrist] before him, and causeth the earth and them which dwell therein to worship the first beast."*[2]

Once again, the failures of the previous phases of the Roman Empire will appear to have been overcome in its revived form. Indeed, it is under the rule of the Antichrist, with the help of the False Prophet, that the concept of universality will finally have taken hold. But looks can be deceiving.

Deception in the Global Kingdom

Deception is key to the kingdom of the Antichrist. First of all, we know that God Himself is going to send a delusion upon the world after the true church has been raptured:

God shall send them strong delusion, that they
should believe a lie:

That they all might be damned who believed not
the truth, but had pleasure in unrighteousness.[3]

We also know that the Antichrist is going to be able to
perform "signs and lying wonders"[4] and that the False
Prophet will literally be able to make "fire come down
from heaven on the earth in the sight of men."[5] Such factors will indeed be central for the appearance of universality in the new world order.

However, there will be another factor that will be instrumental in establishing a sense of universality: the
media. For one, it will aid in giving the masses a final sense
of being united in one world. Second, it will be used as a
tool by the Antichrist in maintaining a façade of truth behind which he is actually conducting a campaign of deception. Indeed, Daniel 8:25 says the Antichrist is going
to "cause *craft* to prosper." The word translated "craft"
means *fraud*, or *deceit*. And the tool used to carry out this
campaign of fraud could very well be global telecommunications.

The Global Village and the Mass Media

Interestingly, the second reason that Henry Kissinger
gave for the failure of the Holy Roman Empire was "the
lack of adequate transportation and communication systems, making it difficult to tie together such extensive territories."[6]

Unlike its predecessor, the Revived Roman Empire
will definitely not be hindered by such a problem. Indeed,
the advancement of technology and telecommunications
in these last days would make the head of anyone from

previous generations spin. Technology and telecommunications today are responsible for having, at least partially, created a world without borders. Jacques Attali, former aide to French President Francois Mitterand, predicted that the world of the future will be:

> girdled by a dense network of airport metropolises for travel, and wired for instant worldwide communications. Money, information, goods, and people will move around the world at dizzying speeds.

> Severed from any national allegiance or family ties by microchip-based gadgets that will enable individuals to carry out for themselves many of the functions of health, education, and security, the consumer-citizens of the world's privileged regions will become "rich nomads." Able to participate in the liberal market culture of political and economic choice, they will roam the planet seeking ways to use their free time.[7]

Telecommunications may also play a role in a global transformation cosmically as well. In the fall of 1992, *Time* magazine published a special issue on the year 2000 and the next millennium. There were, of course, a number of interesting articles and quotes, like the following: "The passage into a new millennium will occur this time in the global electronic village. It will be the first (obviously, given the state of technology in the year 1000) to be observed simultaneously worldwide, with one rotation of the planet. Almost every human intelligence will be focused for an instant in a solidarity of collective wonder and vulnerability—Mystery in the Age of Information."[8]

The first taste that mankind had of being in a "global village" was during the Persian Gulf War. People across

the globe—all at the same time and all in real time—
watched as an international force led by the U.S. unleashed
its military might on a defiant Iraq. Their eyes were glued
to CNN, which was responsible for bringing life to this
global event. Indeed, it was CNN's coverage of the Persian Gulf War that brought this somewhat obscure news
network and its owner, Ted Turner, to the fore of world
attention. It earned Ted Turner the honor of *Time*'s Man
of the Year.

In its special Man of the Year issue, *Time* magazine
noted:

> The very definition of news was rewritten—from
> something that has happened to something that
> is happening. . . . A war involving the fiercest air
> bombardment in history unfolded in real time. . . .
> These shots heard, and seen, around the world
> appeared under the aegis of the first global TV
> news company, Cable News Network. Contrary
> to the dictum of former U.S. House Speaker Tip
> O'Neill that "all politics is local," CNN demon-
> strated that politics can be planetary, that ordi-
> nary people can take a deep interest in events
> remote from them in every way—and can respond
> to reportage in global rather than purely nation-
> alistic terms.[9]

Indeed, Ted Turner had achieved the goal of media vi-
sionary Marshall McLuhan, who dreamed of a global village made out of a network of telecommunications that
would transcend national borders; a global telecommunications network that would bind man together for the
common good. Of course, with power over such a global
telecommunications network comes the responsibility of
ensuring that it would be used for the "common good."
In the wrong hands, such power could bring disaster.

The Propaganda Wars

Just imagine the power of the worldwide telecommunications infrastructure falling into the hands of the Antichrist. Unlike any other leader who has tried to establish world hegemony, he would have at his disposal the most powerful weapon ever devised for control and deception. After all, using the mass media as a propaganda tool is nothing new.

When you think of propaganda, it is probably the former Communist Soviet Union that comes to mind first. There is no question that propaganda is very much a part of Soviet history. It is a well known fact that the Kremlin had firm control over the media, and any attempts at "free thinking" by intellectuals were squashed. The nation that probably least likely comes to mind when you think about propaganda is the U.S. However, the U.S. propaganda machine used to wage a war of disinformation against the Soviets was a very worthy opponent for the Communists. Indeed, in the end it was the victor. A very good history and insider account of the American and Soviet propaganda war during the Cold War years is given in a book titled *Warriors of Disinformation* by Alvin A. Snyder. Snyder, who from 1982 to 1988 was the director of the U.S. Information Agency's Television and Film Service, is the former director of Worldnet Television, the USIA's satellite television service.

The USIA was the successor to the Office of War Information, established by President Roosevelt in 1942. In February of that year, the first "Voice of America" radio broadcast was sent over the airwaves into Europe with the help of the BBC. That first program was broadcast in the German language, and was, of course, a war propaganda weapon during World War II. When the war ended, the OWI was no longer used for "psychological warfare." Following the war Truman initiated his "Campaign of Truth" to counter Soviet propaganda, which was now making an appearance. American libraries and educational exchanges were established in foreign countires to dispel Soviet myths about America. To further the efforts initiated by Truman, President Dwight D. Eisenhower created the United States Information Agency in 1953.

It wasn't until the Reagan years, however, that the role of the USIA really flourished, according to Snyder. Reagan brought in Charlie Wick, a long-time friend who had also been involved in the entertainment industry, to help him get the propaganda machine rolling. Reagan and Wick, says Snyder:

> often discussed how the media could be used to further foreign policy objectives. When Wick arrived in Washington, Reagan gave him a *New York Times* article about how television might be used to undermine the Polish Communist government's crackdown on striking labor unions. Said the article: "Imagine the reaction if the average laborer knew of the latest happenings inside Poland. Picture what an effect TV images of the Polish strikers would have!" Charlie Wick could imagine it. His first USIA-TV satellite show to slam the Communists would be a Polish-language musical starring Frank Sinatra and Pope Paul II, entitled, "Let Poland Be Poland".[10]

It took a couple of media insiders to see the power of TV images in the battle against the Communists. Indeed, TV turned out to be the most powerful weapon of the Cold War. In the beginning of the disinformation campaign, the Soviets successfully managed to disrupt American short-wave radio broadcasts through their noise factories, or "jamming centers." The jamming stations successfully blocked out the radio broadcasts in urban centers, but rural areas were out of the boundaries of the noise created. Also, the U.S. propaganda mill frequently changed the timing of its broadcasts, which made blocking them more difficult for the Soviets. Then the arrival of satellite-TV images created a whole new problem for the Communists:

> Although the Americans weren't rushing to take advantage of the technology, the prospect that TV satellites might someday beam programs from space directly into small home receivers filled the Soviets with cold fear. "The Soviet Central Committee was absolutely paranoid about the prospect," remembers Victor Sheymov, a former KGB operative who defected to the West in 1980. "They saw TV satellites as a huge threat."[11]

Snyder added that Sheymov quotes Brezhnev as saying, "If they [the USIA] pull this off, all our propaganda efforts will be worthless."[12]

Eventually the USIA did pull it off. The Worldnet TV satellite network, which reached into Eastern Europe and the core of the Soviet Union, broadcast speeches by Reagan in their entirety. Interviews with VIP guests such as Henry Kissinger, then Vice President George Bush, and Secretary of Defense Caspar Weinberger were sent over the airwaves. Topics included Soviet aggression in Afghanistan and Soviet pressure on Poland. The USIA made sure that the Eastern bloc knew that NATO was a strong military allied force, capable of, and willing to, back up any efforts at détente. The most damage the USIA created for the Communists was with its broadcasts of a five-minute audio clip of the air-to-ground communication with the pilot who shot down the Korean civilian airliner KE-007.

"The Kremlin was reeling from all the bad press it was getting worldwide," says Snyder.[13]

The Soviets used the 1984 Summer Olympics held in Los Angeles to get back at the USIA. The Soviet propaganda mill claimed that the event was actually organized by the U.S. Federal Bureau of Investigation as a sinister plot to further its own goals. Furthermore, the Soviets claimed that leaflets were being distributed by the Ku Klux Klan in America, threatening any black athletes from Africa planning to compete in the Olympics. Through Worldnet, however, the USIA managed to successfully counter the attack by broadcasting an interview with Peter Ueberroth, who was president of the Los Angeles Olympic Organizing Committee, and Los Angeles' black mayor, Tom Bradley.

Then there was the rumor started by the Soviets that the U.S. developed the AIDS virus as a weapon for biological warfare. The Soviets warned that the U.S. was breeding killer mosquitoes to carry the AIDS virus and that U.S. servicemen were also carriers of the disease. They also claimed that Americans were kidnapping and butchering Latin American children to sell their organs for medical research. While such propaganda was damaging, in the end, the USIA won the propaganda war.

The clincher in the battle were reports on Reagan's Strategic Defense Initiative (SDI), better known as Star Wars. Snyder wrote: "As damaging as Soviet disinformation was, when it came to heavy-duty disinformation with the biggest 'return on investment' (in crass, commercial terminology), no one could top the American government." President Reagan was a firm believer in being tough with the enemy to win their hearts.

> Borrowing an idea from the movie *Star Wars*, the former actor made his grab and the Soviets

snapped to attention. Star Wars, America's disinformation pièce de résistance, had been hatched ...

Snyder noted that SDI was actually a con job that came
at a critical time:

> The Pentagon planned to put bombs aboard the
> missiles that were to be hit by incoming Star Wars
> projectiles, so that the explosion would prove that
> test firings were "successful," thereby conning the
> Soviets into thinking that American missile tech-
> nology was more developed than was actually the
> case....
>
> The Pentagon had pulled it off....

Snyder claims that it was then that Soviet President
Mikhail Gorbachev, realizing that the U.S.S.R. would be
economically crippled if it were to continue in this com-
petitive arms race, decided to end the Cold War.

> The U.S. government's bluff about Star Wars was
> part of another round in the high-stakes propa-
> ganda poker game. Eventually, the Russians
> would fold their hand.[14]

Shaping Society

While Mr. Snyder's book on the propaganda game
during the Cold War years demonstrates just how powerful the influence of images are on society, many Hollywood insiders continue to insist that the images they
portray—often images of violence and sexual promis-
cuity—have no influence on society. While conservative
groups insist that the violent and immoral images are
adding to the decay of society, many in Hollywood just
sneer smugly at them. But the smugness seems hypocrit-
ical when you consider the billions of dollars they accept

each year from advertisers. If TV images have no influence on people, why are they wasting advertisers' money?

On the other hand, the media likes to accept credit for the successes of global media events such as *Live Aid* or *Our Common Future*. Indeed, it even likes to take credit for its role in the release of Nelson Mandela from prison and the disintegration of apartheid in South Africa. It's becoming increasingly difficult for anyone, even Hollywood, to deny that TV shapes culture. As journalist John Lippman observed:

> Asked once what had caused the stunning collapse of communism in eastern Europe, Polish leader Lech Walesa pointed to a nearby TV set. "It all came from there." . . .
>
> The rapid inroads of satellite-based "borderless television" are changing the way the world works, the way it plays, even the way it goes to war and makes peace. . . . Conversely, history is now shaped by television, a reality eloquently symbolized by East German youths when they hoisted MTV flags over the Berlin Wall as it was torn down.[15]

It's very clear. TV images shape society. Danger arises with the possibility that such images could be part of some propaganda campaign. Just ask the relatives of the six million Jews who were murdered during the Nazi Holocaust about the dangers of propaganda. We have visited Israel a number of times, and each time we have visited the Holocaust memorial museum Yad Vashem in Jerusalem. The exhibits are simple. There's a large room with black and white photos and news clippings of the history and atrocities of the Nazi regime. The memorial to the more than one million children who died is a dark room of mirrors with a candle burning in its midst. There are more than one million reflections, one reflection for each child that died. As you walk through the hall of children, an audiotape reads out the names and birthplace of each child. It takes about three years to complete the reading of the list before the audiotape starts again.

Then there is the memorial dedicated to all six million Jews who died. It's a simple room with a concrete floor. On the floor are plaques listing each of the concentration camps and how many died in each one. An eternal flame burns in the midst of the plaques. Again, the exhibit is simple. Yet each and every time we have visited Yad Vashem, especially in the hall of children, our throats have become choked up and tears have rolled from our eyes. The emotional experience each visit brought forth never diminished. It boggles the mind to understand how a whole society could be deluded into participating in such a horrific nightmare, either by active involvement, or by simply ignoring it. Propaganda had a great deal to do with the Holocaust. A book available at Yad Vashem explains how important propaganda was to the Nazis:

> According to Nazism, the German people constituted the highest stratum of the Nordic-Aryan race, while the Jews were a sub-human race who perpetually undermined the sound structure of world affairs and sought to usurp the authority and leadership of the superior race. . . . This doctrine, which Hitler repeatedly and loudly affirmed, had its own laws and lines of development. The mere insistence upon a state of racial war in which there could be no compromising, helped create the background for the "Final Solution." Obviously, if the Jews posed such a serious danger to society, then any measures taken against them, including exterminations, were justified. . . .

During the short period he spent in prison, Hitler wrote his well-known book, *Mein Kampf* ("My Struggle"), in which he outlined the programme of his movement. Hitler and his close associates displayed a remarkable talent for propaganda....

In *Mein Kampf*, in the Nazi Party Press, and in Nazi publications, racist doctrines were openly espoused. Anti-Semitism was one of the most powerful propaganda weapons used by the Nazis to gain the support of the masses.[16]

It is unthinkable to imagine what Hitler could have done if he had the power of a sophisticated visual media like we do today at his disposal.

Unfortunately, Anti-Semitism did not die completely with the disintegration of Nazi Germany at the end of World War II. Today conspiracy stories about the Jews trying to control international banks, the media, and the world, are still making the rounds. Jews are hated by groups in Russia, South America, and, of course, in the Arab Middle East. There have even been some displays of Anti-Semitism in North America and Europe. The world, it seems, has a natural animosity towards God's chosen people. And it is the natural enemy of God's other children as well—Christians. To be hated by the world in the last days, however, is merely a sign of the times. Jesus told His disciples, "Ye shall be hated of all men for my name's sake" (Matthew 10:22).

If They Hated Me

For a number of years, through our research, we have watched a growing animosity towards Christ and Christians in North America. This animosity has been reflected in the educational system. First, prayer was removed from the schools. The role of Christianity in American history began to be papered over in textbooks. Christmas plays and programs were changed to "Winter Solstice" programs. While the excuse was that religion had no place in the public school system, occultism was being quietly slipped in under the guise of relaxation techniques and accelerated learning exercises. As conservative Christian parents began to openly protest, they were painted in the media as narrow-minded bigots who didn't know what they were talking about. Hollywood began to become more brazen about its depiction of Christians and preachers as sleazy liars and cheats in movies like *A Handmaid's Tale*, *Fletch*, and *China Blue*, and on television programs like *The Simpsons*, and *Roseanne*. Indeed, an entire book can be written on this subject alone.

An animosity towards Christianity began to be reflected in church/state issues. The courts started mandating that any statues of religious symbols, like the cross, be removed from public parks. City halls were ordered to take down nativity displays in front of their buildings during the Christmas season. Schools were ordered to take down any crosses or pictures of Christ that were hanging in their hallways. Teachers and students were forbidden to bring Bibles to school or pass out religious tracts.

As Christians began to bring their concerns forward, and to fight their battles in the courtroom, the debate over Christianity began to take on a political and legal appearance, giving the secular world more reason for its animosity. Then, as Christians began to become actively involved in the political arena, more fuel was added to the fire.

In 1994, candidates for the leadership of the Republican party started to hit the campaign trail. Liberals feared that someone from the religious right could actually take over the leadership of the Republican party, or worse, could become the next president. Immediately a barrage of anti-religious right propagandists hit the campaign trail. According to California Representative Vic Fazio, chairman of the Democratic Congressional Campaign Committee, a voter backlash against the "Christian Right" would help Democrats in the 1996 elections. Fazio told *U.S.A Today* that the "stealth campaigns" waged by the "fire-breathing Christian radical right" would alienate the average voter.

Before we proceed any further, it is necessary to clarify our views on politics and Christianity. We do not believe that Christians have been mandated to be politically active. By the same token, we do not believe that it is wrong for Christians to be politically active, depending on the motive behind their actions. For many Christians, being involved in politics, actively or through their vote, simply means voicing their opinion through the political process. They are simply trying to make the world a safe and comfortable place to live in while we remain on earth. Others are fighting for the freedom to continue to proclaim the gospel. But others have different motives.

The "Christian Right," the "Religious Right," or the "Conservative Right" are all broad terms that cover a lot of different beliefs, and a lot of different people are involved in it for various reasons. Some conservative Christians, for instance, believe that we must take over the world's governments before Christ can come and set up His millennial kingdom. Theologies such as "Kingdom Dominion" or "Reconstructionism" go against biblical prophecy, which clearly tells us the condition of the world is going to grow worse in the last days. The Bible is clear that this planet is headed for destruction; it's destined for fire. Nowhere does the Bible say that Christians have to take over the world and subdue the enemy. Indeed, the enemy is going to be allowed to run rampant for seven years during the tribulation. Our victory is not in the world. Our victory is over the world, through the shed blood of Jesus Christ.

Indeed, Jesus told us that we are "not of the world" (John 15:19). We have also been instructed to obey the governments of this world while we are yet pilgrims here. The Apostle Paul instructed Titus: "Put them in mind to be subject to principalities and powers, to obey magistrates, to be ready to every good work."[17]

The only real mandate we received as Christians is to go into the world and preach the gospel. We should be concerned about the salvation of souls. Yes, it would be nice to live in a moral society, as long as we don't lose sight of the fact that moral people do not receive eternal salvation. Only those who have been washed in the blood of the Lamb do through faith in Jesus Christ alone.

With the increasing force of the Christian Right in American politics, the onslaught of verbal attacks has increased as well. The Christian Right was accused of trying to force its moral views on all of society. For instance, Marianne Means, the Washington, D.C., columnist for Hearst Newspapers, wrote:

> Ominously, the politics of religious hate steadily intrudes into our public life. It threatens to engulf the Republican Party and turn the 1996 presidential election into the nasty "cultural war" demanded by Pat Buchanan at the 1992 GOP convention.

> "Hate" is a harsh word. More politely put, it means intense hostility and aversion. That is what we see in the emotions of religious-right activists, who are determined to force everyone to live by their own narrow biblical view, an ultimate moral truth only they can define.

Increasingly, we see its counterbalance in the resistance of others who don't like being told how to behave by people professing to be holy and all-knowing.[18]

From Mean's portrayal of the religious right, one could almost envision that we are on our way to some type of oppressed society controlled by religious bigots similar to those in the movie *A Handmaid's Tale*. Indeed, Christians are no longer being portrayed as merely bigots, but as dangerous bigots.

In a book review of *On The Psychology of Fundamentalism in America* by Charles B. Strozier, Martin E. Marty reported that the book deals mainly with religious sects that believe the end of the world is fast approaching. In the review, the Christian Right was also referred to as fitting under the category of apocalypticism, and suffering from a "kind of collective illness." In the review Marty noted:

> The fastest-growing portion of global Christianity is apocalyptic and millennial. Hundreds of millions of believers, some millions of them in North America, prepare for Armageddon, an end-of-the-world battle between God and the forces of Satan. They hope for a millennium in which a returned Christ will rule. And they have political clout. . . .
>
> They really do want the world to end as prophesied with Jesus in command. But they mix their desire with "a very human kind of hope that the world will not self-destruct." Working for the long pull, many of them now enter politics. The author says that we heard some of them at the 1992 Republican National Convention.[19]

Verbal attacks against the religious right have come from White House staff. Joycelyn Elders, former Surgeon

General, had been unpopular with the Christian community because of her endorsement of the distribution of condoms in the public schools and because of her calls for the decriminalization of drugs. Her popularity amongst the religious right declined even further when in June of 1994 she told an audience at the Lesbian and Gay Health Conference in New York that it was time to fight the "un-Christian religious right" because of its opposition to "health" education and condom distribution. She told her audience that they must "take on those people who are selling our children out in the name of religion."

Those who opposed Dr. Henry Foster as her replacement were called "extremists" by some in the White House, including Vice President Al Gore, even though Dr. Foster admitted performing hundreds of abortions, then was caught in a lie regarding his actions. Jesse Jackson likened the religious right to white supremacists and Anti-Semites. He refused to apologize when a retraction of his comments was requested:

> Jesse Jackson refused to apologize for calling the conservative Christian Coalition a "strong force" in Nazi Germany and a racist influence in the slave-holding South. The civil rights leader expanded on his remarks he made in Chicago and New York, saying that "there is an ideological and historical connection" linking the Christian Coalition today to the white supremacists and anti-Semites of yesteryear.[20]

Indeed, the media campaign against the religious right has made fundamentalist Christians look like a bunch of power-thirsty despots. As Marianne Means said, the religious right is "determined to force everyone to live by their own narrow biblical view, an ultimate moral truth only they can define." However, many involved in the religious right are simply on the defensive, not the offensive. They are trying to defend a society and culture they see moving further away from the traditional values that once made up the American nation. They are defending a nation that was once free to proclaim the gospel without hindrance.

Since the Clinton administration came to power, there was an extensive push to support and expand gay rights. The pro-life movement has pretty much been silenced. It became a federal crime to protest in front of abortion clinics. Some appointees to the Clinton administration have called for a narrower definition of child pornography, which will make prosecution next to impossible. Some have suggested teens should enjoy sex, as long as they use condoms. The U.S. Department of Housing and Urban Development tried to ban religious symbols from public advertisements by housing providers, such as senior citizens residences owned and operated by religious denominations. The Chairman of the Equal Employment Opportunity Commission tried to push through regulations banning all types of religious expression in the work place. The wording of the proposed legislation was so vague that even wearing a cross pendant on a necklace could have been construed as illegal activity. Also, the Justice Department decided that a Minnesota church was not protected under the Religious Freedom Restoration Act in a case before the U.S. Court of Appeals for the Eighth Circuit. The church, according to the Clinton administration, had to pay back $13,450 that was donated to it a year before by a couple who were attending the church and had claimed bankruptcy. If the money had been spent on entertainment, or for personal items like lottery tickets, there would have been no request for the money to be returned. The Clinton administration tried to cut funding for Title XX Adolescent Family Life, the only source of federal funding for programs that supported infant adoption in the case of teen pregnancies. These are only a few examples of what has taken place under the Clinton administration and moved the religious right to become more actively involved in politics in defense of a nation in crisis.

Nonetheless, the anti-religious right media blitz, as well as the numerous anti-Christian parts in movies and TV programs being pumped out of Hollywood, have done some lasting damage. They have changed the way the population views the fundamentalist Christian.

Of course, it is only fair that all the blame not be placed on the doorstep of others. The immorality that has inflicted the church over the past several years, and our own poor personal behavior as Christians at times, have added to the damage as well. But the fact remains that the world at large, and particularly our nation's leaders, have been attacking biblical Christianity as a societal evil.

The Final Display of Hatred

The ultimate propaganda campaign against the followers of Christ will not be waged until the tribulation period. Imagine the hatred that can be incited against God's people by the Antichrist, who will have sophisticated media technology at his disposal. Indeed, as writer Lofti Maherzi observed about the global telecommunications network put in place by the USIA:

> The purpose is in fact an ambition of astronomical proportions: the conditioning of billions of human minds, through direct access to their television

screens. This is the new empire of the superpowers, no longer territorial, but audiovisual and informational. Whoever controls information governs the world. It is a battle which takes place in the skies, with blows struck by satellites. The message is no longer obvious; instead it is impressively seductive.[21]

Through fraud and deceit, the Antichrist will convince the world to persecute and kill the saints of the tribulation period, those who have come to a saving knowledge of Jesus Christ after the church has been raptured out of the world. He will convince the armies of the world to gather at the battle of Armageddon to attack the Jews out of hatred for them and their God. And in an ultimate display of man's rebellious pride and hatred, the Antichrist will convince the armies of the world to turn their weapons against Jesus Christ, very God Himself, Who returns to save His chosen people Israel.

9

Signs and Wonders

In the last chapter, we discussed the fact that deception will be prominent in the false kingdom of the Antichrist. Indeed, it will be so prominent, the Antichrist is going to cause fraud and deceit, or "craft" (Daniel 8:25), to prosper. The global telecommunications infrastructure being constructed today will likely prove to be an indispensable tool for him to spread deceit to its fullest. But such a man-made propaganda machine will only play a part in the deception of the false kingdom of the Antichrist. The deception of the tribulation period will also be highly supernatural and occultic in nature as well.

The fullness of the Antichrist's "craft" will not occur until after the rapture has taken place. Indeed, the Antichrist himself will not be revealed until after the rapture, according to II Thessalonians 2. While the Church is in the world, it acts as a light, exposing sin and evil, which lurk in the darkness. When this light is gone, there will be darkness and wickedness such as the world has never known. Unfortunately, the world will not see it as a time of evil because God is going to send a strong delusion:

> Now ye know what withholdeth that he [the Antichrist] might be revealed in his time.

> For the mystery of iniquity doth already work: only he
> who now letteth will let, until he be taken out of the way.
>
> And then shall that Wicked be revealed, whom the Lord
> shall consume with the spirit of his mouth, and shall de-
> stroy with the brightness of his coming.
>
> Even him, whose coming is after the working of Satan
> with all power and signs and lying wonders,
>
> And with all deceivableness of unrighteousness in them
> that perish; because they received not the love of the
> truth, that they might be saved.
>
> And for this cause God shall send them strong delusion,
> that they should believe a lie.[1]

After the church has been raptured, the Antichrist will
be revealed and he will further the delusion sent by God
with "signs and lying wonders." Although this prophecy
will not be fulfilled until the tribulation period, even today
we see the world being prepared for delusion through a
belief in signs and wonders.

The Search for Miracles

Many in the world and in the professing church today
are fascinated by signs and wonders. Indeed, hardly a day
goes by without seeing some current news story in the
media about visions of the Virgin Mary, statues of Jesus
that bleed or cry, statues of Hindu gods that drink milk,
or of miracles being experienced at any number of "signs
and wonders" church services taking place across the nation. In the spring of 1995, *Time* magazine, for its Easter
edition, asked people if they still believe in miracles today.
Time's poll concluded:

69% said yes; and the fastest-growing churches in America are the Charismatic and Pentecostal congregations whose worship revolves around "signs and wonders." Tens of thousands of people gather in a pasture in Georgia or a backyard in Lubbock, Texas, because of reports that the Virgin appears in the clouds. . . .

The quest for an understanding of miracles is by no means confined to Catholic pilgrims or Protestant Fundamentalists or New Age stargazers. Author Dan Wakefield, a lapsed Presbyterian turned Unitarian, sometime TV scriptwriter, and now itinerant theological investigator, has just finished a book, *Expect a Miracle*. . . . He was amazed by what he learned. "We all read these silly things, the man who saw the Virgin on the fender of his Dodge Dart," he says. "What I found, which is more interesting, is people you'd think of as very conservative. . . . The stories I have are not all religious, and they are from all different religions. It is very vast, and serious. People like to dismiss it as the fringe, but there is a real, mainstream thing."[2]

Divine Miracles

Many in the professing church today place a heavy emphasis on signs and wonders, believing that miraculous displays and performances will increase their faith in God. Considering the history of the Jews, given to us as an example (Romans 15:4), however, the belief that faith is increased by miracles is questionable.

The Israelites in both the Old and New Testaments were witness to many divine miracles. Indeed, no other people on earth have been witness to more miracles than

God's chosen people. While they were slaves in Egypt, Moses was sent to lead them into freedom, but because of the hardness of Pharaoh's heart, he refused to set the Israelites free. Pharaoh needed some coaxing, so God, through the hand of Moses, sent miraculous signs in the form of plagues and famines to demonstrate that He meant business. What was even more miraculous was that all those plagues affected only the Egyptians. The people of Israel remained unscathed.

Instead of believing that Moses was sent by God, however, each time their Egyptian taskmasters made their lives more difficult, the Israelites blamed Moses for making things worse for them. Even after they were finally set free, the Israelites still questioned Moses' divine mission, which was continously proven by God's miracles. God led them by the protection of a cloud during the day and a pillar of fire at night. When the Egyptians were following them into the wilderness, God parted the Red Sea so that they could cross over on dry land. Then God closed the walls of the Red Sea on Pharaoh's army and completely destroyed it. Still the Israelites had a difficult time believing that God was for them and not against them. They complained about insufficient food supplies, so God sent them quails and manna from heaven. Yet they continued to complain and disbelieve. Because of their lack of faith, they were forced to walk in the wilderness for forty years until the disbelieving generation had died out.

In the New Testament, the Jews were witness to the miracles of Jesus Christ, their Messiah. They watched Him cause the lame to walk, the blind to see, and the deaf to hear. They even saw Him raise the dead. But these signs and wonders were not enough for them to faithfully believe He was their chosen Messiah. After all the miracles they had seen, they still did not believe Jesus was sent to them by God. Many even claimed that he was acting on behalf of "Beelzebub the prince of the devils" (Matthew 12:24). Jesus answered them:

> Every kingdom divided against itself is brought to desolation; and every city or house divided against itself shall not stand:
>
> And if Satan cast out Satan, he is divided against himself; how shall then his kingdom stand?:
>
> And if I by Beelzebub cast out devils, by whom do your children cast them out? therefore they shall be your judges.
>
> But if I cast out devils by the Spirit of God, then the kingdom of God is come unto you.[3]

Then some of the scribes and Pharisees in the crowd even had the audacity to ask Him for more signs to prove that He was indeed telling them the truth (Matthew 12:38). This time Jesus replied:

> An evil and adulterous generation seeketh after a sign; and there shall no sign be given to it, but the sign of the prophet Jonas:
>
> For as Jonas was three days and three nights in the whale's belly; so shall the Son of man be three days and three nights in the heart of the earth.
>
> The men of Nineveh shall rise in judgment with this generation, and shall condemn it: because they repented at the preaching of Jonas; and, behold, a greater than Jonas is here.[4]

Indeed, the Jews had been given the greatest sign of all: the death and resurrection of their Messiah. And yet they still did not believe. We have been instructed to not make the same mistake:

> To whom sware he [God] that they should not
> enter into his rest, but to them that believed not?
>
> So we see that they could not enter in because of
> unbelief.
>
> Let us therefore fear, lest, a promise being left us
> of entering into this rest, any of you should seem
> to come short of it.
>
> For unto us was the gospel preached, as well as
> unto them: but the word preached did not profit
> them, not being mixed with faith in them that
> heard it.[5]

So the Jews, even though they had been witness to
many miracles throughout their history, still lacked faith.
Even after all the the signs and wonders, they still didn't
believe what God had told them.

Our faith in God should be strong simply based on the
fact that we can trust in Him. We can believe the promises
made in His Word simply because of who made them. We
shouldn't need to ask God for signs to prove that His Word
is indeed true. "Now faith is the substance of things hoped
for, the evidence of things not seen. . . . But without faith it
is impossible to please *him*: for he that cometh to God must
believe that he is, and that he is a rewarder of them that
diligently seek him."[6]

Hebrews chapter 11 is the key biblical passage on faith.
Indeed, it is a record of the biblical Hall of Fame:

> By faith Abel offered unto God a more excellent sacrifice
> than Cain, by which he obtained witness that he was
> righteous, God testifying of his gifts: and by it he being
> dead yet speaketh.
>
> By faith Enoch was translated that he should not see
> death; and was not found, because God had translated

him: for before his translation he had this testimony, that he pleased God. . . .

By faith Noah, being warned of God things not as seen yet, moved with fear, prepared an ark to the saving of his house; by the which he condemned the world, and became heir of the righteousness which is by faith.

By faith Abraham, when he was called to go out into a place which he should after receive for an inheritance, obeyed; and he went out, not knowing whither he went. By faith he sojourned in the land of promise, as in a strange country, dwelling in tabernacles with Isaac and Jacob, the heirs with him of the same promise: For he looked for a city which hath foundations, whose builder and maker is God.

Through faith also Sara herself received strength to conceive seed, and was delivered of a child when she was past age, because she judged him faithful who had promised.[7]

Each of these biblical characters made it to God's Hall of Fame, so to speak, and yet Hebrews 11 tells us that all these faithful servants of God "died in faith, not having received the promises, but having seen them afar off, and were persuaded of them, and embraced them, and confessed that they were strangers and pilgrims on the earth" (verse 13).

Unfortunately, it seems that many in the church today have placed a greater emphasis on signs and wonders—things that can be seen—rather than on a simple faith in the promises of God's Word. Jesus even went so far as to ask, "When the Son of man cometh, shall he find faith on the earth?"[8]

Indeed, the Apostle Paul warned in a letter to Timothy:

> Now the Spirit speaketh expressly, that in the
> latter times some shall depart from the faith,
> giving heed to seducing spirits, and doctrines of
> devils.[9]

Some in the professing church would consider it blasphemy to even suggest that professing Christians could be deceived by seducing spirits or doctrines of devils. But, remember, it was the Apostle Paul, through the revelation of Jesus Christ, who said it. Furthermore, the Apostle Paul warned:

> I fear, lest by any means, as the serpent beguiled
> Eve through his subtilty, so your minds should be
> corrupted from the simplicity that is in Christ.[10]

He added that any who preach another Christ or another gospel:

> are false apostles, deceitful workers, transforming
> themselves into the apostles of Christ.
>
> And no marvel; for Satan himself is transformed
> into an angel of light.
>
> Therefore it is no great thing if his ministers also
> be transformed as the ministers of righteousness;
> whose end shall be according to their works.[11]

The risk of deception is so great that when the disciples asked Jesus what would be the sign of His return, the very first part of His answer was, "Take heed that no man deceive you." (Matthew 24:4). He wasn't talking to the world here. He was talking to those who knew Him. His own disciples were susceptible to being deceived.

Why have we said all this? Don't we believe that God can still perform miracles today? Of course we do. We don't believe, however, that all miracles are divine miracles. It is imperative that Christians know the Word of God inside and out in these last days of deception. It is only by His Word, our measuring stick of truth, that we can know whether any doctrine being preached, or any miracle being performed, is indeed from Him. If we do not know His Word, we leave ourselves wide open to spiritual deception. While some miracles may appear to be divinely inspired, note that Jannes and Jambres, two of the sorcerers in Pharaoh's court, were able to imitate some of God's miracles demonstrated through the hand of Moses (Exodus 7:10-12, 19-22; 8:5-7, 16-19; 2 Timothy 3:7-9).

Now let's turn our focus to the spiritual deception coming upon the world.

Seeing is Believing

The Bible says that for the Christian, "faith is the substance of things hoped for, the evidence of things not seen" (Hebrews 11:1). The world, however, has no such faith. The world doesn't consider things "not seen" as evidence. Take Shirley MacLaine, for example. She has written several books on her studies of and experiences in the metaphysical, which led her along a path to becoming a firm believer in the paranormal. In *Out on a Limb,* she explained that as a youngster her parents used to send her to church on Sundays. But she never took God seriously because she saw no evidence for His existence:

> I really never had any feeling one way or the other whether there was a God or not... I couldn't believe in anything that had no proof.[12]

Indeed, in this scientific and technological age, people place stock in evidence, not faith. Even for those in the

New Age movement, who tend to believe in signs and wonders, belief seems to have come through something that has directly happened to them. Their belief in strange phenomena, or miracles, has come only through first-hand experience. Experience is their evidence.

Take the experience of UFO sightings and contact with extraterrestrials, for example. At one time, spaceships and men from Mars were the subjects of children's cartoons and comic strips. Anyone who seriously claimed that spaceships or spacemen existed were the subject of psychiatric studies. Today that is changing. Perhaps one of the more famous alien "abductees" is author Whitley Strieber. He wrote of his experiences with alien abduction in his books *Transformation* and *Communion*, which was also made into a movie. Like MacLaine, Strieber has based his firm belief on first-hand experience:

> I did not believe in UFO's at all before this happened. And I would have laughed in the face of anybody who claimed contact. Period. I am not a candidate for conversion to any new religion that involves belief in benevolent space brothers, or in unidentified flying objects as the craft of intergalactic saints—or sinners.
>
> And yet my experience happened to me.[13]

Strieber is not alone. Many in the world today claim to have had the same experience. Of the evolution of UFOs, Strieber wrote:

> Seeming encounters with nonhuman beings are not new; they have a history dating back thousands of years. What is new in this latter part of the twentieth century is that the encounters have taken on an intensity never before experienced by humankind . . .

What may have been orchestrated with great care has not been so much the reality of the experience as public perception of it. First the craft were seen from a distance in the forties and fifties. Then they began to be observed at closer and closer range. By the early sixties there were many reports of entities, and a few abduction cases. Now in the mid-eighties, I and others—for the most part independent of one another—have begun to discover this presence [abduction by ETs] in our lives.[14]

According to a 1993 Roper Poll, the number of people worldwide who believe they have been abducted by aliens could be in the millions:

In a recent Roper poll of nearly 6,000 American adults, specially commissioned by those who accept the alien abduction story at face value, 18% reported sometimes waking up paralysed, aware of one or more strange beings in the room. Something like 13% reported odd episodes of missing time and 10% claimed to have flown through the air without mechanical assistance. From these results, the poll's sponsors concluded that 2% of all Americans have been abducted, many repeatedly, by beings from other worlds. If aliens are not partial to Americans, the number for the whole planet would be more than 100 million people.[15]

Indeed, in the 1990s the possible existence of extraterrestrials seems very plausible. Movies like *ET* and *Independence Day*, and TV programs like *Star Trek: the Next Generation*, *The X-Files*, and *Third Rock from the Sun* reflect this seeming plausibility. The concept has become so realistic that even space agencies such as NASA and SETI have funneled millions of dollars into technology searching for ETs. Emergency and rescue agencies have begun to take aliens seriously. *OMNI* magazine reported:

> It only makes sense that civilian emergency personnel from police to firefighters may be called to the scene of a close encounter.... Our country's "first responders" have never been given any kind of background on the UFO phenomenon, until now....
>
> For a detailed briefing on the topic, all professional rescuers need do is refer to the new, second edition of the *Fire Officer's Guide to Disaster Control* (Fire Engineering Books and Videos). Used by the Federal Emergency Management Agency (FEMA) in its National Fire Training Academy Open Learning Program, the book covers, in addition to more traditional fire fare, the ABC's of UFO's: In practical language, the manual examines potential problems like disruption of transportation and communication, possible psychological and physical impacts, and speculations about government secrecy. To fire up imaginations, the manual also presents a hypothetical alien encounter....
>
> The guide's UFO section is primarily informational, says [William M. Kramer, a district chief with the Cincinnati Fire Department], "intended to get fire officers thinking. Nearly everyone has told me they were impressed that a mysterious subject was taken out of the closet, and many believe we are, somehow, eventually going to make contact with other forms of intelligent life."[16]

Of course, many believe that this contact is not some future event. Indeed, many people believe they have already been in contact with other forms of intelligent life.

Contact

In the New Age, these "intelligent life forms" have come in many different shapes and sizes. For some, like Whitley Strieber, they have come in the form of extraterrestrials. For others, they have come as guardian angels. "Have you noticed?" asked a *New York Times* article:

> It is a strange and subtle little trend, this one, but pervasive. Look at the kids. Amid the typical gaggle lined up outside the rock venues or fooling around on the subway platform—mostly clothed in T-shirts emblazoned with unprintable sentiments and unsavory gestures—you can spot a jarring exception. Angels.
>
> Raphael is possibly the hottest new artist around. His dimpled cherubs adorn not only the apparel of the young but the walls of their dorms and the night stands of their trendier elders. Books on angels are big sellers, including one that ended up on the The Time's best-seller list. The Metropolitan Museum shop has trouble keeping up with the demand for reproductions of angel art: angel posters, pins, statuary, stationery and literature.
>
> Most of the angel books flying from the shelves of the bookstores are accounts of visitations. Many people, it turns out, still believe that in their hour of need—stranded in a blizzard or hounded by bill collectors—the mysterious stranger who came to their rescue was no earthly friend but another kind of guardian. . . . [17]

For others, intelligent beings have come in the form of wise persons, or spirit guides, which have been visualized during guided imagery exercises for healing or relaxation. Such guides are the focal point of many such exercises used in medicine, psychiatry, and even in education. While some choose to believe these spirit guides are simply one's inner voice, others, with a knowledge

of shamanism, claim they are indeed actual spiritual entities, not our own inner voice.

Michael Harner was a teacher of anthropology on
the graduate faculty of the New York School for Social
Research. He was also co-chairman of the anthropology
section of the New York Academy of Sciences. A number
of years ago he decided to research shamanism, which
led him to actually become a "white shaman." In his
book *The Way of the Shaman,* he wrote:

> From the Conibo I especially learned about the
> journey into the Lowerworld and the retrieval of
> spirits. . . .
>
> To perform his work, the shaman depends on spe-
> cial, personal power, which is usually supplied by
> his guardian and helping spirits. Each shaman
> generally has at least one guardian spirit in his
> service, whether or not he also possesses helping
> spirits. In her classic work on the concept of the
> guardian spirit in native North America, Ruth F.
> Benedict observes, shamanism "is practically
> everywhere in some fashion or in some aspect
> built around the vision-guardian spirit complex . . ."
>
> Outside of North America, the guardian spirit is
> similarly important, but is often called by other
> names in the anthropological literature, such as
> "tutelary spirit" in works on Siberian shamanism,
> and as "nagual" in Mexico and Guatemala. In the
> Australian literature it may be referred to as an
> "assistant totem," and in the European literature
> as a "familiar." Sometimes the guardian spirit is
> just called the "friend" or "companion." What-
> ever it is called, it is the fundamental source of
> power for the shaman's functioning. . . .[18]

Interestingly Harner added in the afterword to the book:

> The burgeoning field of holistic medicine shows a tremendous amount of experimentation involving the reinvention of many techniques long practiced in shamanism, such as visualization, altered state of consciousness, aspects of psychoanalysis, hypnotherapy, meditation, positive attitude, stress reduction, and mental and emotional expression of personal will for health and healing. In a sense, shamanism is being reinvented in the West precisely because it is needed.[19]

Others have even been in contact with these spirit entities through modern-day mediums, now known as trance channelers. Indeed, a number of people the world over have opened themselves up as vehicles through which these spiritual entities can speak to us in the physical world. Yang Neang of Cambodia is an example:

> In the Cambodian community, Neang is known as a Kru Khmer, a revered channeler and healer who is said to have the power to contact transcendant realms for information from the spirit world.

> After careful preparation and meditation Neang becomes a 7-year-old boy/god. The Boy, who is said to have lived seven centuries ago in the great temples of Angkor Wat, inhabits her 65-year-old body.

> He is a spirit who can see and sense things mortals cannot. He can figure out the source of family problems. He can cure physical ills. He can offer blessings. He can make friendly predictions. He can tell fortunes. He can even level frightening warnings.[20]

Some of the more well-known North American channelers include J.Z. Knight, who acts as a vehicle for an entity known as Ramtha; Jach Pursel, who channels Lazarus; and Jane Roberts, who acts as a vehicle for Seth.

Interestingly, when you study the accounts of those who have had contact with other beings, there is a connection to mind-altering techniques. Channellers, of course, enter a trance-like state to allow these beings to possess their bodies. Spirit guides are contacted through mind-altering mental exercises such as visualization and guided imagery. Shamans use the same techniques. Sometimes mind-altering drugs are used to quicken the process. For the most part, alien abductees have remembered their stories with the help of mind-altering techniques. Hypnosis is the most common of these. Altered-states-of-consciousness seems to be the common thread that connects human beings to these other entities. Whitley Strieber revealed in his books that he already had a long history with the occult and consciousness-raising techniques before he was contacted by aliens:

> For half of my life I have been engaged in a rigorous and detailed search for a finer state of consciousness. Now I thought my mind was turning against me, that my years of eager study of everything from Zen to quantum physics had led me into some strange and tragic byway of the soul.[21]

It is getting extremely difficult, however, for the world to deny that something seems to be taking place other than mass hysteria. Indeed, psychologists have examined many of these people and have found no reason to chalk their stories up to mental madness. Strieber, for instance, noted:

> I was interviewed by three psychologists and three psychiatrists, given a battery of psychological tests and a neurological examination, and found to fall within the normal range in all respects. I was also given a polygraph by an operator with thirty years' experience and I passed without qualification. . . . In my case there were witnesses, and physical aftereffects that are hard to ignore.[22]

Furthermore, the descriptions of extraterrestrial beings given by those who have been in contact with them are similar. They are described as insect-like beings with almond-shaped eyes. The types of stories contactees have to tell are the same. There are descriptions of paranormal phenomena like levitation, astral projection, ESP, and telepathic communication. There are even stories of sexual encounters, medical examinations, and incubation.

Those who adhere to evidential fact and scientific logic are having a difficult time dismissing the claims of a growing number of men, women, and children the world over who are now saying they have had contact with other-worldly beings. Indeed, the evidence of these entities seems difficult to ignore. The obvious question is then, Are they actually who they claim to be?

Christians believe the answer to this question is no. We believe they are actually demons, Satan's minions sent to deceive the world. Jaques Vallee, astrophysicist, computer scientist, and author of several books on high technology and UFOs, has done a great deal of research on the subject—not as a debunker, but as a believer in such phenomena. Dr. Vallee concluded about contact with such beings:

> As a society, we are developing a great thirst for contact with superior minds that will provide

guidance for our poor, harassed, hectic planet. I think we may be ready to fall into a trap, perhaps a kind, benevolent pitfall. I believe that when we speak of UFO sightings as instances of space visitations we are looking at the phenomenon on the wrong level. We are not dealing with successive waves of visitations from space. We are dealing with a control system. . . .

We are not here dealing with escapism—we are dealing with the next form of religion, with a new spiritual movement.[23]

We too believe that people who have been in contact with other beings *are* the forerunners of a new spiritual movement: the false religion of the kingdom of the Antichrist. Indeed, ET's and UFO's may play a role in explaining the rapture at the beginning of the tribulation period. In an article on the alien invasion of televison programming for the fall 1996 season, *TV Guide* noted "For years aliens have been the top choice for explaining almost all unexplained occurrences—from mysterious circles found in farm fields to freak weather systems."[24]

There is a parallel between all these types of entities that have been said to have been in contact with human beings throughout history: elves, fairies, religious apparitions, ET's, incubi, sylphs, and the like; all denizens of a spiritual realm. The occult phenomena displayed by each is the same. Their message is the same. Why? Because their source is the same: Satan, the father of lies. Indeed, following the rapture of the church, the Bible says that the people who remain on earth are going to believe a very big lie.

The Lie

Second Thessalonians 2 tells us that when God sends a strong delusion upon the earth, those who are left behind will believe "a lie" (verse 11). What is this lie? For the answer to this question, we need to go back to the early days of creation:

> Now the serpent was more subtil than any beast of the field which the Lord God had made. And he said unto the woman, Yea, hath God said, Ye shall not eat of every tree of the garden?
>
> And the woman said unto the serpent, We may eat of the fruit of the trees of the garden: But of the fruit of the tree which is in the midst of the garden, God hath said, Ye shall not eat of it, neither shall ye touch it, lest ye die.
>
> And the serpent said unto the woman, Ye shall not surely die: For God doth know that in the day ye eat thereof, then your eyes shall be opened, and ye shall be as gods, knowing good and evil.[25]

What we see occurring today is an increasing population literally coming in contact with demons, who are spreading the same old lies of reincarnation ("Ye shall not surely die") and human potential ("ye shall be as gods").

Satan's messengers are only too happy to help mankind along this supposed path to enlightenment and godhood. These demons, appearing as channeled entities, angels, ET's, or spirit guides, are all claiming that they are here to help us enter a new age in which man will be mentally and spiritually transformed. Ruth Montgomery, a former journalist and now one of the leading authorities on psychic phenomena, has allowed herself to be used as a vehicle for her "Guides" since 1960. In *Strangers Among Us*, she explained that her guides are entities who have gone through numerous cycles of reincarnation until they finally attained superior enlightenment. Now they are here to help us do the same:

> There are Walk-ins on this planet.
>
> Tens of thousands of them.
>
> Enlightened beings, who, after successfully completing numerous incarnations, have attained sufficient awareness of the meaning of life that they can forego the time-consuming process of birth and childhood, returning directly to adult bodies.
>
> A Walk-in is a high-minded entity who is permitted to take over the body of another human being who wishes to depart.... A Walk-in must never enter a body without the permission of its owner....
>
> The motivation for a Walk-in is humanitarian. He returns to physical being in order to help others help themselves, planting seed-concepts that will grow and flourish for the benefit of mankind.[26]

Spirit guides that have spoken to Shirley MacLaine have likewise told her that reincarnation and godhood are a reality. Trance medium Kevin Ryerson, for instance, told her:

> I say folks have God inside them. The Church says it has God inside of *it*. There's a phrase in the Bible which states that one should never countenance spiritual entities other than God. Most Christians go by that. But then the Bible says nothing about reincarnation either and it's quite well known that the Council of Nicea voted to strike the teaching of reincarnation from the Bible....

The man Jesus studied for eighteen years in India
before he returned to Jerusalem. He was studying
the teaching of Buddha and became an adept yogi
himself. He obviously had complete control over
his body and understood that the body was only
a house for a soul. Each soul has many mansions.
Christ taught that a person's behavior would determine future events—as karma, as the Hindus
say. What one sows, so shall he reap.... Souls that
have died, so to speak, help those who are still in
the body.[27]

This theme of reincarnation crops up again and again
in the teachings of these entities. The teaching has been
given a semblance of credibility through modern-day psychiatry and the use of hypnotic regression. There are
records of some psychiatric patients, often completely by
accident, who have supposedly regressed back to memories of former lives. OMNI reports, for instance:

Treating patients by guiding them through recol-
lections of what appear to be previous lives is
about the last thing Brian Weiss thought he'd be
doing. The South Florida physician, who before
the age of 35 was chief of psychiatry at Mount
Sinai Hospital and a professor at the University
of Miami's medical school, had always taken the
traditional path.

One patient changed all that.

Weiss calls her Catherine in Many Lives, Many Mas-
ters, published in 1988, eight years after her
therapy began. Barely budging her garden-variety
phobias and anxieties with 18 months of conventional therapy, Weiss instructed Catherine while
hypnotized to "go back to the time from which
your symptoms arise." She did: The year was 1863

B.C., and she was a 25-year-old woman named
Aronda.

The article added that "Catherine" revealed a number
of past lives which suggested to Weiss that he had stum-
bled upon some kind of evidence of reincarnation. But this
was only part of it. There were supposed entities speaking
through Catherine as well. OMNI continued:

> Weiss first branded it as mumbo jumbo until "the
> Masters" talked about Weiss's late father and the
> medical condition that caused the death of his
> three-week-old son years before—information to
> which Catherine would have no access.[28]

Indeed, many have come to believe in the teachings
of these entities simply because they know things that
should otherwise be unknown. If they didn't lie about the
facts, why would they lie about the message? Indeed,
haven't they said that they've come to help us? It is by
falling into this trap of deception that many have come to
believe the most blasphemous lie of all: the lie that *we are
God*. Kevin Ryerson claims that four entities speak through
him, the "most highly evolved of all the discarnate entities" being "John." John taught MacLaine:

> The only important knowledge is the spiritual
> knowledge of God within man. Every other
> knowledge flows from that. . . .

> The *self*, however, knows the Divine truth because
> the self is itself Divine. . . . When the human mind
> experiences an expansion of dimensions on many
> levels it becomes more peaceful, more satisfied.
> The skeptic's view of higher knowledge of self is
> most limiting. Your dogmatic religions, for ex-
> ample, are most limiting for mankind because they
> demand unquestioned reverence for authority—

an exterior authority: *You* are God. *You* know you
are Divine.[29]

As the second coming of Jesus Christ approaches,
Satan and his minions know they don't have much time
left to deceive the masses. And so their work has intensi-
fied in these last days. As Shirley MacLaine observed,
"Trance channeling of spiritual entities is becoming more
and more common. It's almost as though the closer we
come to the end of the millennium, the more spiritual help
we are getting if we'd just take advantage of it."[30]

As we mentioned at the beginning of this book, the
people of the world are floating along in the same boat
of life as Christians. They see the same signs of gloom
and doom. They do not have the hope of being rescued
by Jesus Christ in the rapture, however. This is why Satan
has sent these messengers of deception to offer his own
brand of hope: a false hope based on the original lie. He
promises to offer an alternative to Armageddon, which
God has prophesied is the destiny of those who reject His
only begotten Son. Barbara Marx Hubbard, founder of
The Committee for the Future and one of the nominees
for Vice President of the United States at the Democratic
National Convention in 1984, claimed that she had been
given a vision, by a Christ "presence," of an alternative
future for man. This Christ "presence" revealed to her
that:

> Christ-consciousness and Christ-abilities are the
> natural inheritance of every human being now on
> Earth . . . All who choose to be natural Christs will
> be guided from within as to how to proceed. All
> who choose not to evolve will die off; their souls
> will begin again within a different planetary
> system which will serve as kindergarten for the

transition from self-centered to whole-centered being. . . .

Just as any cell, once cancerous, can infect the whole body with destructive growth, every human in the body of humanity can destroy the whole after a certain stage of power has been collectively attained. . . . Only the good can evolve.[31]

Jesus warned that in these days of fraud and deceit:

Many shall come in my name, saying, I am Christ; and shall deceive many. . . .

Then if any man shall say unto you, Lo, here is Christ, or there; believe it not.

For there shall arise false Christs, and false prophets, and shall shew great signs and wonders; insomuch that, if it were possible, they shall deceive the very elect.

Behold, I have told you before. Wherefore if they shall say unto you, Behold, he is in the desert; go not forth: behold, he is in the secret chambers; believe it not.

For as the lightning cometh out of the east, and shineth even unto the west; so shall also the coming of the Son of man be.[32]

10

Mystery Babylon and the Goddess Within

First woman became First Mother and she had many children. She called them her rainbow family. She taught them to live in harmony and balance. She gave them a dream of peace and they were nurtured by her abundance. When First Mother knew her time had come and her tasks were finished she began to change into something other than what she had been. But before her rainbow family spread out across the earth they promised First Mother if she ever needed them, if she were threatened, they would reform the rainbow family, stand together and give their strength to protect First Mother, Mother of us all.

We are part of the rainbow family, you and I. And today the Earth needs protection as never before. As we turn into the 21st century, people everywhere are beginning to recover their reverence for the Earth, to draw meaning from an older world, the world of Gaia, the Earth goddess.[1]

The above, taken from an ancient Celtic tale, was an introduction to a video on the women's spirituality movement, titled *Goddess Remembered*. The ancient tale is being revived today because the time has come, we are being told, for the "rainbow family" to "reform" and to give its "strength to protect First Mother." Indeed, the ancient Celtic lore perfectly sums up the beliefs of the neo-pagan and women's spirituality movement that is emerging in the modern world today. Thousands of women and men everywhere are embracing "the goddess."

> In the beginning, there was no God. There was the Goddess. She peered into the great void and created the Heaven and the Earth, and in this new domain women ruled. The world was peaceful and both sexes worshipped her.[2]

In today's world, with its constant war and environmental degradation, many would like to return to a time in which they believe there was peace and harmony with nature, a time in which Mother Earth supposedly reigned supreme. The need for a return to such a time has become so imperative, we are told, it is critical that we include reverence for the earth as a new spiritual value. Reverence for our planet is to be part of the code of morality in the Revived Roman Empire. The final spiritual church, the religious whore of Revelation 17, is identified as "Mystery, Babylon the great, the mother of harlots and abominations of the earth."[3]

Indeed, the root of the neo-pagan, or goddess worship movement, is found in ancient Babylon. It is there that the goddess first emerged. Dr. John F. Walvoord, former chancellor of the Dallas Theological Seminary, explained:

> The subject of Babylon in the Scripture is one of the prominent themes of the Bible beginning in Genesis 10, where the city of Babel is first mentioned, with continued references throughout the Scriptures climaxing here in the book of Revelation. From these various passages, it becomes clear that Babylon in Scripture is the name for a great system of religious error. Babylon is actually a counterfeit or pseudo religion which plagued Israel in the Old Testament as well as the church in the

New Testament, and which, subsequent to apostolic days, has had a tremendous influence in moving the church from biblical simplicity to apostate confusion. In keeping with the satanic principle of offering a poor substitute for God's perfect plan, Babylon is the source of counterfeit religion sometimes in the form of pseudo Christianity, sometimes in the form of pagan religion. Its most confusing form, however, is found in Romanism....

Of primary importance in the study of Babylon is its relation to religion as unfolded in Revelation 17. In addition to materials given in the Bible itself, ancient accounts indicate that the wife of Nimrod, who founded the city of Babylon, became the head of the so-called Babylonian mysteries which consisted of secret religious rites which were developed as a part of the worship of idols in Babylon. She was known by the name of Semiramis and was a high priestess of the idol worship. According to extrabiblical records which have been preserved, Semiramis gave birth to a son who she claimed was considered a savior of his people and was, in effect, a false messiah, purported to be the fulfillment of the promise given to Eve. The legend of the mother and child was incorporated into the religious rites and is repeated in various pagan religions. Idols picturing the mother as the queen of heaven with the babe in her arms are found throughout the ancient world, and countless religious rites were introduced supposedly promising cleansing from sin.[4]

As Dr. Walvoord noted, goddess worship, which originated in Babylon, was a perversion of God's promise that the Messiah would come from the seed of a woman (Genesis 3:15). The goddess came into being as a usurper of God's authority over man and nature.

> We believe that the goddess we have found [in the form of statues and idols during archaeological digs] in every place is always representing Mother Earth, Mother Nature. And again, when we come to find the male representative, the phallic symbol, we always find it outside the holy of holies. Inside the holy of holies we always find a statue of the goddess of fertility, or her representative, what we call the pubic triangle.[5]

Again, God's Word has been blatantly perverted by such symbolism. While Eve was promised that the Messiah would come from the seed of a woman, she was not promised that mankind, nor the Messiah, would be subject to her. In fact, she was told quite the opposite: "Unto the woman [God] said, I will greatly multiply thy sorrow and thy conception; in sorrow thou shalt bring forth children; and thy desire shall be to thy husband, and he shall rule over thee."[6]

It is only the Messiah Jesus Christ, who offered Himself as our redemptive sacrifice, thereby becoming our High Priest, who has legitimate access to the holy of holies (see Hebrews chapter 9). Nonetheless, the rebellious religion of Babylon spread throughout the ancient world, and as it did, the goddess took on different names: Asherah and Astarte (Canaan); Artemis (Greece); Ala (Nigeria); and Kali (India). By the time Abraham traveled through the land of Sumeria, Mesopotamia, and Babylon, the goddess was known as Ishtar, the Queen of Heaven, as she is referred to in Jeremiah chapter 44.

Women's Spirituality

The women's spirituality movement today is re-embracing the goddess in rebellion against what it calls the patriarchal system. In essence, it is a rebellion against God's redemptive plan for mankind. "Starhawk" is a modern-day pagan, an author, and an instructor at the Institute for Culture and Creation. In one of her books she wrote:

> For the image of the tortured male body on the cross confronts our unconscious hope that maleness itself can remove us from the sphere of mortality, from death and pain. But instead of forcing us through that confrontation to a deeper connection with our own mortal flesh and life, Christianity cheats us with the false promise of an other-worldly resurrection.[7]

In their rebellion against such "maleness," many women the world over are embracing witchcraft and paganism, claiming they are pure traditional spiritualities that have been around much longer than Christianity. They feel this gives paganism some sort of legitimacy, giving it credence as truth. These neo-pagans believe it is time to turn our backs on the "turmoil" caused by the patriarchal Christian era, and return to the more harmonious life of the goddess, at one with the natural world. An example of this type of sentiment is revealed in the following comments made by Karen Toole-Mitchell, a minister with The United Church of Canada:

> I believe that New Age is a return to some very ancient spiritual resources. New Age is really very old "stuff" that has returned in new forms because of our deep spiritual hunger.

> It may be hard for many of us to grasp, but 2,000 years ago Christianity was the "new kid" on the religious block. It was viewed with a fairly healthy level of skepticism by the more ancient religious traditions and hierarchies

of the time. It was seen as a fringe cult with a strange secret fish-like sign, a mystical three-point hand motion,
and emotional gatherings of people who immersed each
other in water.

It seemed to practise some form of cannibalism where
they ate someone's body and drank someone's blood.
No wonder the early Christian leaders were risking arrest and execution! The communion ritual of the early
Christian Church must have appeared like some form of
barbaric human sacrificial rite to those who worshipped
the sun, the seasons, the moon and the beautiful energy
of nature.

New Age stuff has been around for a long, long time.
And in this day and age of deep spiritual longing, people
are resurrecting the nurturing spiritual resources of the
past to fill the void that the more institutionalized religions have left unfulfilled.[8]

Down the Same Old Garden Path

Neo-paganism, which is sweeping the world today,
appeals to the rebellious spirit of mankind. It is tolerant
of diverse spiritual paths, except for what is deemed male-
domineering Christianity. Furthermore, neo-paganism appeals to today's rebellious spirituality in that it recognizes
self-divinity. Pilgrims journeyed from all over the ancient
world to visit the oracle at Delphi. Passing through the
gate of the oracle they would read the inscription "Know
Thyself," one of the central teachings of goddess worship,
both past and present. Christian author Berit Kjos has done
a great deal of research on the subject of paganism's central thought. In *Under the Spell of Mother Earth* she wrote
that the proponents of the movement claim:

It is time to begin writing a new psychology of the feminine, a psychology that returns women to their ultimate roots—a Goddess psychology.[9] In their article, "The Wounded Goddesses Within," Roger and Jennifer Woolger show how this emerging feminine consciousness can lead to the coveted prize, self-actualization: "To know oneself more fully as a woman is to know which goddesses one is primarily ruled by and to be aware of how different goddesses influence the various stages and turning points of one's life."[10]

Once again, it's the same old lie that Satan told Eve in the Garden of Eden: "ye shall be as gods"— or goddesses, as today's eco-feminists would prefer to be called. It is ironic that it is once again the woman, as part of the goddess spirituality movement, who has been deceived by the serpent and is attempting once again to pass on the forbidden fruit to others, just as Eve did to Adam. Indeed, many women today are being caught up in the feminist women's spirituality movement unawares, not realizing there are some hidden issues in the "gender agenda." We are not saying that *all* women caught up in these alternative spiritualities or the feminist movement embrace *all* of the same beliefs. Nor are we saying that it is only women who are being deceived by goddess spirituality and paganism. Unfortunately, many believe that when they are becoming involved with the women's movement, they are simply fighting for issues like job or salary equality. But other issues the movement lobbies for include lesbian and gay rights, and women's reproductive rights, which translates into the right to have an abortion. This is indeed ironic, since those in the women's spirituality movement claim to revere life.

Others think they are learning about their own health and well-being when they become involved in women's issues. While channel surfing one day, Patti noticed a program on women's health and decided to watch for a few moments. The first segment of the program was on breast cancer, followed by another segment on reducing stress with music therapy using New Age music, chanting, and rhythmic drum beating. Women tuning in to the program would think they were getting information on their health and well-being, but in reality, blended with the medical information were basic lessons on neo-paganism and New Age spirituality.

One of the main ways in which women are getting caught up in neo-paganism is through concerns for the environment. They often find themselves indoctrinated in earth-based religions that seek to renew awe and respect for planet earth and Mother Earth, the goddess. They learn that all living things are sacred and interconnected. Grandmother Twila, for instance, an elder of the Seneca Nation tribe, tells women:

> It's a family structure. Everything in nature is a relative and our lives are connected to this relationship. We look at the birds and all the animals as our little brothers and sisters. So you cannot separate a family structure like that. The trees are our teachers and the plants and everything are all relatives. We look at the Earth as our mother.[11]

While it is true that there are biological links and interconnections throughout the ecosystem, there is definitely not a spiritual interconnectedness. The relationship is scientific, not spiritual, as goddess worshippers would have us believe. Once again, neo-paganism twists God's reality and bends truth to fit its own rebellious needs.

Ironically, the word *wiccan* which is used to denote modern-day witchcraft and paganism, is derived from the Anglo-Saxon word "wic," which means to bend or shape. While neo-pagans claim it means to bend or shape one's consciousness or the events of one's life, there is certainly clear evidence that it also means to bend reality and truth. Berit Kjos writes:

> The following 1990 version of the Thanksgiving myth was circulated to about half of all our nation's elementary schools by *Scholastic News*:

> "GIVE THANKS TO THE EARTH: The first Thanksgiving feasts were harvest festivals. People gathered to celebrate successful harvests and *to thank the Earth* for its fruits. You can celebrate the earth every day by always taking care of the environment." [emphasis added][12]

This is an obvious perversion of the historical account of the pilgrims' Thanksgiving feast. And it is a clear perversion of God's Word, which tells us the earth was cursed because of the sin committed by Adam and Eve:

> Unto Adam [God] said, Because thou hast hearkened unto the voice of thy wife, and hast eaten of the tree, of which I commanded thee, saying, Thou shalt not eat of it: cursed is the ground for thy sake; in sorrow shalt thou eat of it all the days of thy life; thorns also and thistles shall it bring forth to thee; and thou shalt eat the herb of the field.[13]

God's Word goes on to say:

> In process of time it came to pass, that Cain brought of the fruit of the ground an offering unto the Lord.

> And Abel, he also brought of the firstlings of his
> flock and of the fat thereof. And the Lord had re-
> spect unto Abel and to his offering: But unto Cain
> and to his offering he had not respect.[14]

Cain brought God an offering from the ground, which
had been cursed because his mother and father had been
beguiled by the serpent to eat the forbidden fruit. The serpent is still subtly at work with his same lies today. And
the entire world is his modern Garden of Eden.

Sorcerers, Soothsayers, and Searching the Stars

It is not without coincidence that as we approach the
rapture and the tribulation period, goddess worship,
which originated in ancient Babylon, is being revived as
Mystery Babylon of the Revived Roman Empire. Nor is it
a coincidence that we are seeing the same spiritism that
dominated ancient Babylon being revived in Mystery
Babylon as well.

Nimrod was the founder of ancient Babylon. His name
literally means "let us rebel." Indeed, in just a few generations he had the people worshipping gods and goddesses, which they assigned to the elements of the heavens:
the sun, the moon, and the stars. They pieced together
their new system of pagan worship as the zodiac. The
rulers of Babylon would turn to their seers and sooth-
sayers, who would consult the zodiac for direction. Guidance by pagan deities, which were linked to the hosts of
the heavens, replaced guidance by God.

Today people continue to seek help outside of God for
guidance, and the sources of this outside help find their
roots in the same spiritism that ruled ancient Babylon:

To learn more about supernatural beliefs of Americans, don't ignore the ads in tabloids lining supermarket check-out stands, say scholars who are exploring areas that have often been considered beneath academic inquiry.

"They (the tabloids) speak for a large number of people," said Elizabeth Bird, a sociologist at the University of Minnesota. . . .

Historian Leda Ciraolo, who spoke on "Check-out Stand Charms" at a recent regional meeting of the American Academy of Religion in St. Paul, Minn., studied 162 products promised to alter the purchaser's life through some miraculous means appearing in supermarket tabloids from March to November last year.

What she found was a variety of charms, amulets, beads, pins, dolls and spells promising everything from wealth to weight loss, new love to hex removals.

While the claims are often grandiose, customers are not asked to make a significant investment: The only product surveyed that cost more than $30 was a Triple Power Mojo Bag [used by Native American spiritualists] selling for $100.

But the eclectic natures of the products and the fact advertisers spend up to tens of thousands of dollars pitching them to a national audience indicates a willingness on the part of many Americans to believe in a variety of supernatural means to bring instant success.[15]

Today we can start each morning with coffee, toast, and one of the horoscope updates that appear daily in newspapers across North America. For many, it's just something that is read for fun, like the fortune in a Chinese cookie. Others, however, take astrological charts and readings much more seriously. When Ronald Reagan served as U.S. president, a brouhaha arose over the fact that his wife was trying to influence the White House through the direction of the stars. The revelation of this White House secret led others who were serious about consulting astrologers or psychics out into the open, including many Wall Street financiers and stockbrokers. Since then it has been learned that other world leaders believe in the occult as well. A *Toronto Star* article, for instance, revealed that Saudi Arabia's royal family regularly consults soothsayers:

> An Amman soothsayer's prophecy has thrown Saudi Arabia's royal family into turmoil and caused an outcry in the kingdom.
>
> At the heart of the controversy lies King Fahd, the aging sick ruler of the desert monarchy, and his youngest son. The rise of Prince Abdulaziz bin Fahd an Saud, 22, is attributed by Saudi insiders to a soothsayer who warned Fahd he would die unless he viewed his son's face at least once a week. . . .
>
> Fahd, 73, is obsessed with the occult. Another prediction—that he would meet his end in the royal capital of Riyadh—is the reason the king spends nearly all his time in the provinces, or in Jeddah.
>
> "The habit of consulting witches and wizards has spread like an epidemic," said a Saudi businessman who frequently travels outside the kingdom. "Although strictly forbidden by Islam, every prince has his own witch or wizard living with him. They are either Saudis or Ethiopians or Moroccans."
>
> It is widely believed in the kingdom that one of Fahd's nephews has a room in his palace dedi-

cated to the black arts, and another royal employs a witch full-time to promote his favorite football team by casting spells on rival players.[16]

According to a *Washington Post* news item, politicians and professionals in India are also flocking to "godmen" for advice:

> They cough up religious icons from their mouths, walk barefoot on red-hot coals, and cause written messages to appear on blank paper with all the pizzazz of cheap nightclub magicians. India's top politicians—including the prime minister—seek their counsel and pay homage by bowing to touch their feet. . . .

> Among those listed who flock to the gurus are "judges, doctors, businessmen, stockbrokers and foreigners."[17]

Even Kremlin policy has been suspected in recent years of being dictated by the occult:

> Behind the carefully orchestrated parade of Russian pomp, an almost Stalinesque paranoia and hysteria is gripping the country's top officials.

> The president's [Yeltsin] men are now reduced to communicating via slips of paper which they burn in ashtrays, while the entire staff lives in terror of the man known as the Black Magician—a KGB general who apparently studies the occult in order to determine national policy.

> He is General Georgy Georgievich Rogozin, who is said to prepare daily horoscopes for top Kremlin officials, as well as scanning space to determine budget issues, using spinning saucers in his Kremlin office and punctuating his working day with repeated mantras. He also goes to great lengths to create favourable magnetic fields around

the president, even to the extent of determining an exact north-south position for Yeltsin's bed. The general is reported to decide appointments to high office by consulting black magic tables.[18]

In the early summer of 1996, there was controversy over the fact that First Lady Hillary Clinton had visualized, with the help of psychologist Jean Houston, former First Lady Eleanor Roosevelt. It was said that Hillary Clinton held a conversation with the vision of Eleanor Roosevelt for her book *It Takes a Village*. Perhaps in an effort to save face for the Clinton administration in light of the November presidential elections, Jean Houston told the news media there were no spooks or seances involved. The conversation was just the First Lady's imagination. Houston claimed that, next to herself, Hillary Clinton was the least psychic person she had ever met.

Given Houston's past history of involvement with New Age spiritualism under the banner of visualization and guided imagery techniques, it is difficult to believe that occultism was not involved in Hillary Clinton's conversation with a dead Eleanor Roosevelt. Nonetheless, while some are more open about it than others, it is increasingly becoming public knowledge that many high-profile politicians and professionals highly endorse soothsayers and the occult, just as the rulers of ancient Babylon did.

Sorcery

Goddess worshippers and neo-pagans do not see the goddess as a separate supreme being from ourselves. Instead, they see the entire universe as a living entity, known as the goddess, with mankind being a part of that living entity. Starhawk explains:

For me the goddess is imminent. She is the world. She is us. She is nature. She is the changing of the season. She is the Earth herself. It's as if the whole universe were one living being that we are part of. And that's what we call goddess.[19]

As such, neo-pagans see this goddess as a life force to be manipulated through occult practices. They claim to call on the forces of nature by casting spells, so that they can direct their own will in a certain way. Ruth Montgomery's "guides" told her that we can indeed manipulate forces and cause miracles to happen:

The Guides say that we are all swimming in an inexhaustible sea of energies, and that those who seemingly perform miracles simply know how to utilize the energies. It's apparently as simple as the law of gravity, if we understand the principles....[20]

In other words, today's neo-pagans believe they are ruling their own destiny, creating their own reality. The manipulation of reality plays a key role in sorcery, or shamanism. Michael Harner, anthropoligist and white shaman, explained:

The ability of the master shaman to operate successfully in two different realities is seen as evidence of power.... The shaman moves back and forth between two realities deliberately and with serious intention....

Both personal realities of the shaman, the nonordinary and the ordinary, have their correlative states of consciousness. Each reality may be coped with successfully only when one is in the state of consciousness appropriate to it. Thus, if one is crossing a busy city street, the proper state of consciousness is different from that to be employed in entering the shamanic Lowerworld. A master shaman is fully aware of the appropriate consciousness for each situation with which he is faced, and enters into that state of consciousness as needed.[21]

Like Michael Harner, Carlos Castaneda was also a young anthropologist who, in the early 1960s, subjected himself to an intense apprenticeship into shamanism. Castaneda, who was taught by Yaqui Indian Don Juan, wrote:

> In order to teach and corroborate his knowledge Don Juan used three well-known psychotropic plants: peyote, Lophophora williamsii; jimson weed, Datura inoxia; and a species of mushroom which belongs to the genus of Psylocebe. Through the separate ingestion of each of these hallucinogens he produced in me, as his apprentice, some peculiar states of distorted perception, or altered consciousness, which I have called "states of nonordinary reality." I have used the word "reality" because it was a major premise in Don Juan's system of beliefs that the states of consciousness produced by the ingestion of any of those three plants were not hallucinations, but concrete, although unordinary, aspects of reality of everyday life. Don Juan behaved toward these states of nonordinary reality not "as if" they were real but "as real."[22]

Interestingly, the word translated "sorceries" in the New Testament (Revelation 9:21) is the Greek word *pharmakeia*, from which we get the English word *pharmaceuticals*, or drugs. Sorcery is associated with Satan in both the Old and New Testaments, and will apparently become much more prevalent and acceptable as we approach the last days.

The Tower of Babel Reconstructed

Over the years, God watched the rebellious people of Babylon follow after their own lusts, participating in the same occult practices we see being revived today. God also watched the people of ancient Babylon try to build for themselves a tower "whose top may reach unto heaven" and "make [them] a name, lest [they] be scattered abroad upon the face of the whole earth."[23] And when God saw them building this tower, He said:

> Behold, the people is one, and they have all one language; and this they begin to do: and now nothing will be restrained from them, which they have imagined to do. . . .

> So the Lord scattered them abroad from thence upon the face of all the earth: and they left off to build the city.

> Therefore is the name of it called Babel; because the Lord did there confound the language of all the earth; and from thence did the Lord scatter them abroad upon the face of all the earth.[24]

Today the world is trying to reverse this Babel effect. It is making an attempt to unite under a one-world system of government, economy, and spiritualism. The spiritual Tower of Babel, whose top would have reached up to heaven, is being reconstructed today.

This time God is going to let mankind continue with its construction. He is going to watch this new tower and its united world order crumble on its own. He will allow man to see that, despite his pride and arrogance, he cannot create a kingdom of heaven on earth without God. Man will have tried and failed. Then God will begin to pour out His wrath upon the earth, to crush the pride of man.

Will man at that point turn to God and say, "We're sorry. You were right all along"?

No. Instead, mankind will blaspheme God for the terrible things coming upon the earth during the tribulation period, and will refuse to repent of its sins, and its sorceries:

> The rest of the men which were not killed by these plagues yet repented not of the works of their hands, that they should not worship devils, and idols of gold, and silver, and brass, and stone, and of wood: which neither can see, nor hear, nor walk.
>
> Neither repented they of their murders, nor of their sorceries.[25]

Indeed, the peoples of the earth during the tribulation period will be prideful and overconfident. There will be peace, unity, signs and miracles—at least for a little while. Mystery Babylon, the spiritual whore and mother of religious harlots, will be riding high and proud on top of the political beast.

Who Is Able to Make War with Him?

While political and spiritual unity will give cohesion to the Antichrist's false kingdom, it appears from Scripture that, just as the ancient Romans had, he too will rely on some military strength to maintain *Pax Democratica*. It is no coincidence, therefore, that we are beginning to see a change in the power structure that has existed for much of this century.

Until the beginning of the twentieth century, a policy of isolationism prevailed in the United States. One of the factors that eventually propelled America into foreign affairs at the beginning of this century was the disintegration of the international stability of Europe. Its disintegration, of course, resulted from Europe's constant wars. Recognizing that instability in Europe and elsewhere in the world placed its own nation at jeopardy, America decided it was time to get involved in world affairs. As President Theodore Roosevelt stated to Congress in 1902, "More and more, the increasing interdependence and complexity of international political and economic relations render it incumbent on all civilized and orderly powers to insist on the proper policing of the world."[1]

181

Having been dragged into the affairs of Europe, especially during two world wars, the U.S. became a major actor on the international stage. It was the aftermath of World War II that created the balance of power that existed during the Cold War years: a counter-balance between the military might of the capitalist U.S. and the communist Soviet Union. It was during the Cold War that the views of these two world powers dominated the views of their respective alliances. And it was the views of this century's two dominant world powers that determined world policy.

Today, in the post-Cold War years, we are seeing a disintegration of both these world powers, though particularly in the former Soviet Union. And it is our belief, in accordance with Bible prophecy, that it will be the European Union, the center of the Revived Roman Empire, that will fill the vacuum left by the diminishing role of the world's two former superpowers.

It is no coincidence that today in the U.S., while there is a definite trend for this great nation to find its prominent place in the global order, there is also a desire for isolationism. The first real sign that isolationism was to be an important part of U.S. foreign policy at the close of the twentieth century was evidenced by Bill Clinton's 1992 campaign for the U.S. presidency. The two previous presidents, Ronald Reagan and George Bush, were very much at the heart of world affairs. Bill Clinton, however, promised the electorate he would focus more on domestic concerns, starting with a reduction in the U.S. military budget. Indeed, Clinton didn't even have a foreign policy to speak of during his campaign.

This is not to say that under the Clinton administration America has washed its hands completely of foreign affairs. The U.S. continues to play a role in world affairs today. However, as the twentieth century approaches its end, the world seems less inclined to follow American desires. Furthermore, the world is beginning to question U.S. foreign policy. For instance, the U.S. has been the dominant sponsor of the Madrid peace process since it commenced in the fall of 1991. Five years into the peace process, however, many Arab nations began to insist that America is Israel's uncritical supporter, thereby questioning the U.S. role as an unbiased mediator. Take the "Operation Grapes of Wrath" mishap in April, 1996, as an example. Northern Israel has for years been the target of terrorist attacks originating from southern Lebanon. In retaliation for a series of terrorist attacks just prior to April, 1996, Israel launched what it called "Operation Grapes of Wrath" against what was supposed to be a terrorist target. Unfortunately, Israel shelled a United Nations post located in southern Lebanon, killing 102 Arab civilians in refuge there. The incident ignited verbal hostilities against Israel, and it ignited hostilities against America as well. As the *Islamic Affairs Analyst* observed in the aftermath:

> The outcry throughout the Arab world at the Israeli actions was further fueled by America's blocking of anti-Israeli resolutions at the U.N.

> Syria complained vigorously about the U.S.'s acceptance of Israel's explanation for the bombing of the U.N. camp in Lebanon, saying: "The U.S. administration's position regarding the Israeli aggression contradicted its role as a basic sponsor of the peace process in the region. . . ."

> The furor over Israel's Operation Grapes of Wrath and the U.S.'s refusal to condemn the shelling of the U.N. camp (let alone the whole operation) has

led to renewed calls in the Arab world for a balance to America's regional omnipotence.[2]

One of the candidates being proposed by the Arabs to take America's place as the key mediator is France, one of the European Union's more dominant member nations. The *Islamic Affairs Analyst* article explained:

> If the Arab world has been infuriated by America, it has been well pleased by an apparent change of policy by France's President Chirac. "The renewed Arab interest in France predates Operation Grapes of Wrath and stems largely from President Chirac's early April visit to Lebanon.
>
> Traditionally France has supported Lebanon's Maronite Christians. Most recently it supported their opposition to the 1989 Taef Accord, that ended the 15-year civil war and handed Syria de facto control of Lebanon, and their boycott of subsequent elections. President Chirac's visit, however, indicated a reversal of this policy and pointed to a French move to reassert its influence in the region by supporting Syria's position in Lebanon. In particular, Chirac supported an Israeli withdrawal from Lebanon ahead of any Syrian withdrawal.
>
> Chirac's visit to Lebanon indicated a major change in policy and has been welcomed by many in the region as providing clear evidence that France wishes to become a major player again—on the Arab side.[3]

In addition, Chirac became the first international leader to address the Palestinian Authority, thus furthering his popularity over the Americans amongst Arabs. Another sign of America's declining popularity in determining world policy came in the summer of 1996. The U.S.

launched an air attack against Iraq, which had ignored the international community's "no-fly zone" regulations when it attacked a pro-Iranian Kurdish faction operating in northern Iraq. Reporting on the world's reaction to the U.S. move, *Intelligence Digest* observed:

> In military terms, the United States can do pretty well what it likes to Iraq. It has the firepower, and no one can stop it. But the largely adverse international reaction to the launch of 27 cruise missiles against Iraq early on 3 September highlights the difficulties the U.S. faces in maintaining a Pax Americana in the Middle East.
>
> No one likes Saddam Hussein, but there was condemnation of the U.S. action not only from predictable sources such as Libya but also from Russia and China. . . .
>
> Important European allies such as France and Spain withheld their support; and, in the Middle East, only Kuwait could be said to be enthusiastic. The Arab League condemned the U.S. attack as infringing the sovereignty of an Arab country.[4]

It is becoming obvious that U.S. popularity as *the* voice of world policy is waning. It is also becoming apparent that Arab parties to the peace process, as well as Arabs at the street level, are beginning to hold strong resentment against American involvement in the Middle East. Arabs are looking for a replacement for the U.S. as the central mediator in the peace negotiations. In the coming days it is very possible that France, as a representative of the EU, could become a dominant force, if not *the* dominant force, in the peace talks. This would obviously place the European Union in a very key spot in world affairs.

Already the EU has surpassed the United States in the global economic realm. The U.S. was once the dominant player in the global economy, as evidenced by the fact that the U.S. dollar has been the deciding currency of world trade for years. However, the growing U.S. deficit has diminished its role in the global marketplace, as well as the fact that U.S. industry has been on the decline. American economic prosperity is on a downward spiral, while the EU's is on an uphill climb. Again, such a trend fits right in with Bible prophecy.

Still, many have a difficult time believing that the U.S. will be anything other than the dominant world superpower that it was, especially considering its military. Such thoughts are cited in consideration of Washington's victory over Baghdad during the Persian Gulf War in 1991. However, while the U.S. is still a strong military power, since the Gulf War its military machine has shown signs of fatigue. For one, under the Clinton administration military expenditures have been cut. In addition, there have been public embarrassments, such as the time American soldiers were killed and publicly dragged through the streets of Somalia by a bunch of Somalian thugs. That unfortunate incident left the U.S. populace reluctant to keep sending its children off to wars that seem to have nothing to do with America. Furthermore, the U.S. military has been drained financially as well as in manpower as a result of its many "peacekeeping" partnership efforts around the world. As global conflicts continue to surface each day, the recognition has come that the U.S. cannot, and perhaps will not, be the world's only global cop. Others have been urged to start contributing their fair share.

Recognizing that the U.S. military might is being stretched, Europe has finally realized it is time to grow up and be prepared to fight its own battles. As the twentieth century comes to a close, the EU is taking its place of prominence in the world. It is coming together in united harmony, based on the same principle that made America great: the democratic union of states. Now the EU is ready to evolve into the final world power system, with a military infrastructure of its own.

The Alphabet Soup of European Defense

Following the end of the Cold War, it was realized that a new face was needed for European defense. NATO (North Atlantic Treaty Organization) and the Warsaw Pact, both products of the Cold War, were no longer appropriate for a Europe that could finally be united, east with west. As the Cold War ended, the idea of a common European defense organization fit snugly with the idea of a common Europe. Indeed, it appeared that the time had come for an independent, pan-European defense organization; one that would cooperate with the U.S. and Russia, but at the same time would greatly reduce their place of military dominance in Europe.

Some European defense organizations were already in existence during the Cold War years, but they were hidden by the overpowering shadow of NATO. One of these existing organizations was the Western European Union, which had been created in 1954. The WEU had remained inactive until 1984, when it became a part of the drive for European unity and common defense. At the 1991 summit during which the Maastricht Treaty was signed, the WEU was defined as the defense arm of the European Union. The groundwork for a common European defense policy is now being laid at the Intergovernmental Conference which commenced in Turin, Italy, in the spring of 1996. The goal is for the WEU to be a separate European defense identity, while at the same time supplying forces when needed in cooperation with NATO, the U.N. Security Council, and the Organization for Security and Cooperation in Europe.

Likewise, "Eurocorps," created by France and Germany in 1992, maintains that its goal is to be an unique European defense force that cooperates with other defense organizations for conflict prevention and resolution in the area. The Germans have said their goal is for Eurocorps to bring France, which had resigned from NATO under the leadership of Charles de Gaulle, closer to the alliance. France, however, envisions Eurocorps as the center of a future pan-European defense force separate from NATO.

Others see NATO as maintaining the prominent role in Europe's defense, but with Europe building stronger defense capabilities of its own so that the burden will not remain entirely on U.S. shoulders, as has been the case in the past. Indeed, with a new look in Europe, a new look for NATO is seen as a natural evolution. Eastern European countries, which had once been ruled by the iron fist of Russia, now want to join NATO. This move is deemed as a strategic step in protecting themselves from a Russia that may one day turn into a predator regime again. Of course, the immediate acceptance of the former Soviet satellites into the alliance would more than ruffle a few feathers in Russia. In fact, some extreme nationalists have claimed such a move would ignite a third world war.

The temporary solution to this dilemma thus far has been the creation of the Partnership for Peace. This branch of NATO was created as an intermediate step for Eastern European nations wanting to join NATO. Eastern European nations have been able to cooperate with NATO in joint military training exercises, with the hope of one day being fully accepted into the alliance. Even Russia was invited to join. At first it refused, then changed its mind, then changed its mind again, and then again.

Joint peacekeeping with Russia has been seen as a way to remove any paranoia over U.S. desires to strengthen NATO by adding new members right next to Russia's doorstep. One of the first joint military training exercises between the two former Cold War enemies took place in Kansas in the fall of 1995. For nine days, 150 Russian and 150 American troops participated in a mission called "Peacemaker 95," simulating peacekeeping operations under a U.N. truce in the fictional land of Kanza.

Another organization being promoted for European defense is the Organization for Security and Cooperation in Europe. The OSCE, originally the Conference for Security and Cooperation in Europe, had been created in 1972 as a forum for East-West dialogue. In 1992 at the CSCE summit, it was decided that the organization should be the main forum for dealing with security threats in a united Europe. In January, 1995, the CSCE changed its name to the OSCE, and with the name change came the promise of an expanded role in peacekeeping. *The Toronto Star's* foreign affairs writer, Gordon Barthos, reported:

> The organization, which groups the U.S., Canada and 50 European nations, used to be little more than a vehicle for the West to take the Soviets to task over security and human rights. No longer. In Budapest, Russia was an active and often cooperative player.
>
> • The CSCE agreed to send 3,000 peacekeepers to the Armenian enclave of Nagorno-Karabakh in the former Soviet republic of Azerbaijan, the first mission of its kind.

- The CSCE also agreed to monitor European countries for hate campaigns against minority groups, aiming to avert war.

- Clinton, Yeltsin and other leaders used the CSCE venue to sign into force the Strategic Arms Reduction Treaty, paving the way for a new round of nuclear weapons cuts.[5]

The Russians even allowed an OSCE fact-finding mission to take place concerning its conflict with Chechnya. Indeed, it appears that the OSCE is the organization with whom the Russians seem most interested in cooperating. Nonetheless, the OSCE is just one of the many organizations hoping to be in charge of European defense—WEU, NATO, OSCE, the U.N., and Eurocorps. Indeed, European defense has begun to look like an alphabet soup. The fear now is that too many cooks are going to spoil the broth. For example, *The European* newspaper reported, following the decision to make the CSCE the prime forum for European security:

> There is a danger that events in ex-Yugoslavia could lead to an uncontrolled escalation of military action, regardless of the political positions adopted by the CSCE participants.
>
> There have already been reports of Canadian U.N. troops returning sniper fire in Sarajevo. The more military forces that are sent to the area—and more French troops have been committed—the greater the risk of such incidents, possibly leading to more serious clashes, and even to direct military intervention by other countries. It has happened many times in history.
>
> Given this dangerous backdrop what, if any, are the CSCE's chances of success in preventing war

in Europe? It joins a bewildering array of over-lapping bodies pledged to defend Europe's security.[6]

The ideal would seem to be for only one of these defense organizations to come out the victor. While it is too early to tell which, if any, of the existing European defense organizations will be in charge of Europe's security in the future, it is interesting that in 1992 it was the OSCE that was named the "regional organization" under the U.N. Charter used for coordinating U.N. peacekeeping efforts. The creation of regional defense organizations operating under the banner of the U.N. is a trendy, growing idea. *The Washington Times* reported in the fall of 1994:

> The State Department's No. 2 man was sweating it out in such African backwaters as Ghana and Malawi.
>
> Burundi, Zimbabwe, Zaire and Ivory Coast—all countries unaccustomed to visits from such a high-ranking American diplomat—were also on Deputy Secretary of State Strobe Talbott's African itinerary.
>
> What gives? Diplomatic and congressional sources say Mr. Talbott was sent by his close friend Mr. Clinton to explain and promote a new U.S. policy for the continent.
>
> After his administration burned its hands in Somalia and sat through genocide in Rwanda, the president determined to find a way not to let it happen again, the sources said. To that end, he sent his No. 2 diplomat to six African nations to urge them to launch peacekeeping missions in their own neighborhoods. . . .
>
> Because the United Nations is "overburdened" with peacekeeping missions, Mr. Talbott said, the

United States is backing peacekeeping and conflict resolution efforts by the Organization of
African Unity and by smaller groups of nations
within Africa.[7]

The Washington Times article went on to add:

In a New York Times article, Mr. Boutros-Ghali
echoed the call for peacekeeping by the neighbors
of troubled states, saying local peacekeeping offices may cost less, respond more quickly, and be
familiar with the culture and geography.[8]

Mr. Boutros-Ghali would, of course, endorse such a
concept of regional defense. As we mentioned earlier in
the book, the trend today is for the creation of regional
governments overseeing the economy, politics, and global
defense, yet operating under the United Nations. The U.N.
Charter was written with regional governance and security in mind.

The Global Enforcer . . . NOT!

In the aftermath of the Persian Gulf War it appeared
that the United Nations was going to be given a prominent position as the global enforcer of the new world order.
But as ethnic conflicts began to increasingly surface in the
post-Cold War years, it became evident that the U.N. was
not up to the task. Take peacekeeping efforts in Somalia
as an example. With head held high, the U.N. sent peacekeepers to Somalia to squash civil unrest and bloodshed.
The U.N. went home a short time later with its tail between its legs.

We were told that much was expected of the U.N. in
the new world order, while too little was being given to
it—too little money, too little military manpower, and too

little authority. The time had come, we were told, to give the U.N. beast some teeth. "There may never be a better time," reported Ron Lowman, "to form a world police force."

> With the carnage in Rwanda and Bosnia and most countries battling huge deficits by slicing defence spending, a standing United Nations army, navy and air force could be the answer to many of the world's woes.
>
> Currently, the U.N. is a toothless lion, which roars when confronted by human savagery, but has to wait for its members to pop in its dentures before it can bite. Even then, the international legislative process toward a first chomp is interminable and there's a built-in reluctance by many nations to commit troops, some of whom might never see home again. . . .
>
> But obviously, if the U.N. does acquire military muscle all its own and financial contributions are received punctually from member states, a subtle transfer of loyalty from national flags and anthems to the blue banner of the U.N. would begin.[9]

Heavy emphasis was placed on the fact that the U.N. does indeed lack teeth to bite, as became especially evident during the Bosnian crisis. The Bosnian Serbs made a mockery of the U.N. peacekeeping mission on several occasions. After two French snipers were killed in Bosnia, the French government gave the U.N. a 48-hour ultimatum to enhance security for its peacekeepers or else its troops would be removed from the mission. At about the same time, a U.N. plane attempting to make its way to Sarajevo was turned back two days in a row by Bosnian Serbs. The Serbs prevented medical and food supplies from getting through by U.N. peacekeepers. NATO was called in for air strikes, but had to back off because Russia, which is pro-Serb, was offended by the attacks. This gave the Bosnian Serbs even more confidence to make a mockery of U.N. peacekeepers.

Even though Russian President Boris Yeltsin had said he would be appalled by any more air strikes against the Serbs, NATO obviously felt confident enough that Russia would not retaliate, and moved in to finish the job the U.N. had been sent to do.

Some of the most embarrassing moments for the U.N. followed the first of the NATO air strikes. Bosnian Serbs captured over 200 U.N. peacekeepers as hostages, chaining them to potential military targets as human shields against further NATO air strikes. Headlines such as "West Has 'No Guts,' Defiant Serbs Say,"[10] "Serbs Use Canadians as 'Shields',"[11] and "Serbs Capture 'Safe' Bosnian Town"[12] began to appear in the papers on a regular basis.

One problem in resolving the Bosnian crisis resulted from the fact that U.N. peacekeepers were essentially sent to the region to ensure that food and medical supplies were getting through. U.N. peacekeepers, dubbed "soldiers without enemies," were sent into a war zone without the authority to get involved in the conflict.

The main problem, however, in resolving the Bosnian crisis was the fact that Russia and the U.S. were on opposite sides of the issue. Indeed, since the beginning of the Cold War many ostensibly minor conflicts have turned into bloody massacres because the two domineering superpowers were not able to come to an agreement on how to resolve them. In turn, world consensus could never be reached when it was needed most to save lives. This has been one of the greatest failures of the United Nations since its creation, and that of its predecessor, the League of Nations. Harlan Cleveland explained the failing philosophy behind these two organizations:

> The founders of the League of Nations and the United Nations—and most of the other advocates of governing institutions for One World—shared some bedrock ideas. Their "world order" would be peopled with universal organizations that would administer and, if possible, enforce universal rights and duties. They would reflect a near-universal political will to band together to restrain and discipline outlaws and aggressors....
>
> As things turned out, the kinds of institutions that emerged from these noble conceptions didn't fit in the kinds of world community that have begun to emerge in the last decades of this century. Why? The ideas were universal and the institutions unitary; but the emerging real-world community was pluralistic.
>
> For the League of Nations to have succeeded would have required a club of the like-minded... [13]

The ideal solutions for the democracy of a new world order would seem to be, logically, to diminish the role of the two superpowers (which are still trying to shape world policy in the post-Cold War world), to diminish the authority of nation-states, and to give the U.N. the authority to act as the head of a global government and military force. This is just what many hope will occur.

Creating a Global Army

Revelation 13:4 tells us that the peoples of the world are going to worship the Antichrist, saying, "Who is like unto the beast? Who is able to make war with him?" It would seem likely from this Scripture reference that the Antichrist is going to have the backing of a global military to enforce the laws of his false kingdom as it expands across the globe.

Of course, such a military machine on a global scale does not exist today. But we believe that in addition to a global government being pre-fabricated for the Antichrist, a global army is being pre-fabricated for him as well. Indeed, the U.N. peacekeeper force, known as UNPROFOR, as well as the regional defense organizations which are rising into positions of prominence, could very well be the embryo of this global army. At minimum, they could serve as a model of what to do and what not to do for a future global military machine.

When the U.N. was created in 1945, its mission, according to the first paragraph of *Article 1* in its *Charter*, was "to maintain international peace . . . and to that end to take effective collective measures." During the Cold War years, however, this mandate was ineffective. Indeed, it essentially remained dormant. In the post-Cold War years, the world has changed. So too must the U.N. Arnold Simoni, who was involved in the founding of the Canadian Peace Research Institute and who works with the Centre for Strategic Studies at York University in Toronto, wrote:

> If the United Nations is to fulfill its mission set forth in the *Preamble* of *Chapter 1* of its *Charter*, it will have to be thoroughly reformed. Its first priority should be the formation of an effective and viable Peace Force. Without such a force at its disposal, the U.N. cannot assure the conditions essential to make and maintain peace.[14]

He then went on to point out several difficulties that are going to have to be overcome in the existing world if the U.N. is to fulfill its mandate by creating a peace force:

Sovereignty: The creation of a Peace Force as an effective arm of the U.N. will necessarily entail some degree of infringement of national sovereignty.

A Reformed International Court of Justice: To establish the rights and limitations of the U.N. Peace Force, a code of international law will be required, and the parties responsible for implementing them will also have to be clearly defined. This code furthermore will determine the framework under which the U.N. Peace Force could and should intervene. Such a reformed International Court will have to be neutral.

Military Peace Force and Its Responsibilities: An essential element for establishing a U.N. Peace Force will be the establishment of a model demonstrating how a military department at the U.N. might work. Such a department would be responsible for the recruitment, arming, training and stationing of the Peace Force . . .

Personnel: The Peace Force should comprise volunteers. They will have to renounce their nationality for the period of their service, which might be about two years.[15]

Of course, if nation-states gave up their sovereignty and eventually ceased to exist, this point would be moot. Simoni went on to add:

Funding: Funding for the military forces, including armament and operational costs, will have to be obtained through taxes, which should be imposed on all nations in proportion to their wealth. These contributions will, to a degree, represent a partial transfer of expenditures that are now allocated to national defence budgets; the existence of an effective U.N. Peace Force would enable nations to reduce their own military forces, and with it their defence budgets. A possible source of armament would be the arms rendered surplus by national military forces.[16]

In such a scenario, nation-states, while they continued to exist, would be demilitarized. At the same time, the U.N. would have under its command a global army. To avoid abuses of such an army, Simoni said we would need:

> **Checks and Balances:** To prevent the misuse of U.N. forces, checks and balances will have to be clearly defined and imposed. The increase in military power required to make the Peace Force effective will also make it dangerous if misdirected.[17]

He gave no suggestions as to what these checks and balances would be if nation-states have given up their sovereignty and their national defense forces.

Indeed, while global planners are promoting the idea of a U.N. army, they are at the same time suggesting, as did Mr. Simoni, that the nation-states should be demilitarized. Ron Lowman reported, for example:

> Disarming nations relies on decisions by governments to surrender some of their sovereignty to the U.N. Security Council.

> Respect for and allegiance to U.N. international symbols might take a decade or two and there would be great difficulty in persuading such powers as the U.S., Britain, Germany, and France to eliminate their conventional and nuclear forces and leave the global protection job to the U.N. But this must be the goal if anarchy is to end.[18]

While nations are making an effort today to reduce the numbers of conventional and nuclear weapons in their possession, it would be extremely difficult to convince them to completely disarm themselves. It may, however, be the appearance of the Antichrist, which will likely occur during a time of global crisis, which will be the catalyst for putting the finishing touches on such a global military machine, and for convincing the nation-states to give up their sovereignty and national defense forces. They would likely be convinced to become a part of regional defense organizations operating under the command of the U.N. As Simoni observed:

> Because the changes required are so profound, it might be argued that one will have to wait for action until cataclysmic crisis conditions occur that undermine the status quo.[19]

Once such a military is under the command of the Antichrist, the way will be paved for the prophecy in Revelation 13:4 to be fulfilled: Who indeed will be able to make war with him?

In the meantime, however, while nation-states feel more secure with their weapons than without, there is another trend occuring that may also help to fulfill this prophecy. Many nation-states are now mandating that their national citizenry hand over their weapons under the banner of "Gun Control Laws." On June 13, 1995, for example, the Canadian Parliament passed a controversial gun control law known as Bill C-68. Canadian Prime Minister Jean Chretien had lauded it as the toughest gun control law in the world. The bill stipulated that by 1998, the three million Canadians who own firearms would be expected to register the seven million firearms they are estimated to possess. And there would be very stiff penalties for those who refused. Bill C-68 also stipulated:

- At 5-year intervals, gun owners will have to produce a good excuse for possessing a weapon—i.e. hunting, collecting antique guns, or target shooting.

- The sale of small, snub-nosed revolvers will be outlawed.

- Military and para-military weapons like AK-47s will be banned. Present owners would be able to keep such weapons, but after January 1, 1996 the sale of them will be illegal.

- Cross-bows will also have to be registered.

- Small, single-hand cross-bows will be banned.

The Canadian law is just part of a trend taking place around the world. Other nations have already passed similar gun laws, and others are working on passing them, the U.S. included.

Disarming the Populace

The physical shock waves reverberated over 50 kilometers away. The emotional shock waves resounded much further.

The world sat stunned, eyes glued to CNN, watching live coverage of injured toddlers and federal workers being rescued from the rubble of what was once the Alfred P. Murrah Federal Building in Oklahoma City. Over 200 were killed and more than 400 injured.

The federal building housed the Social Security offices and the Drug Enforcement Agency, as well as several other government service agencies. It also housed a day-care center. Many of the dead were innocent children and infants. The target of the attack were the offices of the Federal Bureau of Investigation (FBI) and the Bureau of Alcohol, Tobacco and Firearms (ATF).

Swift investigation by federal agents led to the arrest of Timothy McVeigh. According to a federal affidavit,

McVeigh was obsessed with the April 19, 1993, showdown between Branch Davidians and ATF and FBI agents. The Oklahoma bombing occurred two years to the day following the inferno at Waco. According to media reports, correspondence was found in McVeigh's vehicle that "threatened retribution" against the FBI and ATF.

There is no question that the Branch Davidians were members of a misguided cult who posed a possible threat because of their stockpile of firearms. At the same time, there is also no question that the FBI and the ATF mishandled the situation, as was revealed in public hearings. Their mismanagement of the situation eventually led to the mass suicide of Branch Davidians who remained in the compound, some of whom were children. What McVeigh had allegedly done, however, was the worse crime.

Immediately following McVeigh's arrest, it was revealed by the media that he was linked to the rising militia/patriot movement. With this revelation, one of the key issues of contention between the government and the militia movement rose to the surface—gun control. Indeed, gun control has proven to be one of the most controversial issues of our time.

Each side seems to have some valid arguments, but history has shown there are some very good reasons to oppose gun control laws. "Since 1900," reports the group *Jews for the Preservation of Firearms Ownership, Inc.,* "there have been at least seven major genocides." And according to the group, each case of genocide was preceded by gun control laws. According to their report, *Lethal Laws,*[20] 1 to 1.5 million Armenians were killed between 1915 and 1917 by the Ottoman Turks. The government of the Ottoman Turks had earlier passed two gun laws, in 1866 and in 1911, preventing Armenians from defending themselves.

In the former Soviet Union, 20 million anti-Commu-
nists and anti-Stalinists were murdered between 1929 and
1953. The Soviet Union had passed its gun control law the
same year the massacres began.

In Nazi Germany and the European nations which
came under its control, 13 million Jews, Gypsies, and anti-
Nazis were murdered in the years 1933 to 1945. The Nazi
"Law on Firearms & Ammunition" and the "Weapons
Law" had been passed in 1928.

China had three periods during which genocide was
committed, starting in 1949 and extending to 1976. Twenty
million people were killed following strict gun laws that
had been made. (This record of genocide does not include
the massacre that took place at Tiananmen Square in 1990.)

One hundred thousand Mayan Indians were killed in
Guatemala from 1960 to 1981 as a result of two different
gun control laws, which kept the Indians from protecting
themselves.

In Uganda, 300,000 Christians and political rivals were
murdered between 1971 and 1979 as a result of the 1955
"Firearms Ordinance" and the 1970 "Firearms Act."

And finally, a 1956 gun control law in Cambodia
opened the door for war and the eventual massacre of one
million "educated persons" between 1975 and 1979.

The total killed in the 1900s as a result of gun control
laws? 55.9 million people. In every case, gun control laws
precluded the citizenry from defending itself against an
aggressor government.

Keeping this history in mind, there seems to be a very
good case for opposing gun control legislation. Furthermore, there are many *responsible* citizens in America, and
in other parts of the world, who possess firearms.

Unfortunately, there are also a lot of loose cannons like
Timothy McVeigh. Following the Oklahoma incident, a

paranoia over the militia movement's paranoia began to spread. The actions of Timothy McVeigh seemed to warrant such public concern. Daniel Pipes, editor of the *Middle East Quarterly*, wrote:

> News reports about the Michigan Militia and other extreme-right groups belonging to the so-called Patriot Movement, allegedly connected to the bombing in Oklahoma City, portray them as a phenomenon of the past few years. But their political views and psychology are part of a much longer history. Only by seeing the groups in this light can we understand who they are, what menace they pose, and how to deal with them.
>
> The Patriot groups primarily see the world in terms of conspiracy theories: The federal government is conspiring to deny Americans their constitutional freedoms; Zionists are conspiring to control the government, as are foreign states; the federal government staged the Oklahoma blast, as a way of winning sympathy and justifying a crackdown on Patriot groups.[21]

The controversy over gun control laws comes from the dilemma of wanting to prevent loose cannons like McVeigh from possessing or building weapons, while at the same time not wanting to trample on the constitutional rights and civil liberties of responsible people who may need to defend themselves someday. The big question is, "What cost in freedom will people be willing to pay in exchange for an assurance of their safety?" Indeed, fear is the biggest motivator for accepting a loss of freedom in exchange for peace and safety.

A Call to Arms, or a Call to Prayer?

For some, the issue of gun control legislation seems like one of those issues that never really come to a clear resolution. However, our main concern over the issue is, "What should my response as a Christian be?" For the answer to this, we must go back to the illustration at the beginning of this book and visit our Christian friend floating along in the boat of life.

Remember that our Christian friend had been warned by God that things in the world were going to get increasingly worse. God told him that he would see signs, meaning that the boat was getting closer to a point where a world dictator was going to present himself to the world as a false savior over a global government. At first, the Antichrist will seem to be a friend to God's chosen people, but he is going to convince the armies of the world to try to destroy these people. Our Christian friend was told that this same Antichrist is going to persecute the saints of God and kill them.

However, these prophecies were given for the tribulation period. God told our Christian friend in the boat of life that he would be taken out of the boat before it reached this brink. Now, this is not to say that Christians won't face any physical persecution in the world. Indeed, many Christians in other nations have been or currently are being physically persecuted. We in North America have been blessed not to have suffered this kind of persecution on a wide scale.

But the fact is that the McVeighs of the world, the Branch Davidians, and many others in the militia/patriot movement see these same signs. They think their hope is in the boat. They have decided it is imperative that they do what they can to salvage it from government control.

Hence, they oppose virtually everything to do with the government from birth certificates to marriage licenses to taxes. They believe they have to protect themselves from a world dictator and from the loss of civil freedom. Their whole foundation is built on the sand of mankind's improvements rather than upon the Rock, who is Christ.

Jesus told us that when we see all of these things coming upon the world, we are to look up, because our redemption is drawing nearer.[22] He did not give us a call to arms against our governments. He called us to prayer and fasting. The Apostle Paul reminded Titus to "put them in mind to be subject to principalities and powers, to obey magistrates, to be ready to every good work."[23]

As Christians, our battles are not physical. They are spiritual. We are reminded that "we wrestle not against flesh and blood, but against principalities, against powers, against the rulers of darkness of this world, against spiritual wickedness in high places."[24]

And for this battle we need the armor of God, with our:

> loins girt about with truth, and having on the breastplate of righteousness;
>
> And your feet shod with the preparation of the gospel of peace;
>
> Above all, taking the shield of faith, wherewith ye shall be able to quench all the fiery darts of the wicked.
>
> And take the helmet of salvation, and the sword of the Spirit, which is the word of God.[25]

Fighting with weapons will only encourage more government control and intervention, not less. Indeed, by fighting the prophesied new world order with weapons, it only seems to bring it about that much quicker. As Christians, we are not to fear this coming world order. We should be rejoicing in it, for it means we are that much closer to being present with our Lord and Savior.

The Russian Bear in Prophecy

The mighty Soviet bear once threatened to devour the entire world, satisfying its hunger for communist domination. But the predator instinct of this Soviet bear was kept in check for the most part by its Cold War enemy, the United States. In the post-Cold War years, the Soviet bear faces new enemies: enemies of internal chaos. It suffers from economic disease and environmental decay. The head of the former Soviet family, Mother Russia, has therefore released her cubs. She is now seeking to find a less prominent place in a new world order.

This is to be expected in light of Bible prophecy. God's Word prophesies that it is the Revived Roman Empire that is to be the final world power system. And it is now, as Russia fades from superpower status, that the Revived Roman Empire is rising to its place of world dominance. This does not mean, however, that Russia is going to fade into the pages of history. God still has a plan for Russia that is yet to be fulfilled.

The Lord told our Christian friend floating along the river in his boat that one of the signs he was going to see along the shoreline was a bear. This bear, according to God, is going to spot a big fat fish in the river. It is going to grab

207

hold of that fish, not realizing it is actually bait on a hook. And when the bear attempts to swallow the bait, God said He is going to set the hook in the bear's jaw and reel it in for the kill. What does this warning mean? It is necessary to take a look at Russia today to understand this prophecy of the bait and the hook.

Don't Underestimate the Bear

Intelligence sources agree that Russia will never be a threat on a global scale as it was during the Cold War years. Nevertheless, this does not mean Russia's ability to create trouble for the world should be underestimated. *Intelligence Digest*, for instance, noted:

> Our sources insist, there will be no return to the Cold War....

> All military power is ultimately based on the strength of a country's economy, and the latest CIA figures on the Russian economy show just how far it is from being a superpower....

> However, the fact that Russia could not again mount a *global* challenge to the Western powers is a very long way from meaning that it is no longer a problem.

> Russia, with an economy more than 10 times the size of Iraq, with a population of 150 million, with the largest land area of any country in the world at 17 million square kilometers (China, Canada, and the U.S. all have around 9 million square kilometers), and with over 8,000 strategic nuclear warheads at its disposal, is hardly a negligible force. If Russia wants to make trouble, it can make trouble.[1]

Other sources reveal that even though the Cold War is over, it should not be forgotten that the bear still has claws. A report in *The Wall Street Journal* pointed out, for example, that Russia is still placing a heavy emphasis on its submarines, completing construction of those that had been started during the days of the Cold War, "on about the same timetable as the Soviets produced them."[2] The article revealed that Russia "will enter the next century with the largest nuclear submarine fleet in the world."[3]

In 1995 Russia possessed 120 nuclear subs and 60 diesel subs. *The Wall Street Journal* article noted, however, that the U.S. expected these numbers to decline to 80 nuclear and 40 diesel submarines by the turn of the century because Russia cannot afford to maintain them. Even so, continued the article:

> A submarine force of 80 nuclear ships in the year 2000 could be a world-class force. (The U.S. will have fewer than 70 nuclear subs at that time.) But numbers alone don't make you world-class. Quality matters. One significant determinant of a submarine's quality is the amount of noise it radiates. Noisy submarines are more easily detected, and detectable submarines risk being destroyed by an adversary.
>
> The Russian nuclear submarines decommissioned recently were older and noisier. The newest Russian subs are not noisy; indeed . . . in important ways they are quieter than many of our submarines. . . .
>
> The best explanation for this ambitious program, although it doesn't fully explain the size of the submarine force, is that Russia is trying to protect its nuclear forces and its nuclear position established under the START treaties.[4]

A few months after *The Wall Street Journal* report, it was announced that Russia was buying from the Ukraine a number of bombers and strategic missiles that would help it hold on to its "nuclear potential at an appropriate level until 2009."[5]

What makes Russia even more dangerous than the fact that it intends to maintain its nuclear potential for years to come is the fact that it is an unstable nation, politically and economically. Even though Boris Yeltsin won the 1996 summer presidential elections, meaning the majority of the Russian population voted to continue on with painful democratic and economic reforms, international observers agreed that Russia's future was still uncertain. For one, most believe that because of poor health, Yeltsin will not complete his full term as Russian President. (Indeed, we wondered whether he would make it to the printing of this book.) One of the big questions is who will become the next Russian leader if Boris Yeltsin is unable to finish the job. Regardless of who is in charge of Russia, its political future remains critical. While it is true that the majority of the population in the 1996 presidential elections voted to continue with democratic reforms, it should not be forgotten that Communist Party leader Gennady Zyuganov came very close to becoming Russia's next leader. This says something about the Russian sentiment at the time of the elections.

Since the fall of communism, the road to democracy and economic prosperity has been long and rocky. Many look at the potholes in the road and think back to the days of communist rule, when things appeared to be more stable. After all, many believe the state was providing for them. There were jobs and there was food. Furthermore, many look back with longing to the days of Russia's superpower status, which had been created by Stalin.

Hedrick Smith had spent three years in the early 70's as the Moscow bureau chief for *The New York Times* in Russia. When communism collapsed, he decided to go back to Russia and see what changes had taken place, in the nation and in the people. In his book *The New Russians* he noted:

> People's views of Stalin are a touchstone for the political loyalties and their attitudes toward the Soviet future. For if there are millions like [Byelorussian archaeologist] Zenon Poznyak who believe Stalin was a demon, there are still millions of others who revere him as a demigod.
>
> It was Stalin, they declare, who built the Soviet Union into a superpower. It was Stalin who industrialized a peasant country, took it from wooden plows to atomic weapons, thrust it into the twentieth century, and made the West tremble at the might of Russia. Above all, it was Stalin who won the war, destroyed Hitler, beat the Germans. As they talk of Stalin, his admirers romanticize the exploits of their own youth, when, with Stalin at the helm, they were building a Brave New World.[6]

Others, however, remember the years of terror under Stalin and the atrocities of cold-blooded murder committed at his command. Stalin was responsible for the deaths of 50 million of his own people. He sent millions to prison camps on trumped-up charges in order to steal their gold and possessions. Millions died from starvation and exhaustion in these concentration camps, or *gulags*. Stalin claimed to implement his collectivization program for agriculture as a share-the-wealth policy. The move was actually a ploy to steal the people's land and force them to obey his whims, while at the same time threatening to withhold food from them if they didn't obey. Peasants who resisted Stalin's policy of collectivization were starved to death in order to break their will. The result of his collectivization was a famine that was responsible for the death of eight million lives.

Many also remember that Stalin only defeated Nazi Germany after having collaborated with Hitler to take control of all of Europe, and eventually the entire world. To fulfill their lust for power, Stalin and Hitler together marched over millions of corpses with no regrets.

Stalin's successor, Nikita Khrushchev, vowed to continue Stalin's policy of terror. At the Twentieth Party Congress on February 24, 1956, Khrushchev proclaimed:

> The questioning of Stalin's terror, in turn, may lead to the questioning of terror in general. But Bolshevism believes in the use of terror. Lenin held that no one was worthy of the name Communist who did not believe in terror.[7]

The memories of many Russians are apparently short-lived. Just one year after the collapse of communism, many were longing for those good old days. *The Buffalo News* reported in the summer of 1992:

> Almost a year after the collapse of communism, the mood in the great Russian heartland is decidedly bleak.
>
> "Life was better during the so-called days of stagnation," said Valentin Novkov, who belongs to the emerging class of private farmers that has supposedly benefited from free-market reforms, referring to the period of hard-line Communist rule in the 1970s and early 1980s. "If I had the possibility, I would gladly return to those days. You could buy chocolate then. Now you work from morning to night and end up under a mountain of debt."

"The label 'democrat' has become a worse term of abuse than 'Communist,' " said Yevgeny Kovalyev, a journalist who helped organize some of the first protests against Communist Party rule in this Volga River city of 600,000 people [Yaroslavl]. "They said that prices would go up three times. Instead, they have gone up 40 times. People's patience is at a breaking point."[8]

An ominous example of what can happen when the Russian patience reaches the breaking point is their support of extreme nationalists like Vladimir Zhirinovsky. When he first came on the political scene, Zhirinovsky had done quite well in Russian politics, despite his virulent anti-Westernism and neo-fascist beliefs. His support from the Russian populace surprised, and perhaps for a time alarmed, the international community. Foreigners perceived Zhirinovsky as a mad clown making outrageous and dangerous promises of restoring the Soviet Union. Some even feared he could become Russia's next freely elected president. The fear was further fueled when his inappropriately named Liberal Democratic Party of Russia (LDPR) did extremely well in the December 1995 parliamentary elections. The Communist Party also did extremely well. The message had been sent: Much of the Russian public was fed up with democratic reforms and longed for the fulfillment of nationalist and communist promises of a Soviet empire restored to its former glory.

Another ominous sign, linked to the large support of leaders like Zhirinovsky and Zyuganov, is the fact that much of the Russian population is looking for a scapegoat for its problems. They are unwilling to blame their own forefathers. In a conversation with Hedrick Smith, film director Andrei Smirnov told him:

I agree with Solzhenitsyn that without repentance, we cannot change ourselves or our society. We must feel responsibility for our history. Who was it who made Stalin's terror? It was we—our fathers—and we must now pay for our fathers. But this is repulsive to most people. They want to blame others. They accuse Jews or someone else. They do not want to accept responsibility.[9]

Anti-Semitism in Russia

There has been a long history of anti-Semitism in Russia. Under the Czars it was policy. Under the Soviets it was a battle against "Zionism." And today it is a battle against a "Jewish-Masonic plot" designed to destroy Russia. While it is true that anti-Semitism has declined somewhat since the fall of communism, there is no question that it is still a part of life in Russia. Anti-Semitic comments are common from the general populace, and even from politicians. Venomous anti-Semitic comments from Vladimir Zhirinovsky have appealed to hard-line nationalists. They heartily agreed when Zhirinovsky claimed that while "the Jews controlled all the wealth," it was the Russians who were getting poorer. And although Communist Party head Gennady Zyuganov, just prior to the presidential elections, had called for an end to "nationalism, separatism, anti-Semitism and chauvinism," he too has suggested in his own writings that the Jews control the world's economy. International observers agreed that anti-Semitism played a key role in the 1996 presidential elections. Julia Rubin from the Associated Press, for instance, observed:

> Anti-Semitism remains part of the anti-Western nationalism that helps unite the Communist-led coalition of hard-line groups, the "National Patriotic Bloc."

Many of the coalition's leaders are overtly anti-Semitic. Zyuganov dances around the edges.

Many of his followers wave signs at rallies calling Yeltsin and his government "Yids," and the whole past 10 years of market reforms the work of a "Jewish-Masonic conspiracy" aimed at Russia's destruction.

"It is shocking that after a period of greater liberation . . . the situation's now reverting and major Russian political parties are using anti-Semitism as part of their program," said Adrian Karatnycky, director of Freedom House, a New York-based group monitoring democracy and human rights.

Russian anti-Semites traditionally equate Jews with Western influences, in particular capitalism, they consider alien and dangerous.

Now, when Western culture seems triumphant, anti-Semites blame Jews for their country's economic collapse.[10]

While many agree that Jews are experiencing a time of greater freedom in Russia since Soviet-era restrictions, there are some who are warning that it could only be a temporary lull. Rubin further observed:

A recent poll by the American Jewish Committee supported the impression anti-Semitism is in decline, saying Caucasus mountain ethnic groups such as the Chechens are now the main targets of prejudice.

But the pollsters warned widespread ignorance about Jews, along with general intolerance, means anti-Semitism could rebound "should the situation in Russia seriously worsen in the future."[11]

The warning bodes ill, since most agree that it will be a long while before the Russian economy improves. Indeed, the fire is being stoked for the Russian invasion of Israel, which was forewarned by the prophet Ezekiel.

Identifying Russia in the Bible

Those of you who have read the Bible from cover to cover know that the word "Russia" does not appear anywhere in its pages. So how can we say that the prophet Ezekiel forewarned that Russia would one day try to invade the State of Israel? First, it must be remembered that Ezekiel would have identified "nations" in his day by their ancient tribal names. Today, of course, these nations are identified with twentieth-century names.

Ezekiel 38 (verses 2-6) and 39 tells of an army coming from the north of Israel to invade it. We'll look at all of the various ancient tribes mentioned in these passages of Scripture, but for this chapter we want to focus on "Gog, of the land of Magog, the prince of Rosh" (Amplified Version, verse 2). Bible scholars agree that "Gog," also described as the "prince of Rosh," is the leader of what is modern-day Russia. The *Smith's Bible Dictionary* explains:

> The whole sentence, thus rendered . . . "Magog the chief prince of Meshech and Tubal," ought to run, "Magog the prince of Rosh, Meshech, and Tubal." The meaning is, that Magog is the head of the three great Scythian tribes, of which "Rosh" is thus the first. By Rosh is apparently meant the tribe on the north of the Taurus, so called from the neighborhood to the *Rha*, or Volga, and thus in this name and tribe we have the first trace of RUSS or RUSSIAN nation."[12]

Not only is Russia, therefore, mentioned in Bible prophecy, but also it is described as a people that displeases God because of its prince. Ezekiel warns this prince:

> Thus saith the Lord God; Behold, I am against thee, O Gog, the chief prince of Meshech and Tubal: And I will turn thee back, and put hooks into thy jaws.[13]

Why would God be so opposed to modern-day Russia that He is going to deliberately set a trap for it? Well, for one, Russia has a long history of persecution against God's chosen people, the Jews.

Second, Russia is a nation that, by its very doctrine, has defied God Himself. Using the occasion of the 70th anniversary of the Bolshevik revolution, Michael Johns, then assistant editor of *Policy Review,* decided to take a look at the seventy-year history of terror and evil that took place in the former Soviet Union starting in November, 1917. As for the Soviet Union's doctrine of atheism, Johns recorded:

> **January 13, 1918**—A decree denies churches all property and legal rights, in effect outlawing their existence. Soon after, religious marriage is abolished and the family is declared obsolete. Family is criticized for preventing women from doing work useful to the state and declared irrelevant, since the state will gradually take over childrearing.

> **October 2, 1920**—Lenin defines "Communist ethics" in opposition to morality of "bourgeoisie, who declared that ethics were God's commandments. We . . . do not believe in God. . . . We say that our morality is entirely subordinated to the interests of the class struggle of the proletariat. For the Communist, morality consists entirely of

compact united discipline and conscious mass struggle against the exploiters."

1922—Atheist publishing house begins operations along with weekly newspaper of same name. By 1923, monthly Soviet magazine, *The Godless at the Workplace*, begins publishing crude anti-Semitic cartoons later used by the Nazis.

May 15, 1932—A five-year anti-religion plan [initiated by Stalin] proclaims: "By the first of May 1937 not a single house of prayer will be needed any longer in any territory of the Soviet Union, and the very notion of God will be expunged as a survival of the Middle Ages and an instrument for holding down the working masses."[14]

Let My People Go

When the Israelites had finally been released from slavery in Egypt, God, through His servant Moses, led them on a journey to the land He had promised to Abraham, Isaac, and Jacob. God warned the Israelites, however, that if they refused to obey His commandments, He would expel them from the land and scatter them to other nations, where they would be persecuted:

> The Lord shall scatter thee among all people, from the one end of the earth even unto the other; and there thou shalt serve other gods, which neither thou nor thy fathers have known, even wood and stone.

> And among these nations shalt thou find no ease, neither shall the sole of thy foot have rest: but the Lord shall give thee there a trembling heart, and failing of eyes, and sorrow of mind:

> And thy life shall hang in doubt before thee; and thou shalt fear day and night, and shalt have none assurance of thy life.[15]

We know, of course, from the history of the Jews, that this is exactly what happened to them for over two millennia. When not restricted by slavery, they would flee persecution and would settle down for a time. Then they would be forced to flee again as new rounds of persecution erupted. Sadly, millions of Jews throughout their history never escaped the persecution.

However, God also promised that this would not be their eternal destiny. He told His chosen people that in the last days He would bring them out of the nations of the world to which He had scattered them, and would lead them once again to the promised land. This generation has seen the fulfillment of this prophecy. Israel became a nation again in 1948, for the first time in over two millennia. Since then, Jews have been returning to the promised land, modern-day Israel, just as God promised:

> For I will take you from among the heathen, and gather you out of all countries, and will bring you into your own land.[16]

One of the places the Jews had fled to, in an attempt to escape centuries of persecution in Europe, was Russia and other areas of the former Soviet Union. With nowhere else to go, many Jews remained in the area of the former Soviet Union, despite the intermittent eruptions of persecution. With the rise of communism, the Jews were hindered for decades from leaving the region, even if they had wanted to. But God's Word also specifically promised that this would be an area from which His chosen people would be set free in the last days:

> But, the Lord liveth, that brought up the children of Israel from the land of the north, and from all the lands whither he had driven them: and I will

bring them again into their land that I gave unto
their fathers.[17]

As the Lord promised in this passage of Scripture,
the Jews have been released from captivity in "the land
of the north." As a result of Soviet-American détente,
which reached its peak in 1978, the Kremlin rulers
agreed to let some of God's chosen people go. From 1978
to 1979, about 200,000 Soviet Jews fled to Israel. Then
the Iron Curtain closed once again, and the remaining
Soviet Jews were held captive for another decade until
the fall of communism. With its fall, the Iron Curtain
was removed and Soviet Jews were free to leave in mass
exodus. God's prophecy for His chosen people in the
last days was free to be fulfilled.

However, just as the Egyptian pharaoh regretted let-
ting God's chosen people go and followed after them, so
too will the Russians one day. Indeed, there are many par-
allels in the story of the exodus of the Israelites from Egypt
and the exodus of the Jews from Russia in these last days.

The Plagues of Russia

The Egyptians had immediately regretted releasing
their slaves, and followed them into the wilderness. Egypt
was in ruins, having suffered from God's plagues sent
upon it because of the Jews. Indeed, the Israelites were the
reason Egypt had been left in such a disastrous state. Similarly, Russia today lies in a state of disintegration since
the fall of communism. Embarrassed by and angered over
the loss of superpower status, many are now blaming the
Jews for the poor state Russia now finds itself in..

Since the fall of communism, things have not gone
particularly well for the Russians. Thinking back to the
early days following the collapse of the Soviet Union, we

remember seeing on the daily news, night after night, numerous line-ups of frustrated Russians waiting for lengthy periods of time to get into their local shops to purchase food. They were even more frustrated, we learned, when, having finally gained entrance into the shops, they discovered that not only were there no choice items left, but there was virtually no food to be purchased at all.

Such scenes of Russians queuing up for long hours no longer flash across our TV screens on the nightly news. Nonetheless, things have not greatly improved in the years since. 1995, for instance, was a very bad year for most Russians. At the beginning of 1995, *Intelligence Digest* reported that Russia's prospects for the coming months were pretty bleak:

> The economic crisis in Russia is reflected in a monthly inflation rate that has rocketed from around 5% last August to 17.8% in January. That equates to an annual inflation rate of over 700%....
>
> The prospects for 1995 are further clouded by the racing certainty of a major crisis in agriculture. Some 80% of all farm machinery is in need of repairs which the farms cannot carry out because of the delay in the payment of subsidies. During January, meat and butter output was down by over 40% on last year, and sources say that Russia's 1995 harvest could also be 40% down on 1994.
>
> To crown it all, life expectancy in Russia is now just 65 years (it might be as low as 64.1 years according to some calculations), four years lower than it was at the beginning of the decade.[18]

In the months that followed, current events stories backed earlier warnings about Russia's poor prospects for

1995 as one crisis after another seemed to crop up. In the spring of 1995, an earthquake measuring 7.5 on the Richter scale hit Russia's Sakhalin Island, one of the most earthquake-prone regions in that area. What made the earthquake even more of a disaster, according to some, was Russia's poor supply of cash. Reporting from *The Toronto Star's* Moscow bureau, Olivia Ward wrote a short time after the quake:

> Irresponsible Soviet planning, economic collapse and unlucky geography all contributed to the worst earthquake disaster in modern Russian history on remote Sakhalin Island.
>
> "In the past seismic monitoring stations were placed along the edges of Sakhalin," said Grigory Kireyev, head of the Pacific territory's newspaper and information agency.
>
> "Last year, three were closed down near Neftegorsk for lack of funding."

As a result, Sakhalin's 3,200 sleeping residents were unprepared for the earthquake, and most were killed.

In the summer of 1995, another crisis was taking place, this time in Russia's banks. Many feared that the bank crisis could fuel a return to dictatorship. Miranda Anichkina reported for *The European*:

> In the past three years, said Mikhail Berger, the influential economics editor of *Izvestia*, the Russian interbank market has developed into a fairly efficient mechanism through which the country's estimated 3,000 banks buy and sell currency. As such, it has provided the liquidity essential to their survival. But bankers fear that if they stop lending to each other, banks will be unable to meet client obligations.

> A run on the banks by depositors demanding their money back would effectively paralyse the monetary system. Businesses would then be unable to pay wages, taxes or debts; the state, without taxes, would be unable to meet its obligations, and, he added, 'some sort of Pinochet would step in to restore order,' an allusion to the former Chilean dictator. . . .

> Interbank trading stopped at the end of last week when several banks failed to pay their debts, prompting panic among banks over one another's ability to settle. Overnight interest rates soared from 30 per cent to more than 1,000 per cent.[19]

Of course, the Russians survived the crisis and avoided a return to dictatorship—this time.

Just as the Russian economy was facing a shortage of cash, fears of a grain shortage were starting. As the International Wheat Council was warning that the world's wheat supplies were falling to a worrying low, Russia's deputy prime minister was boasting that, not only would Russia not need to import grain in 1995, but instead it would be able to export it. *Intelligence Digest* warned, however, that its intelligence sources "in Moscow are warning that the entire Russian agricultural sector is close to collapse as a result of the low prices paid for agricultural output and the lack of state support."[20]

Furthermore, it was revealed a few weeks later that:

> Russian farmers have received only 50% of the promised amount of fertilizer this year.

> As a result of the shortfall, only 1.1 million out of the 7 million hectares of winter crops have been top-dressed.

> Some 3 million hectares of winter crops are reported to have perished because of lack of fertilizer, and spring

crops covering "considerable areas" have also been killed by frost.

A further problem is the lack of fuel which means that many machines are standing idle although the weather in many areas is ideal.[21]

Come fall, the Russians were facing a frightening shortfall. A Reuters press release announced:

Russia faces a shortage of 15 million tonnes of grain, including 7 million tonnes of breadmaking wheat, Interfax news agency quotes agriculture ministry specialists as saying.

Interfax said Russia, expected to record its lowest grain harvest in 30 years, will experience "a significant deficit" of grain.[22]

As if these critical situations the Russians were facing in 1995 were not enough, a gas pipeline explosion occurred near the town of Ukhta. The disaster brought to the world's attention the decrepit state of Russia's oil and natural pipeline infrastructure. *The Wall Street Journal* reported that:

Russia boasts the largest energy-transportation system in the world. Unfortunately for Western oil companies, it's also one of the most decrepit, a drawback underscored by yesterday's spectacular explosion in a natural-gas pipeline 800 miles northeast of Moscow. . . .

The domestic pipeline network, built by the Communists and neglected since the Soviet Union dissolved, is in such bad repair that the government reports there are more than 700 major leaks a year.[23]

At the same time, Russians near Usinsk had been dreading spring thaw, which would bring with it the results of a major oil-spill that took place the previous year. The Usinsk spill was said to have affected an area about the size of seventy football fields. Another *Wall Street Journal* article on the same day reported:

> Spring thaw is usually a welcome time in the Russian north. But this year, residents are bracing for warm weather that could let loose a flood of oil frozen into the ice over the winter after last year's 100,000-ton spill.
>
> Unchecked, the spill would poison their drinking water, kill their cattle and reindeer and wipe out their local fishing industry. They may have a fighting chance now, because after months of delay a vigorous cleanup effort is finally under way. Despite driving snows, intermittent freezes and rising rivers, a consortium of Russian, American and Australian workers is striving to contain one of the world's largest spills, three times the size of the Exxon Valdez disaster off the coast of Alaska.[24]

As Russia continues to face one crisis after another, the news that comes from the south of Russia is sometimes much rosier.

The Grass *Is* Greener over There

Russia occupies more land than any other nation in the world. It is virtually double the size of China, Canada, or the United States. Furthermore, Russia possesses more natural resources than any other nation in the world. It holds 13% of the world's crude oil, 35% of the world's natural gas resources, 12% of the world's coal supply, 32% of its iron ore, 27% of its tin, and 11% of the world's copper resources.[25] Despite such benefits, however, Russia just cannot get its economic act together.

On the other hand, the news that comes from Israel is much different. While it certainly cannot be said that Israel does not face problems of its own, economic degradation and starvation are not among them. While Israel is one of the tiniest nations in the world, without the benefits of mineral resources like crude oil or natural gas, it is quite successful agriculturally.

When the first Jews began arriving in the land following World War II, it was nothing but barren desert that had laid waste for centuries. But with a lot of hard work and ingenuity, the Jews began to reclaim the land. Areas along the Jordan River were swampy, so they planted Eucalyptus trees to dry up the wet land. They planted millions of other trees in the desert areas. Thus began the process of desertification of the land, including the design of irrigation systems that would not waste precious water in order to produce food for its inhabitants. Former Israeli Prime Minister Shimon Peres wrote that the early Jewish settlers:

> increased agricultural yield by twelve times in twenty-five years—from 1950 to 1975—virtually without increasing the size of the arable land. The estimate is that 95 percent of the increase was the result of science, technology, and planning.[26]

Israel has continued to increase its agricultural yield over the years, so much so that it actually exports some of its products. Mr. Peres also interestingly noted, when speaking of Israel's agricultural prosperity, that:

> When Russia renewed diplomatic relations with Israel in 1991, among the first things the Russians

did was buy cows from us. It came out that an Israeli cow provides three times more milk than a
Russian cow. Actually, it is the same cow, with the
same horns; the difference is the system—scientific and technological—that we have applied to
our stables.[27]

On the economic front, Israel has been equally successful. In the spring of 1996, an article in *The Jerusalem
Report* noted Israel's economic progress from the time of
the first Zionist settlers to today:

The change is palpable everywhere, not only in
the high-tech island between the garages. It shows
in fact that 40 percent of adult Israelis travel out
of the country for a week or more every year, in
the cars that they drive (sporty Mazdas and Jeeps,
a yuppie favorite everywhere), in their sunglasses
(Cebe brand, from France, is the preference of Jeep
owners), in their $200 Timberland hiking boots,
and in their restaurants they frequent for tofu-
burgers and sushi.

In today's Israel, where the free market rules, the
growing number of people with more money have
plenty of places to spend it. . . .

Car sales, in fact, are a good indication of con-
sumption patterns. . . . "If everyone was satisfied
with a Volkswagen or a Renault in the old days,"
says sociologist Shalve, "now cars are bigger and
more expensive."

An increasing number of Israeli families have not
one car, but two or three.[28]

The Jerusalem Report article also noted that while no
one in Israel is quite sure when it was that the economic

change began, many say it commenced "with the start of the aliyah from the former Soviet Union that brought 600,000 new immigrants—jump-starting the economy with a major increase in the number of consumers and a huge supply of highly educated workers."[29]

Indeed, some of the most brilliant thinkers in the former Soviet Union were Jews. They took their intellectual skills with them when they emigrated to Israel. In an interview with *This Week in Bible Prophecy*, former Israeli Economic Minister Pinhas Dror was asked about the phenomenon of "brain drain" experienced by the Russians when Soviet Jews emigrated to Israel, where many intellectuals were already in abundance. He told us:

> Israel, if you cover the bases, is the highest educated country in the world. If you talk about the publicizing of PhDs, Israel is first in the world on a per capita basis, number eighth in the world in absolute numbers. So this is the kind of thing you see out of Israel. Countries that are falling behind unfortunately, are even Europe. Eastern Europe is definitely falling behind. The ex-Soviet Union is terribly behind . . .

> I would say that about when the Russian immigration started to Israel, I was at that time serving in the government. We were all quite hysterical and apprehensive about it because, just to give you an idea, a country of four and a half million people that is supposed to absorb 600,000 people in two or three or four years is just like me telling you that in Canada you are supposed to absorb five million people in three years. Nobody knows even how to react to that. How do you do it? And I remember we were quite apprehensive. We were thinking that the Israeli economy would sink . . .

> But it became an unbelievable blessing. I would think it's a miracle. There is no other way to describe it but as a

miracle. If a country of four and a half million people can absorb 600,000 people in four years—and people are not going hungry in the streets, and most of them, I wouldn't say all of them, but most of them, are now absorbed in the mainstream of the Israeli economy—this is a miracle by itself.

So what is happening right now is, Israel is the only country in the world in which Russian scientists, promoters, engineers, you name it, are working in the Israeli economy and have become something called "incubators." The incubators are places in which Russian scientists and Israeli scientists can work together, to come together with new technological processes. This has become a great success.... The fact that it was brain drain, well, I admit it was. But whom are they going to blame for that? That is the question. Whom are they going to blame?[30]

Hook, Line, and Sinker

Indeed, the bait before Russian eyes is beginning to look more tempting with each passing moment. While Russia's future remains bleak, God had prophesied that not only would He bring the Jews back to their homeland, but also in the end He would make them prosper.

> He shall cause them that come of Jacob to take root: Israel shall blossom and bud, and fill the face of the world with fruit.[31]

This prophecy is starting to come to life today, and the Russians are going to look with envy upon the prosperity of their southern neighbors. Indeed, some modern-day observers claim that envy is a common temptation in Russian society. Many Russians are envious of, and even venomous against, those who are more prosperous than themselves. Hedrick Smith, former Moscow bureau chief for *The New York Times*, for example, observed this when he returned to Russia following the collapse of communism—and he noted this as someone who likes the Russians, not as their enemy. Smith recorded in his observations that many Russian workers tended to be lazy because they had never been brought up with entrepreneurial competitiveness in mind. The state always took care of them, equally, and there was no incentive to work harder or strive for more. With this ingrained in so many for so long, the tendency was to assume that no one should strive for more than their neighbors have. In many instances, as capitalism is slowly being introduced in the Russian nation, this assumption has led to a collective, virulent jealousy. Smith wrote:

> Traveling around the country, I came to see the great mass of Soviets as protagonists in what I call the culture of envy. In this culture, corrosive animosity took root under the czars in the deep-seated collectivism in Russian life and then was cultivated by Leninist ideology. Now it has turned rancid under the misery of everyday living.

> The Soviet ruling class, with their cushy cars, clinics, and country homes, are a natural enough target for the wrath of the little people. But what is ominous for Gorbachev's reforms is that this free-floating anger, the jealousy of the rank and file, often lights on anyone who rises above the crowd—anyone who workers harder, gets ahead, and becomes better off, even if his gains are honestly earned.[32]

Then Mr. Smith went on to give some examples of destruction that had been caused by this collective jealousy.

One story had been related to him by a Soviet diplomat: Some farmers in a small town outside Moscow had set the barn of a neighboring farmer on fire after setting all his cows and horses loose because they were jealous of his prosperity.

When we heard about this, we were reminded of Patti's grandparents, who had emigrated to Manitoba, Canada, from the Ukraine when they were young. After they were married, they were considered to be prosperous because they had been given a cow and a horse as a wedding gift. But one of their neighbors, who was also from Russia, was extremely jealous. Though it was never proved, that person was probably responsible for setting their barn on fire and destroying their livestock.

It could be this same kind of jealousy that will one day lure the Russians as a whole to take God's bait and mount an attack against Israel. Indeed, the prophet Ezekiel tells us they are going to "think an evil thought" (38:10) as they prepare to invade Israel. Specifically they will think to:

> take a spoil, and to take a prey; to turn [their] hand upon the desolate places that are now inhabited, and upon the people that are gathered out of the nations, which have gotten cattle and goods, that dwell in the midst of the land.[33]

And when Gog has taken the bait, God said He will set the hook in his jaw and reel him in for destruction:

> Thus saith the Lord God; Art thou he of whom I have spoken in old time by my servants the prophets of Israel, which prophesied in those days many years that I would bring thee against them?

> And it shall come to pass at the same time when Gog shall come against the land of Israel, saith the Lord God, that my fury shall come up in my face....

And I will turn thee back, and leave but the sixth part of thee, and will cause thee to come up from the north parts, and will bring thee upon the mountains of Israel:

And I will smite thy bow out of thy left hand, and will cause thine arrows to fall out of thy right hand.

Thou shalt fall upon the mountains of Israel, thou, and all thy bands and the people that is with thee: I will give thee unto the ravenous birds of every sort, and to the beasts of the field to be devoured.

Thou shalt fall upon the open field: for I have spoken it, saith the Lord God.

And I will send a fire on Magog, and among them that dwell carelessly in the isles: and they shall know that I am the Lord....

And it shall come to pass in that day, that I will give unto Gog a place there of graves in Israel, the valley of the passengers on the east of the sea: and it shall stop the noses of the passengers: and there shall they bury Gog and all his multitude: and they shall call it The valley of Hamongog.[34]

Interestingly, this prophecy notes that Gog and his followers are going to fall on the mountains of Israel, where they will be left to be devoured by ravenous birds. In the winter of 1995, an article that appeared in a bird-watchers' magazine about large predator birds that migrate through Israel caught our eye in reference to this prophecy. The author of the article wrote:

As we stand under the warm sun, the desert landscape stretches in all directions as far as the eye can see. A strong northerly wind cools our skin, as we count the birds that fly around us in eerie silence. The sky above us is filled with so many

birds it looks as if it is in constant motion. The at-
mosphere of the desert heat and the surreal sky is
spellbinding to the point that after a few minutes,
I turn to my partner and make a trivial remark
just to break the unnerving quietness. This is an
example of spring migration at Eilat.[35]

According to Dr. Yosef, the author of the article, he and
his partner had counted "tens of thousands" of steppe
buzzards making their way across Israel into Europe and
Asia. Other large birds that covered the sky included black
kites, ospreys, and steppe eagles. According to Yosef:

During spring, some *two million* soaring birds tra-
verse Israel on their way to nesting areas. . . .
During the spring of 1994, staff and volunteers
from the International Birdwatching Center in
Eilat (BCE) recorded a total of 1,022,084 raptors
comprising 29 species. . . . Would you believe an
average of 11,110 raptors were counted each
day! . . . In my opinion, the best place in the world
to see large numbers of birds of prey during spring
migration is Eilat.[36]

Broken Promises

God's Word is not clear about when this Russian invasion will take place. Bible scholars have differing opinions about when the attack will occur in relation to the
tribulation period, and offer good points for their conclusions. Although we cannot be certain of the order of
events regarding the invasion, it is possible it will occur
at the mid-way point of the tribulation period. We do not
believe the invasion takes place at the end of the tribulation period, coinciding with the battle of Armageddon.
The armies of the *entire* world will gather against Israel

for the battle of Armageddon, we are told in Revelation.
For the invasion in Ezekiel 38, however, only a few nations are listed.

The prophet Ezekiel tells us that when the Russians
get it in their minds to go after the goods and cattle of the
Jews, Israel will apparently be at peace: "Thou shalt say,
I will go up to the land of unwalled villages; I will go to
them that are at rest, that dwell safely, all of them dwelling
without walls, and having neither bars nor gates."[37]

It makes sense, therefore, that Israel has already signed
the peace covenant with the Antichrist at this point because she feels secure enough to have open borders. This
is certainly not the case today. Even a stroll along the
Mediterranean beach of Tel Aviv is hindered by military
security structures, as we observed on our many visits
there. The first time we visited Israel, we were frustrated
by the many barbed-wire fences that obstructed our walk
along the beach, until we finally realized the reason for
their presence. After having been deceived by the false
messiah along with the rest of the world, Israel will one
day feel secure enough to remove such obstructions from
its borders.

The possibility that Russia would ignore this peace
treaty during the tribulation period doesn't seem surprising. Consider the following:

> **August 23, 1939**–Soviets sign nonaggression pact with
> Nazi Germany, paving way for Hitler's and Stalin's in-
> vasion of Poland and allowing Germany to attack Britain
> and France without fear of an eastern front. Stalin-Hitler
> treaty violates earlier nonaggression treaty Stalin signed
> with France, promising that in event of aggressive war
> against France by a third nation, Soviet Union would not
> "give aid or assistance, either directly or indirectly, to the
> aggressor."

September 17, 1939–Soviets invade Poland, violating Treaty of Riga between Warsaw and Moscow.

November 30, 1939–Soviets begin aggression against Finland, violating Treaty of Dorpat.

June 1940–Soviets invade and occupy the sovereign countries of Lithuania, Latvia, and Estonia, violating nonaggression treaties signed with each nation.

June 27, 1940–With their invasion of Romania, the Soviets violate both Kellogg-Briand Pact and Pact of Paris for sixth time in less than a year.

October 2, 1944–Violating a defense alliance agreement with Britain, Soviets deny Britain and United States the use of shuttle bases in Ukraine to drop supplies for Polish Home Army fighting Nazis. Refusal paves way for slaughter of 200,000 non-Communist resistance fighters.[38]

Although other violations of treaties and broken promises are mentioned as well in this brief history given by Michael Johns of *Policy Review,* this list is enough to reveal a pattern. Even following the fall of the communist regime, it appears that Russian officials are still not averse to ignoring treaties if it suits them. In the fall of 1994, *In telligence Digest* reported:

> In further signs of the times, Russia's chief of the general staff General Kolesnikov has said that, if the U.S. does not agree to a renegotiation of the 1992 Conventional Forces In Europe (CFE) treaty to allow Russia to station more arms in the North Caucasus and Leningrad military districts, Russia will break the treaty anyway. But, as the general remarked none too subtly in an interview with *Nezavismaya Gazeta* on 5 October. "We hope that . . . our Western partners will see the need to amend the . . . treaty as a major condition of its viability."[39]

The threat was kept alive in the months that followed as a warning against further discussions in the West over allowing Eastern European nations to join the ranks of NATO. *The Washington Times* observed:

> The Clinton administration confirmed the president of Belarus has stated that his country will not honor its commitments under the Conventional Forces in Europe treaty because of NATO expansion eastward....
>
> In a little-noticed statement, Belarus President Alexander Lukashenko announced that Belarus had suspended its program of scrapping large numbers of conventional weapons under the CFE treaty, which has been signed by 30 nations.
>
> His comments came only a day after Russian President Boris Yeltsin visited the Belarus capital, Minsk, for two days.[40]

Former Russian Defense Minister Pavel Grachev had also warned that Russia would not honor the CFE treaty if NATO expanded eastward. Therefore, our suggestion that the Russian invasion could very well take place after the covenant of the Antichrist poses no problem for the biblical scenario.

Other points to consider are that, after having signed the covenant with the Antichrist at the beginning of the tribulation period, Israel and the world are deceived into believing that he is a messiah who has come to save them and lead them into an age of peace and prosperity. Under this delusion, the Jews obviously do not believe God is the supreme ruler. However, the prophet Ezekiel tells us that when the Russian invasion occurs and God destroys their armies, the world is going to know God is responsible for their destruction:

> Thou shalt come up against my people of Israel, as a cloud to cover the land: it shall be in the latter days, and I will bring thee against my land, that the heathen may know me, when I shall be sanctified in thee, O Gog, before their eyes.[41]

Furthermore, Israel will recognize God at this point: *"So will I make my holy name known in the midst of my people Israel."*[42]

Thus, it is possible it will be in the midst of the tribulation when Israel recognizes that God is who saved her from the Russian army. It therefore follows that Israel will then recognize that the Antichrist is not her true messiah. Interestingly, at the mid-point of the tribulation period the Antichrist is going to break his covenant with Israel, and put an end to Jewish temple worship:

> In the midst of the week he shall cause the sacrifice and oblation to cease for the overspreading of abominations he shall make it desolate, even until the consummation, and that determined shall be poured upon the desolate.[43]

Jesus warned in Matthew 24:15,16 that when the Jews see "the abomination of desolation, spoken of by Daniel the prophet, stand in the holy place, (whoso readeth, let him understand:) Then let them which be in Judea flee into the mountains."

What is this abomination of desolation that the Jews are warned to watch for? Second Thessalonians 2:4 tells us it is the act of the Antichrist entering the temple of the Jews, telling them that he alone is god:

> Who opposeth and exalteth himself above all that is called god, or that is worshipped; so that he as God sitteth in the temple of God, shewing himself that he is God.

The Jews are warned that when they see this abomination of desolation take place, they are to flee into the
mountains, because all hell is going to be cast upon the
earth for the final three and one-half years of the tribulation period. The devil, the accuser of the saints, along with
his demons, is cast out of heaven, down into the midst of
the inhabitants of the earth. Angered because of the short
time he has left to deceive mankind, the devil makes war
with anyone who follows after the true God (see Revelation chapter 12).

Revelation also tells us that it is in the middle of the
tribulation that the devil, the dragon, is going to give great
power to the Antichrist for three and a half years: "Power
was given unto him to continue forty and two months."[44]

During this forty-two months, there will be a time of
great evil for which God is going to pour out His wrath.
There will be plagues and pestilences, the likes of which
the world has never known before. The cause for this time
of horror is, of course, man's own wickedness. And the
catalyst could very well be the Russian invasion of Israel,
which finally opens her eyes to the deception she has fallen
under. It will be a terrible time from which escape comes
only through faith in Jesus as Savior and Lord.

The Aligning of Nations Against Israel

N ot only does Russia have a long history of persecution of God's chosen people, it also has a history of backing anti-Jewish regimes. Interestingly, biblical prophecy fore-warned that many of these anti-Israeli regimes with which Russia has alliances will cooperate in the future invasion of Israel. In fact, the alliances formed in Ezekiel 38 sound just like the geo-political and geo-strategic alliances we see developing today.

The nations that will attack Israel are, according to the prophet Ezekiel (chapter 38), Rosh, Magog, Meshech and Tubal (verse 2); Persia, Ethiopia, and Libya (verse 5); Gomer and all his bands, and the house of Togarmah (verse 6). Except for Ethiopia and Libya, we don't see these names on a modern-day map. This is, once again, because Ezekiel was referring to these nations by their ancient tribal names as found in Genesis chapter 10. Looking at historical maps of biblical times, we can determine that Rosh is Russia. Magog was located north of the Caspian Sea, current-day Kazakhstan. Meshech was east of the Black Sea, where Georgia and northeastern Turkey are situated, and Tubal was southeast of the Black Sea, which is where northern Turkey is today. Persia is modern-day

Iran. Ethiopia was part of a tribe known in Genesis 10 as Cush, which also included the area of modern-day Sudan. Libya was known as Phut. The tribe of Gomer covered the areas of today's Ukraine, southern Russia and central Turkey, while Togarmah, which was located southeast of the Black Sea, occupied eastern Turkey. Thus, the nations that are going to invade Israel appear to be Russia, Kazakhstan, Georgia, Turkey, Iran, Ethiopia, Sudan, Libya, and Ukraine.

When communism collapsed, many hoped Russia would become an ally of the West, and that it would become a part of the "common European house" being created in the new world order. Indeed, former Soviet leader Mikhail Gorbachev expressed this desire at the Council of Europe in Strasbourg in 1989. Several years later, his wish was fulfilled as the Council of Europe accepted Russia as a member of its elite club. Indeed, the West has been willing to embrace Russia, even so far as to desire its membership in the ranks of NATO. However, with the increasing popularity of Russian nationalists and communists, Russia's alliances are likely to be made with the East, not the West, as many had hoped. Jack Matlock, Jr. was Ambassador to the Soviet Union from 1987 to 1991. Prior to the Russian presidential elections in 1996, he observed that extremists were popularizing erroneous myths about Russia's relationship with the West. Matlock wrote:

> One of the more portentous developments on the Russian political scene has been the alliance of communist and nationalist forces, which began in the last years of the Soviet Union and has reached near-fusion on the eve of the presidential campaign. . . .
>
> Russian nationalists, including communists, often describe themselves as *derzhavniki*, or proponents of a

strong state. In so doing, they adopt one of the most per-
sistent and erroneous myths in the Russia political tra-
dition—namely, that the security and well-being of the
Russian people depend on a strong state. The usual jus-
tification for a strong, authoritarian state is that it is necessary for protection against foreign invasion.
Throughout history, however, Russians have suffered
more from an overly powerful state than from in-
vaders....

The chauvinists claim that a hostile West, or more often,
the United States brought about the dissolution of the
Soviet Union. Current social and economic dislocation,
they declare, are the result of that collapse, Russia's con-
sequent loss of great power status, and a West determined to keep the country weak and subservient....

Far from attempting to keep Russia weak, the West has
made substantial efforts, including International Mone-
tary Fund (IMF) loans of billions of dollars, to assist it in
its difficult transition.[1]

Matlock also noted that extremists have been mis-
leading the populace to believe that since the West is its
enemy, it is necessary to form alliances to the east. He continued:

Another fallacious geopolitical argument dear to Russian
nationalists holds that Russia is not a Western but a
Eurasian power. At its most benign, this contention im-
plies that Russia's role is to serve as a bridge between
East and West. At its most pernicious, it suggests that the
West is inherently Russia's enemy and thus Russia must
ally itself with the East—whether the Islamic world,
China, or both—in a cosmic East-West struggle.

Both variants approach the absurd. Russia is a Eurasian
power in the geographic sense, just as the United States
is both an Atlantic and Pacific power. But Russia is

primarily a European power, and no amount of wishful thinking can enable it to play off the "East" against the "West." Historically, it has had more conflicts with Islamic peoples than with Europeans, and it extorted much of its Asian territory from China; understandably, the Chinese and Islamic peoples of Central Asia have regarded Russians not as fellow Asians but as colonialists.[2]

It is not just extreme nationalists or communists who seem to be focusing their attention on the East. Even under the leadership of a supposedly democratic Boris Yeltsin, it has been Russian policy to renew its ties with the East. While Russian defense minister Pavel Grachev was warning the U.S. that Russia intended to reopen its "traditional arms markets," namely the Middle East, Victor Posuvalyuk, acting as President Yeltsin's envoy, was stating that Americans had to respect the fact that Russia holds an interest in the Mid-East. According to the observations of *Intelligence Digest*:

> Of particular importance was Posuvalyuk's response to a question about Iraq. He was asked whether Russia should be "throwing a lifebelt to a dictatorial regime, which they say is dangerous and immoral." His reply was a classic statement of *raison d'etat*: "As far as morality is concerned, we serve our own national interests first and foremost. Secondly, we do not interfere in other countries' domestic affairs, and we count on other countries not to interfere in ours."

> This interview, for a Russian audience, was complemented by an article contributed in Arabic to the pan-Arab *al-Hayat* for its 13 November edition in which Posuvalyuk berated Gulf Arab critics of Russian policy towards Iraq. He stated in bold terms that the Gulf states would have to accept a Russian role in their security, saying: "Russia, as the closest neighbour, a major naval power, and as a permanent member of the Security

Council, is developing the aspiration to become a guar-
antor of peace and stability in the Gulf region."[3]

Not long afterwards, President Yeltsin appeared to
confirm Russia's foreign policy concerning the Mid-East.
In its analysis of President Yeltsin's February 17 State of
the Nation address to the Russian Federation's Federal
Assembly, *Intelligence Digest* observed:

> In a run-down of Russian foreign-policy priori-
> ties, Yeltsin first said, with regard to the Middle
> East (or Near East as the Russians call it): "The
> Near East states, where there are strong fears re-
> garding the unipolarity of the new world order
> [in other words, American dominance], see in
> Russia an essential factor of global and regional
> equilibrium." He then went on to say: "The work
> in hand in the Near East has made it possible to
> minimize the adverse consequences of the devel-
> opment of events in Chechnya with regard to the
> entire Muslim world."
>
> We can hardly stress enough how important this
> statement is. First of all, Yeltsin is saying in diplo-
> matic code that the states of the Middle East want
> Russia to play an anti-American role. Secondly,
> he is admitting that Russian diplomacy has
> stepped up its efforts in this direction in order to
> counter Islamic criticism of Moscow's actions in
> crushing Muslim Chechnya's rebellion.[4]

Indeed, Russia is looking east, just as the prophet
Ezekiel had stated.

Moving Eastward

The fact that Georgia and Ukraine will form an alliance
with Russia for the invasion of Israel is not surprising,

THE EDGE OF TIME

given their Slavic ties with Russia. Furthermore, there are approximately 25 million Russians living in former Soviet satellites, many of whom reside in Georgia and Ukraine. The alliance with Kazakhstan is no great surprise either. Although Kazakhstan rests in Central Asia, a large portion of its population is Russian. In fact, President Nazarbayev, who reigns with old Soviet-style policies, has openly favored close ties with Moscow. He has even been pushing other former Soviet satellites in Central Asia to form an Eurasian Union.

Kazakhstan, however, not only holds an interest in ties with Moscow. Being a land-locked nation, it also holds an interest in ties with Iran in order to use its territory for the exporting of oil and other products. Indeed, Kazakhstan, although not deeply rooted in Islam, is Moscow's gateway to the Islamic world.

Russia cannot risk conflict with the Muslim world. Such a conflict could spread through Central Asia and the Caucasus right next door to its borders. As far as the Transcaucasus goes, Russia needs good diplomatic relations with Iraq and Syria, which lie to the south of Turkey. Russia also needs a good relationship with Kazakhstan and Iran. Indeed, Iran would be the key instigator for any Islamic penetration into areas of Central Asia that are under Moscow's control. In light of this, Moscow has ignored American desires to isolate Iran, a sponsor of terrorist activities around the world, with trade sanctions. Moscow has managed to save face over its foreign-policy decisions in the eyes of the international community and continue commercial deals with Iran, including the sale of arms and nuclear cooperation. (The main reason is that other nations, including France and China, have also gone against U.S. efforts for an embargo against Iran.)

The desire for a good relationship between Russia and Iran is not one-sided. Iran wants something from Russia as well. According to *Intelligence Digest*, Iran's motive is simple: "It needs Russian backing in its strategic goal of dominating the Persian Gulf—and it is receiving it. In return, Tehran has undertaken not to spread Islamic fundamentalism in ex-Soviet Central Asia or in Russia itself."[5]

In addition to dominating the Persian Gulf, Middle East observers believe Iran also "has a strong interest in heading up a radical anti-Israeli front. Tehran sees itself not only as the dominant force in the Persian Gulf but also as the head of the pan-Islamist movement; and playing a leading role in the expulsion of the Jews from Palestine and returning Jerusalem to Islamic control would greatly enhance Tehran's Islamist status"[6]

In confirmation of Iran's desires to head a pan-Islamic movement against Israel, and of its goal to eventually liberate Jerusalem, Tehran, in the summer of 1996, brazenly named the war-game exercises of its elite Revolutionary Guards *Tariq al-Quds*, translated, *The Road to Jerusalem*.

Islamic *Jihad*

For the Russian nation, it appears that envy of Israel's prosperity will be a key motivator for the future invasion of Israel. For Russia's Muslim neighbors to the east, however, the motivator will likely be Islamic *Jihad*. As is the case for Iran, which desires to head a pan-Islamic/anti-Israeli force, radical Islamic fundamentalism plays a key role in the shaping of events in the Middle East. And Islamic fundamentalism certainly plays a role in the societies of the remaining nations listed in Ezekiel 38. Ethiopia, for example, has a large Muslim population. Clashes between rival Muslim groups are responsible for much of the turmoil experienced by that nation today.

Sudan also suffers from strife caused by rival Muslim groups. While Sudan is considered an outcast nation by the U.S. because of its backing of Saddam Hussein during the Persian Gulf War, nations such as Egypt, Russia, and Iran support Sudan. Furthermore, Islamist-ruled Sudan is very pro-Iranian, and it has long been suspected that Iran has troops stationed at military bases inside Sudanese borders.

Islamic-ruled Sudan and Iran are also supporters of Libya, which is listed in Ezekiel 38. Libya is considered a pariah nation by the U.S. because of its involvement in terrorist activities. For refusing to hand over the terrorists responsible for killing the passengers on board a Pan Am plane flying over Lockerbie, Scotland, the U.N. has imposed trade sanctions against Libya. Nonetheless, Libya, under the leadership of Moammar Gaddafi, continues to defy the West. As a demonstration of its radical terrorism, Libya, according to the testimony of CIA director John Deutch in early 1996, has been constructing a chemical weapons plant. It was announced that the U.S. was managing to delay its construction by blocking shipment of needed materials from other nations, but the U.S. also claimed it was not able to completely destroy the chemical weapons plant because of its location under the surface of a mountain. Nonetheless, U.S. defense secretary William Perry warned during a trip to Egypt that military action against Libya could not be ruled out. The response from the Arab world to Mr. Perry's comments, according to *Intelligence Digest*, was predictable:

> The Arab League responded with a statement saying: "Libya has repeatedly said it has no intention to produce chemical weapons and has denied having such a programme.

"Members of the international community must work towards making the Middle East a region free of weapons of mass destruction and particularly free of nuclear weapons as Israel is the only country in the region that owns any."

Egypt, one of Washington's principal Arab allies, made the same connection.

In a lengthy editorial, Egypt's semi-official daily *al-Ahram* hammered home the point, saying: "Israel's nuclear capability poses a genuine and acute strategic threat to the Arab countries which cannot be ignored under any circumstances."[7]

It is well known that Libya has posed a danger to Israel for years. Essentially, however, the response to Mr. Perry's comments demonstrated that the Arab League and Egypt simply want to change the subject. Instead of acknowledging that Libya may be in the midst of a dangerous chemical weapons program, they have instead claimed that Israel is the true threat. Furthermore, Russia came to the defense of Libya, sending a warning to the U.S. about any military actions against it. In another *Intelligence Digest* report a week later we read:

Russia has taken Libya's side in the dispute. On 11 April, the Russian Foreign Ministry issued a statement saying that Libya had become the target of "direct threats not backed with evidence."

The Foreign Ministry said that such direct threats by a high-ranking American official "cannot but cause alarm" and would not promote stabilization in the Middle East. . . .

Slowly, slowly, Moscow is rebuilding its post-Cold War foreign policy and its alliances around an anti-Western stance.[8]

Indeed, the alliances of Ezekiel 38 are clearly developing today. Turkey, the final nation left in our Ezekiel 38 list, has not been in an alliance with the other nations. In fact, at the time of writing, Turkey doesn't get along with Russia very well at all. It has instead been a Western-oriented democracy for over seventy years, with memberships in western institutions such as the U.N., the IMF, NATO, and the Council of Europe. Turkey even signed a military pact with Israel in the spring of 1996, for which it received warnings from Syria and Iran. The pact was seen as a stabilizing factor in the Middle East, and Turkey has been a valuable Western ally in an unstable region for many years.

Developing trends in recent years, however, indicate this alliance may come to an end. One event that is likely to shift its loyalties is the European Union's repeated rejection of Turkey as a member. Although granted associate membership to the then EEC in 1963, full membership has not been forthcoming. Many observers have warned it is a mistake to treat such a loyal and key strategic ally in this manner:

> The effect of the European rejection cannot be exaggerated. Turkey's associate membership agreement of 1963 specifically held out full membership as an eventual goal. By applying for full membership in 1987, Turkey was ahead in the queue of Austria, Finland, Sweden, and Norway, all of whose applications were subsequently accepted and expedited. . . .

> There is now a well-founded suspicion in Ankara that the erstwhile Soviet-bloc countries of Eastern Europe will also be accepted as full members more rapidly than Turkey. This is a deep affront to a people that has, for 70 years, so categorically rejected its own past in favour of becoming Western. The EU rejection implies that the

whole 70-year experiment has been wasted and that Turkey is still seen in Western capitals as an oriental nation with no business to be in Europe.[9]

Turkey's Islamic history was erased under the leadership of Kemal Ataturk following World War I. The success of the Islamic Party in elections over recent years, however, indicate that a growing portion of the Turkish population desires a return to its past. In the summer of 1996, Turkey's parliament approved Necmettin Erbakan, leader of the Islamist-oriented Welfare Party, as the new prime minister. The approval of Erbakan marks the first time in Turkey's modern history that the government will be inspired by Islam. While it is too early to tell at the time of writing in what direction Erbakan will take Turkey, it is clear from past comments the direction he would like to go. Middle East observers have noted:

> Left to his own devices, there is little doubt in which direction Erbakan would take Turkey—away from the West and secularism.

> In a typical election speech, Welfare's leader said: "We will set up an Islamic United Nations, an Islamic NATO, and an Islamic version of the EU. We will create an Islamic currency."

> He also said: "I promise I will work for a just order, to liberate Bosnia, Azerbaijan, Chechnya, and Jerusalem."

> The Welfare Party's economic manifesto, written by Erbakan, promises to scrap interest rates and to do away with "world imperialism and Zionism as well as Israel and a handful of champagne-drinking collaborators in the holding companies that feed it."[10]

Erbakan's goals, which appear to line up with the goals of Iran and other nations ruled by Islamic fundamentalism, define Islamic *Jihad*. The goal is to liberate Jerusalem, while annihilating the "Zionist enemy," and other "infidels," namely Americans, who support them. Radical Islamic fundamentalists believe Jews and Americans are trying to control the Middle East for their own greedy purposes, at the expense of the large Muslim population that inhabits the region. But the root of their hatred for Jews and Americans comes mainly from the religious beliefs endemic to Islam. Radical Islamists believe they can enter paradise through the blood of the Jews and other infidels. They are even willing to take their own lives in suicide bombings to obtain entrance into paradise. How can Israel bargain for lasting peace when dealing with this kind of mentality?

In the fall of 1994, a TV special titled "Jihad in America" was aired on PBS. On the program, Palestinian Sheik Tamim al-Adnani was shown at a fundraising gathering in Lawrence, Kansas. "The only politics we understand is tah, tah, tah," said al-Adnani, imitating the sound of a semi-automatic weapon. "This is the best politics. Our problems are solved in the trenches, fighting, not in hotels around tables."[11]

Islamic Jihad requires bloodshed. Fayiz Azzam, another Islamic fundamentalist, was quoted on the program as saying at a gathering in Atlanta, Georgia, in 1990:

> Allah's religion—be he praised—must offer skulls, must offer martyrs. Blood must flow. There must be widows. There must be orphans. Hands and limbs must be cut, and the limbs and blood must be spread everywhere in order that Allah's religion stand on its feet.[12]

It is in the midst of such raw hatred that Israel is being pressured to concede on strategically important issues for the sake of "peace."

Biding Their Time

For those seeking the eventual annihilation of Israel, there are a couple of obstacles to be overcome. For one, there is Israel's military might, which was successfully demonstrated during the Six Day and Yom Kippur Wars. There is also the fact that Israel is suspected of possessing nuclear strike capabilities, although she has never confirmed that she has these capabilities.

Radical Islamic fundamentalists, however, believe these obstacles can be overcome if they patiently bide their time. The best way to counterbalance Israel's alleged nuclear capabilities is to acquire nuclear capabilities of their own. Iran is likely to do so in the future, under the guise of acquiring atomic energy, with the aid of Russia and possibly China. Both nations have said they do not agree with U.S. fears that Tehran will use any materials provided by them for turning atomic energy into atomic weapons. Russia and China have even promised Iran that they would ignore U.S. requests to withhold the needed materials.

Furthermore, many Arab nations turned the occasion of Israel's refusal to sign the Nuclear Non-Proliferation Treaty, up for extension in 1995, into an excuse for acquiring nuclear weapons of their own. Speaking to an audience of the Canadian Club and the Canadian Institute of International Affairs, Prince Khaled bin Sultan predicted that Arab nations will indeed attempt to do so unless Israel comes clean on its nuclear weapons program. The nephew of Saudi Arabia's King Fahd had noted that Arabs were willing to make peace with Israel. But he added, "why should Arabs continue to live in the grim shadow of Israel's bomb? The Arabs feel that Israel's nuclear arsenal threatens the national security of the entire Arab world."[13] Therefore, he contended, it is the duty of the Arab world "to seek to acquire a deterrent of their own."[14]

At about the same time, *Intelligence Digest* published some excerpts from an article which appeared in Egypt's semi-official *al-Ahram* on May 31, 1995. Referring to an article written by Dr. Hassan Nafia of Cairo University's School of Economics and Political Science, *Intelligence Digest* noted:

> Dr. Nafia talks of a "full consensus among the Egyptian elite" that America can no longer be trusted as an honest broker in the Middle East because of its support for Israel's positions on the Nuclear Non-Proliferation Treaty and East Jerusalem.
>
> He goes on to argue that as Egypt pioneered the Arab approach to peace with Israel, and as the direction the settlement process has taken of late "cannot possibly lead to a durable, just, and comprehensive peace," Egypt is "duty bound" to correct the approach....
>
> But the main reasons Nafia gives for the swing in Egypt are Israel's nuclear deterrent and Jerusalem.
>
> He says that Egypt cannot "accept an Israeli monopoly, even a temporary one, on nuclear arms in the region" and that Egypt "cannot possibly accept Israeli sovereignty over East Jerusalem in any circumstances."[15]

Libya's radical leader Moammar Gaddafi claimed he was grateful that a good excuse had been given to the

Arabs for acquiring nuclear capabilities. In a speech commemorating Libyan fighters who had participated in the "Arab Wars for Palestine," he noted:

> We would like to thank the Israelis and the Americans and the entire Western alliance for having provided the Arabs with the excuse and justification to manufacture the nuclear bomb. . . .
>
> It is considered self-defense, because they told the Israelis that the right to manufacture nuclear bombs is self-defense and the maintenance of peace. Based on this, we say to them that peace in the Middle East can only come about if there is mutual nuclear deterrence. The Arabs have a nuclear bomb and the Israelis have a nuclear bomb; this is mutual nuclear deterrence, because they said the peace after World War II only lasted such a long time because there was mutual nuclear deterrence. Russia has nuclear bombs and the Americans and their alliance [NATO] also have nuclear bombs. As long as both had nuclear bombs, no one started a war and the peace lasted for 50 years.
>
> As long as the Middle East is a hotspot liable to explode and they want peace there, there must be mutual nuclear deterrence. . . .
>
> So the Arabs are now thanking the Israelis and the Americans that they gave them the justification so that they can manufacture nuclear weapons, if they have the capability, openly, in broad daylight, considering that to be something legitimate for the sake of peace and self-defense.[16]

As for Israel's abilities in conventional warfare, radical Islamic fundamentalists know this obstacle too can be neutralized if they wait patiently. Indeed, the peace process itself is seen as the way to achieve this end. Iran, for one, is definitely opposed to the peace process, since it would mean ending hostilities with the Zionist enemy. Nevertheless, Iran has remained somewhat passive during the peace process and has not stirred up trouble in the region to thwart the talks from continuing, because Iran knows that if Israel is persuaded to agree to Arab demands, she will be left in a weakened state militarily.

Perhaps the most blatant indication that the goal of the peace process is to leave Israel in a strategically weakened condition were comments made by Palestinian Authority Chairman Yasser Arafat in May, 1994, during a visit to a mosque in South Africa. His comments were made following his agreement with Israel to work towards peace. Middle East observers made note of the comments made by Arafat:

> PLO Chairman Yasser Arafat's now widely-reported private speech in a South African mosque, made during his visit for Nelson Mandela's inauguration, cannot be dismissed lightly. It contained two very specific points that spell trouble for the future.

> The first was that the PLO intends to continue the "jihad" or holy war until East Jerusalem is under full Arab control. As Arafat said: "The jihad will continue . . . Jerusalem is not for the Palestinian people; it is for all the Muslim nation . . . [The] battle is not to get how much we can achieve from [the Israelis] here or there. Our main battle is Jerusalem: Jerusalem, the first shrine of the Muslims."

> The second, and even more revealing, point to be emphasized from Arafat's speech relates to the PLO-Israel accord . . . "This agreement, I am not considering it more than the agreement which had been signed between our Prophet Mohammed and the Quraysh."

This is a reference to the non-belligerency pact Mohammed signed with the Quraysh tribe which controlled Mecca. Two years later, he violated the agreement, conquered Mecca, and killed the leaders of the tribe.

This is the light in which subscribers must view the Madrid peace process as it continues to take its course under Western pressure.[17]

Almost two years later, Arafat gave a similar speech to a group of Arab diplomats in Sweden. Intelligence sources quoted Arafat as saying:

[Israeli Prime Minister Shimon] Peres and [Israeli negotiator Yossi] Beilin have already promised us half of Jerusalem [but] we Palestinians will take over everything, including all of Jerusalem. . . .

Within five years we will have six to seven million Arabs living on the West Bank and in Jerusalem. . . . If the Jews can import all kinds of Ethiopians, Uzbekis, and Ukrainians as Jews, we can import all kinds of Arabs. . . . We plan to eliminate the state of Israel and establish a Palestinian state. . . .

We will make life unbearable for the Jews by psychological warfare and population explosion. Jews will not want to live among Arabs.[18]

At the time of writing, relations between the Palestinian Authority and Israel have reached another low because of newly-elected Prime Minister Netanyahu's firm stance that the Palestinians will not be given a Palestinian state, nor East Jerusalem as its capital. It is too early to tell where the peace process will go from here. Fears are that a return to violence as occurred during the Intifada are a grave possibility. Shortly following Arafat's speech to Arab diplomats in Sweden, his adviser, Nabil Shaath, who has been considered to be a moderate PLO leader, gave a speech at a symposium in the West Bank. In his speech, Nablus warned:

> If the negotiations reach a dead end, we shall return to the struggle and strife. . . . As long as Israel moves forward . . . we observe the agreements on peace and non-violence. But if and when Israel will say: 'That's it. We will not discuss Jerusalem, we will not return refugees, we will not dismantle settlements, and we will not retreat from borders' then all the acts of violence will return. Only this time we will have 30,000 Palestinian soldiers who will operate in areas where we have unprecedented elements of freedom.[19]

In speaking of a 30,000-man army and areas where they have "unprecedented elements of freedom," Shaath was, of course, referring to gains already made from Israel's former Labor government. Indeed, the very weapons provided by Israeli Jews to the Palestinian police were used against Jews during the Temple Mount riots in the fall of 1996.

An Unwelcome Guest

Another obstacle standing in the way of radical Islamic fundamentalists is a U.S. presence in the region. Proponents of Jihad have been working to overcome this as well. While virtually all Arab states have been anti-Israeli at one time or another, and most remain so today, not all have been anti-American. This was demonstrated during the Persian Gulf War, when Saudi Arabia allowed U.S. troops to station there for battle against Saddam Hussein.

Over the years, however, as Islamic fundamentalism has increased, so too has anti-Westernism. This means that a presence of foreign troops in the region is not welcome. Iran has been a key instigator behind radical protests against the presence of Western ally troops. This protest has led to threats and even violence against foreign troops, one of the most recent being the explosion of a U.S. military complex in Khobar, Saudi Arabia. Iran's influence has even gone so far as to deliberately surround Saudi Arabia with nations that are pro-Iranian and anti-Western. The goal is to chase foreign troops home.

At the same time, relations between India and the U.S. have gotten cooler. Although not located in the Middle East, India is strategically located between Iran and China. Noticing signs of a failing friendship between India and the U.S., Iran, as well as Russia, have moved in for a courtship. The relationship between the U.S. and Pakistan also grew colder during the Clinton administration. Pakistan, strategically important to the U.S., is considered to be a haven for Islamic fundamentalist terrorist groups. While remaining friends with Pakistan, the U.S. is able to closely monitor these groups. With the loss of the friendship, however, the U.S. would lose this ability. Even Egypt, which has been considered a Western ally in the Middle East since the signing of the Camp David Accords peace treaty with Israel, has been slowly turning anti-American as Islamic fundamentalism has been gaining popularity.

What all of this reveals is that the U.S. is losing a lot of friends in a region in which Israel has essentially no friends. The U.S. is, for all intents and purposes, one of the few friends that Israel has in the entire world. In helping to broker peace in the region, especially with Syria, the U.S. has promised to provide military aid to ensure Israel's security. If, however, the trend continues as it has, the U.S. will have few friends in the region who will allow her to launch a counter-attack in defense of Israel.

Furthermore, we must consider how long the citizens of America will tolerate attacks against U.S. troops in the Middle East before they start insisting that their politicians bring them home. And how long will U.S. citizens tolerate terrorist attacks on their own soil, as happened with the bombing of the World Trade Center in 1993, before they start insisting that the U.S. quit sponsoring Israel in the peace process? If trends follow this course, Israel will be left wide open for the Russian/Arab attack prophesied in Ezekiel 38. To the natural eye this seems like a strategic nightmare for Israel. That nightmare is further compounded by the fact that the prophet Ezekiel tells us Israel will be a land of "unwalled" cities and towns at the time of the invasion. Through natural eyes, this will be less than an ideal situation for Israel. Through spiritual eyes, however, we can see that trends are turning out perfectly. God said that when the nations of Ezekiel 38 come against His people, He Himself will defeat their armies and rescue Israel. It won't be Israel's military might that stops the invasion, and it won't be the military might of the United States. It will be very God Himself. Israel will know it, and the nations of the world will know it. God alone will get the glory He so greatly deserves.

The Peacemakers

Before we leave the region of the Middle East, we would like to briefly take a look at three other nations in the area that are not part of the list of Ezekiel 38, but that play a very significant role in shaping the politics of the Middle East. They are the nations that come to mind when the term "peace treaty" is mentioned. These nations—Egypt, Jordan, and Syria—we are told, have a place in Bible prophecy.

Egypt

Egypt was the first Arab nation to sign a peace treaty with Israel, in 1979, under the leadership of Anwar Sadat. For his actions, former president Sadat lost his life at the hands of radical Islamists. While a treaty of peace had been formally signed, following Sadat's death the most that could be said was that there was a cold peace between the two countries. Very little progress was made following the signing of the treaty towards close diplomatic ties, and Egypt kept strong restrictions in place concerning Israeli visitors to its nation. Furthermore, Israeli citizens have continually been banned from taking part in international film festivals, book fairs, and other cultural events which have taken place in Egypt.

In 1995, this cold peace began to take on the look of an ice age. When it was clear that Israel would not be signing the Nuclear Non-Proliferation Treaty, up for extension in April of that year, Egypt headed up a campaign against Israel. Pressure on Israel for its weapons programs had started during the opening sessions of talks on multilateral arms control and regional security in mid-December of 1994. David Ivry, then the Director-General of the Israeli Defense Ministry, announced that Israel could not talk about regional arms control until Syria agreed to become a full participant in the talks. A few days later a surprise summit was hosted by Egypt in Alexandria involving Syrian President Hafez al-Assad, King Fahd of Saudi Arabia, and Egyptian President Hosni Mubarak. According to the observations of the *Islamic Affairs Analyst*, the purpose of the Alexandria summit "appears to have been twofold: to halt the uncoordinated Arab rush towards peace with Israel and to agree on a strategy for dealing with Israel's nuclear superiority."[1] As we noted earlier, many in the region believe this Arab strategy should include acquiring nuclear weapons of their own.

Another sign that the diplomatic temperature between Egypt and Israel was about to drop a few more degrees came with the victory of Benjamin Netanyahu as Israel's Prime Minister. There is no question that Arabs were disappointed with Netanyahu's victory. Once again, Egypt played host to an Arab summit, this time to put together a united Arab response to Netanyahu's victory. One of the main results of the summit was an agreement that all Arab states would back Syria's demands for a peace treaty with Israel, meaning Israel's full withdrawal from the Golan Heights and southern Lebanon. Furthermore, the united

Arab response was that Israel must discontinue Jewish settlement of the West Bank and Gaza Strip.

One of the clearest indications of the Egyptian/Israeli ice age, however, came on the eve of Benjamin Netanyahu's first visit to an Arab country as Israel's Prime Minister, in this case Egypt. The front-page headline of Egypt's *El-Dustour* newspaper, deliberately worded in the Hebrew language, read: "We Don't Want You in Cairo." In addition, according to an Associated Press news service report:

> Egypt's opposition government newspapers unleashed a barrage of insulting cartoons and blistering editorials yesterday, portraying him as Public Enemy No. 1. . . .
>
> "Israel's prime minister comes to our country as an unwanted, insufferable guest," *El-Dustour* said. . . .
>
> "Since Netanyahu came to power, we have become closer to each other [a reference to Arab nations following the summit convened in response to Netanyahu's victory] and our differences have dwindled," Mustafa Amin, a leading Egyptian columnist, wrote in the government-owned *Al-Akhbar* newspaper.
>
> "If the Israeli prime minister persists in these foolish policies, the Arabs will head toward violence," he wrote.
>
> Amin was referring to Netanyahu's stated opposition to the underlying principal of Arab-Israeli negotiations since 1991: trading land won in the 1967 Mideast war for peace. Netanyahu also ruled out a Palestinian state and any negotiations over Jerusalem.[2]

While the meeting between the Egyptian and Israeli leaders produced no great breakthroughs in the peace process, it did go more smoothly than many had anticipated. Following it, President Mubarak claimed, "I am very relaxed. I understand his conceptions."[3] Nonetheless, tensions remain between the two nations.

While Egypt's sentiments towards Israel are cool at the time of writing, we know that God has a special plan for Egypt down the road, and it appears that Egypt will follow a difficult path to get there. God's plan for Egypt has been outlined for us by the prophet Isaiah:

> The burden of Egypt. Behold, the Lord rideth upon a swift cloud, and shall come into Egypt: and the idols of Egypt shall be moved at his presence, and the heart of Egypt shall melt in the midst of it.
>
> And I will set the Egyptians against the Egyptians: and they shall fight every one against his brother, and every one against his neighbour; city against city, and kingdom against kingdom.
>
> And the spirit of Egypt shall fail in the midst thereof; and I will destroy the counsel thereof: and they shall seek to the idols, and to the charmers, and to them that have familiar spirits, and to the wizards.
>
> And the Egyptians will I give over into the hand of a cruel lord: and a fierce king shall rule over them saith the Lord, the Lord of hosts.
>
> And the waters shall fail from the sea, and the river shall be wasted and dried up.
>
> And they shall turn the rivers far away; and the brooks of defence shall be emptied and dried up: the reeds and flags shall wither.
>
> The paper reeds by the brooks, by the mouth of the brooks and every thing sown by the brooks, shall wither, be driven away, and be no more.

The fishers also shall mourn and all they that cast angle into the brooks shall lament, and they that spread nets upon the waters shall languish.

Moreover they that work in fine flax, and they that weave networks shall be confounded.

And they shall be broken in the purposes thereof, all that make sluices and ponds for fish.[4]

It is obvious from this passage of Scripture that Egypt appears to be in for some troublesome economic times. It also appears that Egypt is in for a civil war of some kind, at the end of which she will fall under the rule of a "cruel lord; and a fierce king" (verse 4).

Ever since Anwar Sadat signed the peace treaty with Israel, there has been discord between Egypt's secular government and Egypt's Islamic fundamentalist population. Over the years the government has tried to keep Islamic fundamentalists in line by outlawing their groups and organizations. Even the Muslim Brotherhood, which was not known for violence, has been banned. In retaliation, radical Islamists have often resorted to violence. There have even been a couple of assassination attempts against President Hosni Mubarak. Unfortunately, in an effort to hurt the government through its tourist trade, innocent foreign visitors have been killed by terrorist attacks. The government has tried to keep these groups from gaining a foothold in politics by prohibiting them from forming political parties. Nonetheless, Islamic fundamentalism has been gaining popularity with the Egyptian population. During times of tragedy, it has been some of these radical Islamic groups that have beaten the government to the punch in doling out charitable aid. Furthermore, Islamic fundamentalism is becoming increasingly appealing to Egypt's intellectuals and professionals. If today's trends continue, it is not difficult to see that civil unrest could one day occur. The prophet Isaiah also tells us, however, that Egypt is going to go through a time of spiritual shaking and awakening:

> In that day shall Egypt be like unto women: and it shall be afraid and fear because of the shaking of the hand of the Lord of hosts, which he shaketh over it.

> And the land of Judah shall be a terror unto Egypt, every one that maketh mention thereof shall be afraid in himself, because of the counsel of the Lord of hosts, which he hath determined against it.

> In that day shall five cities in the land of Egypt speak the language of Canaan, and swear to the Lord of hosts; one shall be called, The city of destruction.

> In that day shall there be an altar to the Lord in the midst of the land of Egypt, and a pillar at the border thereof to the Lord.

> And it shall be for a sign and for a witness unto the Lord of hosts in the land of Egypt: for they shall cry unto the Lord because of the oppressors, and he shall send them a saviour, and a great one, and he shall deliver them.

> And the Lord shall be known to Egypt, and the Egyptians shall know the Lord in that day, and shall do sacrifice and oblation; yea, they shall vow a vow unto the Lord, and perform it.

> And the Lord shall smite Egypt: he shall smite and heal it: and they shall return even to the Lord, and he shall be intreated of them and shall heal them.[5]

Thus, although Egypt will go through difficulties in the days ahead, in the end God is going to heal Egypt and bless her along with Israel (verse 24).

Syria

The conclusion of the prophecy in Isaiah 19 also says that "Assyria" is going to be blessed with Egypt and Israel:

> In that day shall there be a highway out of Egypt to Assyria, and the Assyrian shall come into Egypt, and the Egyptian into Assyria, and the Egyptians shall serve with the Assyrians.

> In that day shall Israel be the third with Egypt and with Assyria, even a blessing in the midst of land:

> Whom the Lord of hosts shall bless, saying, Blessed be Egypt my people, and Assyria the work of my hands, and Israel mine inheritance.[6]

Who is "Assyria"? Could it be modern-day Syria? Possibly. In her book *Pathways to Armageddon . . . And Beyond*, Betty Lynn noted:

> In Isaiah 19 we have a prophecy about Egypt and "Assyria." While we can all easily identify Egypt on a map, "Assyria" is more difficult. The Assyrians originally lived in an area which is now the much-contested and mythical "Kurdistan." Their empire eventually covered the entire "Fertile Crescent"—the Tigris-Euphrates Valley and the eastern Mediterranean coastline. While the original inhabitants near the northeast Mediterranean coast were called Arameans (sons of Aram) that area soon became known as "Syria," from the name "Assyria." Therefore, in determining the modern identity of Assyria, we can each draw our own

conclusions. However, in that modern Syria began discussing "land for peace" with Israel before the Gulf War began, perhaps it is Syria who will also earn a special place in the messianic kingdom. In any case, God surely knows the peoples with whom He is dealing, and we will be able to identify them as prophecy is fulfilled."[7]

Indeed, at the time of writing, Syria is the only Arab nation that is working on coming to a formal peace deal with Israel, although one has to wonder how seriously she is seeking peace. Several years of negotiations have seemed to provide nothing more concrete than a lot of air miles for U.S. secretaries of state flying between Washington, Damascus, and Jerusalem. At times it appears that the peace negotiations between Israel and Syria are more like game-playing, with one side saying, "You go first" and the other responding, "No you go first." Nonetheless, if Syria is the "Assyria" of the Isaiah 19 passages, we can watch for an eventual peace treaty. As Betty Lynn pointed out, we'll just have to wait for the prophecy to be fulfilled to know for certain.

Jordan

You may be wondering why God left Jordan out of the blessings in the Isaiah 19 passages. Indeed, besides Egypt, Jordan is the only Arab nation formally at peace with Israel. In fact, when looking at diplomatic relations between Israel and Jordan under King Hussein, peace is a lot warmer than it is between Egypt and Israel.

Like much of the world, on October 26, 1994, we turned on our TV set to watch the historic signing of the peace treaty between the two nations. Ironically, the ceremony took place in a mine field on the Israeli/Jordanian border, thus restricting the 5,000 guests and heads of state to a limited area. In his speech, U.S. Secretary of State Warren Christopher noted that on that day the field of mines had been transformed into a field of dreams. It was a touching ceremony, and from all outward appearances it certainly seemed that King Hussein was sincere about making peace with Israel.

Interestingly, in its treaty of peace with Jordan, Israel vowed to recognize that King Hussein should have an administrative role over Moslem holy sites in Jerusalem. Despite the fact that King Hussein holds a special interest in Jerusalem because he is said to be a direct descendant of the prophet Mohammed, Israel's special recognition of him angered many Arabs. Especially offended were Palestinians, who have their eyes set on Jerusalem as the capital of Palestine.

Will peace be lasting between Israel and Jordan? Jordan's diplomatic relations with Israel in the many months following the signing of the peace treaty seem to suggest that King Hussein is indeed sincere, just as his grandfather King Abdullah before him had been sincere in his desires to be at peace with Israel. For this, King Abdullah was assassinated in 1951 on the Temple Mount in Jerusalem by those opposed to peace with the "Zionist enemy."

While King Hussein seems sincere, however, not everyone in his kingdom views peace with Israel through the same eyes. Indeed, King Hussein has become quite unpopular with the Islamic fundamentalist population in his kingdom, many of whom are Palestinian. It is impossible to predict the scenario of events that are going to take place in Jordan regarding peace with Israel. We do know, however, from Bible prophecy, that the enmity between Israel and the peoples of Jordan has ancient historical roots. And for this, we know that Jordan will have a different place in Bible prophecy than Egypt and Assyria, which are to be blessed with Israel. Betty Lynn wrote:

> The nation of Jordan is comprised of three ancient tribes: Moab, Ammon, and Edom. Moabites and Ammonites are the descendants of Lot by his incestuous daughters, and Edomites are the descendants of Esau, Jacob's twin brother.
>
> These nations have always been at odds with the children of Israel. God will ultimately punish Jordan for its treatment of Israel. In fact, numerous prophecies tell us that Israel will ultimately possess Jordan. Today, just the opposite is true. Jordan occupies the East Bank of the Jordan River, which is the inheritance of Israel's son Gad. This is a fulfillment of prophecy:
>
> Concerning the sons of Ammon. Thus says the Lord: "Does Israel have no sons? Or has he no heirs? Why then has Malcam [the national god of the Ammonites] taken possession of Gad and his people settled in its cities? Therefore, behold, the days are coming, declares the Lord, that I shall cause a trumpet blast of war to be heard against Rabbah of the sons of Ammon; and it will become a desolate heap, and her towns will be set on fire. Then Israel will take possession of his possessors," says the Lord (Jeremiah 49:1-2).

This Israeli territory expansion is echoed in the prophecies of Obadiah. In fact the main theme of Obadiah is the destruction of Edom, which lies in southern Jordan:

> Then the house of Jacob will be a fire and the house of Joseph a flame; but the house of Esau [Edom] will be as stubble. And they will set them on fire and consume them, so that there will be no survivor of the house of Esau, for the Lord has

spoken. Then those of the Negev [southern Israel]
will possess the mountain of Esau, and those of
the Shephelah [Judean hills near Gaza] the Philis-
tine plain [Gaza]; also, they will possess the territory of Ephraim and the territory of Samaria [West
Bank], and Benjamin will possess Gilead [East
Bank] (Obadiah 18-19).[8]

Scripture is not clear on when Israel will take possession of this territory that now belongs to modern-day
Jordan, but we do know from Scripture that it will take
place, and that the nation now known as Jordan will not
share in the same blessing as Egypt and Assyria with Israel.

A New World Economy

I n the summer of 1995 we went to see the movie *The Net*, starring Sandra Bullock as a computer analyst. She had been sent a disk that was supposed to hold a new computer game, but actually contained sensitive data bases from agencies like the Federal Reserve Board and the Atomic Energy Commission. Bullock's discoveries ensnared her as a victim in a huge plot to control the world of cyberspace. When the conspirators discovered she had the disk, they turned her life into a nightmare by altering her personal files and identification in government and financial databases. With a few strokes on a keyboard, the conspirators created such an identity crisis for her that she was wanted by the police, she couldn't use her credit-card number or withdraw money from her bank account, nor could she prove her true identity. She was completely locked out of the net.

Prior to the movie's release, a group of VIPs from high-level businesses and government agencies were given a private screening of the film in Washington, D.C., Apparently, the group left the private screening room a bit unsettled by what they had just seen. According to Irwin Winkler, who directed the film, "They told us that

everything in the story was accurate and plausible—
frighteningly so."[1]

What made the plot in *The Net* work was the fact that
Bullock's character was a loner. She worked at home and
communicated with the outside world via fax-modem, e-
mail, and Federal Express. The only relative she had was
a mother with Alzheimer's disease. Her neighbors never
saw her. She had no friends. Such a thing would not likely
happen to us in the real world because we probably all
know at least one person who could give us a positive ID.
Nonetheless the conclusions of those in the private screening room confirm that we are indeed the first generation
in which the prophecy of the "mark of the beast" can be
fulfilled:

> He [the Antichrist, or the Beast] causeth all, both
> small and great, rich and poor, free and bond, to
> receive a mark in their right hand, or in their fore-
> heads:
>
> And that no man might buy or sell, save he that
> had the mark, or the name of the beast, or the
> number of his name.[2]

According to this prophecy in God's Word, the day is
coming when the Antichrist will be able to lock people out
of the net. He will be able to prevent every man, woman,
and child on earth from carrying out any financial or commercial transaction if they refuse the mark. We will look
at some technologies in existence that could possibly fulfill the prophecy of the mark in the next chapter, but in
this chapter we would like to determine *how* the Antichrist
could possibly control the buying and selling of all people
on earth.

When we first started studying Bible prophecy many
years ago, this seemed like an extremely monumental task.

Revelation 13 tells us that the Antichrist will able to control ALL financial transactions, EVERYWHERE in the world, for EVERY person on the planet. Even in the early days of computerized banking technology, the infrastructure that would allow this prophecy to be fulfilled just did not exist. There were bits and pieces of the global economic puzzle, but some of the necessary pieces for the completion of the puzzle were not yet available. This is no longer true. The picture in this prophetic puzzle is becoming much more recognizable.

Puzzle Piece #1—Networking

The key technology driving the world toward the fulfillment of the mark of the beast prophecy of Revelation 13 is the computer. Computers have dramatically changed the world we live in. As seasoned veteran of the computing and communications industries Frank Koelsch observed, the new world order "doesn't just include PCs, but revolves around PCs."[3] Even our wristwatches and kitchen appliances, from the breadmaker to the microwave oven, are computerized. And with each passing year, computer power and speed are increasing exponentially. The average car today has more computing power than the Apollo spacecraft that sent the first men to the moon.

This exponential growth in computer speed and power has enabled today's PCs, miniature versions of their forerunners, to carry out tasks that the giant mainframes of a few decades ago were incapable of doing. In the early days of our prophetic research, there were rumors of the existence of a giant computer in Brussels, Belgium. This giant mainframe computer, nicknamed *The Beast*, was supposedly capable of housing personal information on every individual on the planet. The truth of the matter is, the giant mainframes of yesterday—while capable of much—just couldn't handle this task.

Today's PCs, however, pack more punch than the alleged Beast ever could have. Furthermore, today's PCs are capable of fulfilling the task that the Beast was said to be intended for, without having to store a huge global database on every individual on the planet. Enter the world of networking. In an interview with our ministry magazine, *This Week in Bible Prophecy*, Janlori Goldman, deputy director of the Center for Democracy and Technology, told us:

> Thirty years ago, people were screaming and yelling about a national database, a national data bank, and that there were proposals to create a single computer filled with personal information on all people in this country. Now, that is a ridiculous concept. You can have distributed networks, or distributed systems. You can have millions and millions of computers. They all talk to each other. You can link information. You can share information. You can manipulate it. You can create profiles. It is absurd to talk about a data bank. The information is all over the world. It is in many, many different databases and they can all talk to each other.[4]

Being wired into networks such as the Internet has provided millions of individuals and businesses with the ability to link into numerous databases virtually anywhere in the world. Individuals can now shop in cyberspace, or send their shopping list by fax-modem and have someone else do the shopping for them. They can do their banking in cyberspace. They can even make their own airline or dinner reservations. Businesses can quickly do credit checks on a client or do statistical research for upcoming projects. Their employees can become teleworkers. Thanks to teleconferencing, they can hold business meetings with clients anywhere in the world without having to leave their office.

Police forces and government investigative agencies are now able to tap into each other's crime databases across national or international borders. They can accumulate data for criminal investigations into a large database of their own. One of the largest of these in the U.S. is the FBI's National Crime Information Center (NCIC). It holds over 24 million records, linked to over half a million users. There is also a large database accumulated for suspected crimes in the financial sector, known as the Financial Crimes Enforcement Network (FinCEN).

Other government agencies are also taking advantage of networking. With the ability to connect with each other, they can now easily share and compare information on individual citizens. For example, welfare agencies in neighboring counties can compare files on benefits recipients to locate double dippers. Government agencies can now also search the databases of non-governmental organizations to compare information. In fact, many government agencies such as the FBI and IRS have secretly purchased data marketing lists. One database company, Donnelly Marketing, is said to have files on 125 million individuals in the U.S. With this kind of information at its fingertips, the IRS claims it will now have the ability to easily weed out tax scofflaws. The *Los Angeles Times* reported in the winter of 1995 that:

> A cadre of IRS agents with computers and modems now will be searching records filed with the Department of Motor Vehicles, county tax assessor's offices, credit-reporting companies and the U.S. Bureau of Census in an effort to find

people who are underreporting their business
sales, overestimating their deductions or trying to
hide assets—or themselves—from federal tax col-
lectors.[5]

Indeed, in the technological information age, the New
Age term "interconnected" is taking on new meaning. One
of the latest trends is for whole communities or states to
wire together their banks, businesses, libraries, schools,
and the like, into one network. In a special spring 1995
edition on the world of cyberspace, *Time* magazine reported on one such multipurpose community network:

> For the past 18 months, a partnership between the
> town of Blacksburg, Virginia, Bell Atlantic and
> Virginia Tech University has operated a com-
> munal network called the Blacksburg Electronic
> Village. By the end of 1994, the project had hooked
> up a majority of the town's businesses and 36,000
> citizens, including 24,000 students at Virginia
> Tech, whose campus is situated in town. All these
> people reach the Internet through a local network
> that ties Blacksburgians to the town hall, hospi-
> tals, stores, restaurants and one another. In time,
> participating merchants hope to do business using
> Digicash Corp.'s "E-cash," a form of electronic
> money.
>
> Computer-connected communities, in various
> stages of development, are operating in dozens of
> cities in the U.S. and Canada. The entire state of
> North Carolina has built its own information
> highway based on a fiber-optic system that links
> most of the state's departments and services, its
> public universities and even parts of the penal
> system. In Mecklenburg County, for example, a
> video link permits prisoners to "appear" before

judges without actually making the trek to the county courthouse.[6]

While the U.S. has made the most progress in becoming an electronic village, the rest of the world is catching up quickly. The global electronic village is truly becoming a reality. In fact, what the world is essentially becoming in these last days is one massive computer with a plethora of links.

Without the Shadow of a Doubt

There is no question that computers have made the lives of individuals and businesses much easier. For example, it boggles the mind when one considers that large corporations used to have to manage their accounting books manually. Now computer software programs can easily handle the work that once took twenty or thirty accountants and bookkeepers to do, and do it more accurately.

Our own lives were dramatically changed when we were introduced to the computer. As writers, we had to cope with a typewriter, crossing out mistakes or paragraphs we didn't like. Now we can mark text in our work and move it around from one place to the next with a keystroke. We can erase words and paragraphs, or put them back in a second, all without those messy marks that once spoiled the look of our manuscripts or articles. We also remember the time when we had to use time-consuming cut-and-paste methods for graphically designing our monthly newspaper and newsletter. Again, computers have provided the ability to design and redesign without having to retype and repaste graphics and text. It used to take our secretary over a week to type out names and addresses on envelopes in order to mail the newsletter to our subscribers. As our mailing list has grown, our secretarial pool would had to have grown dramatically if we still did this task manually. The purchase of our first computer changed our lives and work dramatically. Such tasks that once took days are now done more efficiently in just a few hours, or even minutes.

Virtually any information people need today is available at the touch of their fingertips. Information, speedily processed and transmitted, is vital to the developing global village the world is rapidly becoming. In fact, one of the things that defines a developed nation today is one that has mastered the ability to accumulate information, along with the know-how to process it in a meaningful and beneficial way.

While computers have simplified lives, however, at the same time they have made our lives an open book for anyone who cares to take the time to read it. Every time we log on to the Internet, send a fax, make a purchase with our credit card, or rent a video, we leave behind information about our personal lives. This personal information is known as a "data shadow," which starts accumulating almost the minute we are born. It may surprise many to know just how much of an open book their lives really are. In 1993, reporters at *The Ottawa Citizen*, the local newspaper in the Canadian capital, decided to test just how true this is:

> Bill Walther considers himself a very private person.
>
> But maybe he isn't. You can look at the profile the *Citizen* quickly drew up of him, through documents and easily accessed computer files, and judge for yourself.
>
> We learned Walther's birth date, home address and phone number, although the phone is not in his name.

We learned his occupation, education and minimum salary.

We told Walther most of his addresses and phone numbers for the last 30 years. We figured out roughly when his marriage broke up. We learned where his ex-wife lives, what her birth date was and what she paid for her new house.

We know the woman Walther lives with now, when they began living together, and what her occupation was.

We learned that Walther drives a red 1991 Chevy S-10, and has until Nov. 20, 1994 to repay a $21,361 loan to his dealer in Gloucester. Walther's driving and criminal records have been clean for the last three years, a computerized information kiosk told us. He is 183 centimeters tall and wears glasses or contact lenses, it added.

There's more. Through computer databases accessed at the *Citizen's* newsroom we learned Walther's hobbies.

He's a nature-lover whose interests are birdwatching, herbs and wild mushrooms, according to information on the National Capital FreeNet computer network, of which Walther is a member.

Another database told us Walther played Friar Laurence in a 1983 Carleton University production of Romeo and Juliet.

This three-decade sketch of a person's life came after a few days' work and a few dollars spent. . . .

Walther is one of three volunteers who let the *Citizen* probe their personal and financial lives to help determine the bounds of privacy.

The ground rules were simple: find what could be found legally, in documents, public information and databases. There were no interviews with friends, relatives or neighbors—often the first tactic for a reporter. There were no private eye moves, no surveillance, no sorting through trash, no insider sources for credit or financial records, and no misrepresentations. . . .

True, we could not legally obtain credit records, medical records, banking records and social insurance numbers.[7]

While Canadian laws are strict about medical and banking records, such information is much more easily obtained in the U.S. Robert Gellman is a privacy and information policy consultant, and is the former chief counsel to the House Subcommittee on Government Information. In an interview with *This Week in Bible Prophecy*, Mr. Gellman told us that during the Reagan years the issue of privacy had come to the fore. The subcommittee he worked with drafted a bill that would give U.S. citizens privacy over their medical records. The bill, however, died in committee. When President Bill Clinton tried to bring about health care reform, the issue of the privacy of medical records resurfaced. But as the Clinton administration's health care reform proposals died, however, so did the push for medical records privacy. This means there is no law in the U.S. to protect an individual's medical record. Mr. Gellman noted, "The truth today is that medical records are not confidential. Everybody thinks they are. Everybody acts like they are. Everybody talks about them as if they are. But in point of fact, medical records are passed around quite a bit within the health care system. There are very few legal protections for anybody."[8]

As for banking records, let's return to the findings of the reporters back at *The Ottawa Citizen*:

Joseph Apter, Telephonic-Info's president, bragged he could get similar information on *The Citizen's* volunteers, after helping the *Boston Globe* track down a person's unlisted phone number.

Apter said he is connected to the U.S. "collection network," which includes the collection departments of banks, credit card companies, stores and finance companies.

But Apter hit the wall when he tried to cross the border.[9]

The experiment conducted by the reporters at *The Ottawa Citizen* demonstrated just how much information is readily available about our personal lives in Canada. And for our U.S. neighbors, privacy is even less secure. What is interesting is that much of the knowledge collected about us is information that we readily give out. For instance, *The Citizen's* point about not being able to legally obtain a social insurance number for a Canadian citizen is moot. Virtually all Canadians give out their social insurance number as identification freely whenever asked, even though they are not legally required to do so. Every time you fill out one of those warranty cards you give out information. Not long ago we purchased a new kitchen appliance and proceeded to fill out the warranty card contained in the box. When I reached the question about our annual income, I stopped to consider. What did our annual income have to do with a new coffee maker? I decided to read the rest of the way through the warranty card before contributing any further details about ourselves. In very fine print at the bottom of the warranty card I read that it was not even a requirement to fill out the card in order for the warranty to go in to effect. For that matter, it wasn't even required to send the warranty card in the mail!

Every time we enter a contest or fill out a marketing questionnaire, we reveal personal information about

ourselves. When we accept a loyalty card from our supermarket, we are actually allowing them to keep a record
of the types of foods we like to eat. We give clues as to
how many people live in our household, and whether we
have children or pets living with us. If we stop buying
shaving cream and razor blades, we are suggesting that
the marital status of the household now reads "single." If
we start buying diapers we are revealing that a new baby
has entered the family.

Before computers came along, such information was
virtually useless. It was scattered in various files held by
a broad array of organizations, institutions, and businesses, as well as government agencies. With computers,
however, what was once just reams of paper exhausting
to read has become valuable information that can be easily
accumulated, stored, processed, and compared with other
databases. In many instances, such information is used by
marketing companies. This seems harmless enough, except for the fact that we start receiving a lot of unwanted
junk mail. For the most part people just don't care who
knows which brand of coffee or cereal they prefer. Most
of us have nothing to hide.

But the possession of such information can open the
door to Big Brother-style control. In some instances this
appears to be a good thing, but when you stop and think
about it, it is actually a foreshadow of what is to come
under the rule of the Antichrist. Take for instance the issue
of dead-beat dads. In the summer of 1996, a Canadian law
was passed that would allow the government to track
down dead-beat dads, even ones who think they have
managed to disappear, and encourage them to catch up
on past-due alimony payments. How does the government intend to encourage them? By threatening to take
something away from the dead-beat dad that is important

for their survival. A passport can be revoked from a dead-beat dad who uses it on a regular basis for business travel. One newspaper article reported on a woman who was ecstatic when she found out the driver's license of her ex could be taken away, because he was a cab driver. Most of us would applaud such efforts. There are far too many men who have shamelessly ignored their responsibilities as a parent. Unfortunately, innocent children and tax-payers have had to suffer for it. If such issues can be resolved with a bit of infringement on personal privacy, most are willing to say, "So be it."

Canadian privacy commissioner Bruce Phillips has expressed wonder on numerous occasions over the fact that the issue of privacy has not come to the fore of concerns for Canadians. In 1993 he warned that Canadians were being caught up in the advantages of high technology, claiming that "society is caught in a technological trance."[10]

Similarly, Brian Foran, policy adviser to the federal Privacy Commission, warned, "People are being mind-lessly led into an information age without understanding what it means. We're all going to be at a disadvantage when we wake up."[11] Indeed, the world of the Antichrist is one in which it will be extremely difficult to hide. This brings us to puzzle piece #2.

Puzzle Piece #2—Nowhere to Hide

With the growing trend in creating free trade regions, from the European Union (EU) to the North American Free Trade Area (NAFTA) to the Asia Pacific Economic Cooperation (APEC), the world is becoming a world without borders. Increasingly, nation-states are putting up "open for business" signs, welcoming foreign investors and multinational corporations. This trend, combined with advanced telecommunications technology, is bringing the term "one world" to life. As global thinker Harlan Cleveland noted:

> It no longer matters so much where you are if you are electronically plugged into what the buyers and sellers you care about are doing, wherever they are. The notion of a "New York market," a "Tokyo market," a "London market," or a "Zurich market," already sounds quaint. It evaporated before our eyes on Black Monday in 1987, as information about prices and pessimism ricocheted around the globe.... All the really important markets are world markets. Daniel Bell, the premier philosopher of the information society, foresaw long ago "a change in the nature of markets from 'places' to 'networks.' That change has come."[12]

As Mr. Cleveland noted, the world was chillingly made aware of the fact that national economies do indeed interconnect to form a global economy. Following the Black Monday crisis, *The New York Times* commented:

> While the marketplace is global, political constituencies end at the borders of the nation-state... nationalistic concerns, analysts say, set the stage for the collapse October 19 in stock markets worldwide. Now, threatened with global cataclysm, the nations seem to be making concessions.... Though their cooperation has expanded in the last two years these economic super powers still resist yielding enough of their sovereignty to pull together.[13]

Time magazine quoted a German central banker as angrily saying, "No event has ever dramatized the interdependencies of world financial markets quite like the October crash. American policy is determined by domestic considerations, even if it affects the world economy. Such thinking is no longer appropriate."[14]

In this new world without borders, however, it is not just electronic data, goods, and services that are free to move beyond national borders. Increasingly, people are moving about more freely as well. By the year 2000, industry insiders predict there will be 15 million U.S. "telecommuters" working in the world. Telecommuters are employees who are able to take advantage of telecommunications and computer technologies so that they can work at home or anywhere across the globe. Indeed, high-tech gadgets such as satellites, cellular phones, and notebook computers with built-in fax-modem and e-mail capabilities have made it possible not only to reach anywhere in the world, but also to *be* reached virtually anywhere in the world. Furthermore, telecommunications experts and observers can clearly see the day when people will wear their "telephones" like jewelry, with hidden microphones in necklaces or lapel pins. Phillips is working on a sophisticated wristwatch that it hopes to have ready for the year 2002. "The not too distant future," reported *The European* newspaper:

> will see such implements as portable personal intelligent communications with touch screens for pen and finger input, desk-based voice phones with intelligent screens, and handheld personal organisers, which use the global positioning system to guide the user through cities and countries. Advanced integrated circuit products will make these items possible. The list of combinations is endless, and the only limit is the imagination of inventors or the will of companies to manufacture them.
>
> Integrated circuit technology will soon bring creators enough miniaturisation for them to slap a video telephone

together with a camera, a television, and a computer—
all in a package so small you can wear it as a wristwatch.[15]

In this world of high-tech gadgetry, it is the cellular
phone industry that will play a key role in making us accessible anywhere we go. Jon Van, a staff writer for the
Chicago Tribune, observed:

> Another means to track people relies upon the existing
> network of cellular-phone transmitters.
>
> The cellular industry and emergency-response officials
> have proposed standards to the Federal Communications
> Commission that would enable police, fire and ambu-
> lance dispatchers to find people who dial 911 from wire-
> less phones.
>
> At present, nearly one-quarter of the 911 emergency calls
> made in the U.S. come from wireless phones, and half
> the time the callers don't know their location, posing a
> major problem for emergency personnel.
>
> Developing computer systems to track locations of so
> many calls is a daunting task, but it is consistent with the
> phone industry's goal of one day assigning phone num-
> bers to human beings, rather than to equipment. Once
> the phone network becomes sophisticated enough to do
> this, it will smooth the way for widespread monitoring
> of people's whereabouts.[16]

In the fall of 1995, AT&T was already taking reservations for its universal lifetime phone number. According
to the *U.S. News & World Report*:

> AT&T began taking reservations last week for
> permanent personal numbers, called True Con-
> nections, enabling subscribers to be reached any-
> where in the world 24 hours a day by those who
> know the number. Individuals with these num-

bers, which carry a 500 area code, will call a computerized data bank and punch in a phone
number—a car phone, beach home or friend's
house, say—to which calls made to the 500
number are to be forwarded. . . . GTE, MCI and
Sprint, among other long-distance carriers, plan
to offer 500 numbers by the end of the year.[17]

We will discuss the issue of identification numbers
and other tracking methods further in the next chapter,
but suffice it to say that with each passing moment high
technology is making the world vast and wide open to us.
We can now easily move across the globe, physically or
electronically. At the same time, such advanced technology
is creating a world that is no longer big enough to hide in.
There is only one thing left for us that would give us
anonymity or provide us with the ability to vanish if we
so chose. If we were rich enough, we might be able to live
solely on cash. The one thing that can close the open book
on our lives is *cash*. But for how long?

Puzzle Piece #3—A Cashless Society

In our early days of prophetic research, there was a
trend towards a "less cash" society, but many were insisting we would never become a "cashless" society. For
a number of years now, however, bankers, financiers, and
stock market traders have considered money to be nothing
more than electronic bits of information that are passed
back and forth through cyberspace. The only reason physical cash has stuck around as long as it has is to appease
those who feel more comfortable with coins jingling in
their pockets and paper dollars thickening their billfolds
and wallets.

The truth of the matter is, bankers and financiers would like nothing more than for these remaining die-hards to turn over their paper bills and metal coins in exchange for a plastic card, preferably one containing a small microchip. Slowly, such die-hards have been introduced to the convenience of debit cards for large purchases, and prepaid cards for everything from vending machines to toll booths or public telephones. In the fall of 1994, *The New York Times* reported that many industry insiders view cash as a "nightmare." They are just waiting for the day when these consumers who prefer to carry cash wake up and smell the coffee:

> "What consumers want is convenience, and if you look at cash, it's really quite inconvenient," said Donald J. Gleason, president of the Smart Card Enterprise unit of Electronic Payment Services, known as EPS, which runs the MAC cash machine network. "And for merchants, cash is a nightmare. It is expensive to handle, count and deposit, and they have slippage, which is their way of saying theft." . . .

> "Banks estimate that 4 percent of the value of cash that is deposited gets eaten up in handling costs," said Michael C. Nash, a senior vice president with Visa International.[18]

If Canadians are any sign of coming trends, the "nightmare" will soon be over. After Japan, Canada has the highest per capita number of automated teller machines. The acceptance of debit cards has increased many-fold from the predictions of Canadian bankers. Canadians as a whole have taken to the idea of a cashless society. According to *The Edmonton Journal*:

For the first time since Confederation, the number of cheques in circulation has stopped climbing.

Canadian banks have been devoted to the concept of electronic banking since the early 1980s. There are now 5.31 automatic bank machines for every 10,000 Canadians, compared with 3.1 machines for every 10,000 Americans. Only the Japanese are more automated—8.7 machines for every 10,000 inhabitants.

And people use them. In 1990, people paid bills, withdrew or deposited cash, and transferred funds 577 million times on ABMs.

In 1993, 834 million transactions were recorded.

Indeed, consumers seem to love them: More than 20 million debit card transactions worth over $1 billion were buzzed through in December at 80,000 stores across Canada.[19]

By 1995, debit card use in Canada had soared well beyond the dreams of Canadian bankers:

Canadian shoppers "swiped" a lot of plastic in stores during 1995.

The Interac Association reports that plastic banking cards were used for 390 million direct payment transactions last year, 111 per cent more than a year earlier. . . .

Usage surged in December despite a subdued Christmas shopping season, said Jim Kenney, vice-president, marketing and business development for Interac.

"Debit cards were almost as popular as greeting cards," he said, pointing to a near doubling of transactions to 51 million during December . . .

"All the signs are pointing to a continued acceptance by consumers. Quite simply, they love this service," said Kenney.[20]

To further wean the consumer and retailer of cash, bankers have made it easier for them to do their banking at home or the office simply by using computers and telephones. Indeed, it has now reached the point where the only reason for the couch potatoes of North America to head for the nearest ATM is to withdraw cash. Eliminate cash, and you eliminate the need to roll off the couch. More free time on the sofa, speculate cyber retailers, means more time for consumers to spend their electronic dollars. As businesses, financiers, and computer software companies began to recognize that a potential market worth billions of dollars was waiting at home to spend its money in cyberspace, the race was on to become the main supplier of the first secure form of digital global currency. Kurt Kleiner wrote for *New Scientist*:

> Digicash is the brainchild of David Chaum, a former professor of computing at Stanford University in California who now runs the Digicash company from his new home in Amsterdam. The million digidollars he distributed to get the trial going are not real money in the sense that they can be converted back into guilders, pounds or dollars. But they can be used to buy goods and services from the 50 companies that agreed to join in the trial. If the scheme proves successful, then Digicash will be in the running to establish the first global electronic currency.
>
> Digicash may be first but there will soon be plenty of others with their own version of electronic cash. The prize is enormous. Sitting there now are millions of Internet users, all of whom might like to buy something straight from the screen . . .

The software giant Microsoft is developing secure payments systems in league with Visa. With Microsoft's marketing clout this is a partnership to be reckoned with.
Then there's Cybercash of Vienna, Virginia, which has
its own e-money nearly ready to test along with the Wells
Fargo Bank. Not to be left out of the action, Mastercard
and Bank of America have joined forces with Netscape,
the World Wide Web software designer, to pioneer a
secure payment system. And in Britain, the National
Westminster and Midland Banks are preparing to set customers loose with their Mondex smart card e-money
system in Swindon, Wiltshire.[21]

Since this report, the Royal Bank of Canada and the
Canadian Imperial Bank of Commerce agreed to test the
Mondex system in a pilot project in Guelph, Ontario. Bell
Canada, the nation's phone company, agreed to cooperate
and provide the specially-equipped telephones needed
for the pilot project. According to a press release by Bell
Canada:

> The heart of the Mondex system, conceived and
> developed by a large British bank, is a micro-com-
> puter chip embedded in a plastic card which stores
> the electronic equivalent of cash.
>
> "Using this card in combination with a telephone
> that is equipped with a card-reader means you
> virtually have your own personal automated
> banking machine in your home or place of busi-
> ness," said a Royal Bank official.[22]

Indeed, current trends suggest that the new world
order will be a cashless society, not just a less-cash society,
as many thought just a few years ago. From biblical
prophecy we know that under the rule of the Antichrist,
the existence of cash will not be likely. If cash were still

around, how would he be able to control the buying and selling for EVERY man, woman, and child on the planet? Furthermore, the utopian new world order, which man is even now trying to create, will benefit from the fruits of a cashless society. Cash is the cause of many of the crimes that take place today, from muggings to drug trafficking to money laundering. While supposedly ridding the world of the evil created by the existence of cash, the Antichrist will turn around and use the cashless society for his own evil purposes.

No man might buy, or sell . . . or steal?

Those who wish to survive in the Antichrist's new world order will be required to take his mark. What happens if they don't? It is obvious that without the mark, survival will be virtually impossible during the tribulation period. Without the ability to use electronic money, you could not pay rent or a mortgage. You could not buy food at the supermarket or at a restaurant. You couldn't buy an airline ticket or rent a hotel room. In essence, you would be entirely locked out of the system, like that character in *The Net*.

Over the years we have come across some interesting news items that suggest it will even be difficult to fish, steal, or try to grow crops secretly under the rule of the Antichrist. In the spring of 1993, a news report claimed that shop owners in Britain were planning to install tiny electronic devices in food packaging to thwart shoplifters. One of Britain's daily newspapers reported:

> They are to hide tiny electronic devices in foodwrappings in a pilot scheme financed by a consortium of the major supermarkets and packaging companies. The tiny bugs

will set off alarm bells and flashing lights if shoppers try to leave without paying.

Co-Op security supremo John Hall said: "Supermarkets are tired of writing off millions through petty pilfering. It's about time we harnessed new technology to deter these potential thieves."[23]

Also in the European Union, it was announced in 1992 that a spy satellite surveillance system had been launched. What kind of criminals were Brussels looking for? Farmers. An article in *The European* newspaper reported:

Brussels has launched spy satellite surveillance of Europe's nine million farmers in the intensifying war against fraud. In all but two of the 12 member states, the fields of thousands of farmers who make bogus claims for hefty EC subsidies are being detected with pinpoint accuracy.

For the first time, satellite surveillance makes it possible to carry out checks on virtually every farm, largely superseding the cumbersome procedure of random on-the-spot checks by agriculture ministry officials.

In Brussels, the Commission is collating the spy satellite data, then passing it on to national enforcement agencies in readiness for a blitz on fraudsters once the autumn begins. . . .

The first task for EC experts is to give every field a serial number and identify the type of crop being grown. Detailed analysis can then reveal whether the actual plot tallies with a farmer's application for subsidy. . . .

The Commission's response has been an ambitious Ecu 1.15 million scheme centralising records on who farms what. A "Domesday Book" would be compiled listing every field and animal across Europe. It would be policed by satellite surveillance and a new electronic system of tagging livestock.[24]

Closer to home, the same kind of satellite technology has also been used to catch would-be cheats. The culprits in this instance were ones who apparently misinterpreted the meaning of a recipe that called for "poached" fish:

> A tracking system used to pinpoint Iraqi targets in the Persian Gulf war helped nab illegal fishermen on Lake Huron.
>
> Conservation officers used it to pinpoint two ice-fishing holes and determine that four U.S. Indians were illegally fishing in Canadian waters on March 7.
>
> Using a Global Positioning System, a navigation aid that relies on a satellite network, the officers pinpointed two holes in the ice between Sulphur Island in Ontario and Poe Point on Drummond Island in Michigan.[25]

Indeed, satellites and other highly technological tracking devices have made the prophetic picture clearer.

There is another piece of the economic puzzle that will allow the Antichrist to control and monitor the peoples of the world. This piece of the puzzle is also a key part in fulfilling God's prophecy about the "mark of the beast" in Revelation, chapter thirteen. Even as we write, technologies are being developed and tested that could very well play a role in implementing the fulfillment of the prophetic mark. We will take a look at some of these futuristic technologies in the next chapter.

The Mark of the Beast

The year is 2005. Mark Jones and his son, Chip, are passing through customs at the airport, having just returned from a vacation at the popular theme park VR Land. There is no customs official to greet them and ask questions. They simply pass through the checkpoint with their arms raised and hands outstretched. An implant reading device scans the microchip embedded in their hands to verify their ID. A camera checks their facial images for further identification verification. At the same time, infrared scanners are passing over the radio tags on the items in their cart, which is in front of them on the conveyer walkway. The appropriate duty charges for the cart's items are deducted from Mark's financial account. The whole transaction is updated on Mark's microchip implant. He can go over all the financial transactions for their entire trip when he gets home and places his hand under his personal chip-reading device, PCRD for short. The whole process takes a matter of moments. Mark just loves this new technology. Chip likes it too, but like most six-year-olds, is a little impatient with real-life details. He can't wait until they come up with speedier technology. "Dad," Chip says, turning to his father, "what was it like when you were growing up?" Mark pauses to reflect. "How did we get to where we are now?"

For years, Christians have been forecasting such a future for mankind from the teachings of God's prophetic Word about the "mark of the beast."God's Word forewarns that the Antichrist will implement a system using the "mark" by which he will be able to control all consumer transactions for everyone on the planet:

> He causeth all, both small and great, rich and poor, free and bond, to receive a mark in their right hand, or in their foreheads:

> And that no man might buy or sell, save he that had the mark, or the name of the beast, or the number of his name (Revelation 13:16,17).

Many have laughed at such predictions as the ravings of paranoia, but a future like that of our fictional characters Mark and Chip is not as sci-fi as many believed in the past. More and more, people are beginning to realize that such a future is plausible. For instance, Jon Van reported for the *Chicago Tribune*:

> A tiny chip implanted inside the human body to send and receive radio messages, long a popular delusion among paranoids, is likely to be marketed as a consumer item early in the next century.

> Several technologies already available or under development will enable electronics firms to make implantable ID locators, say futurists, and our yearning for convenience and security makes them almost irresistible to marketers.

> "This is currently very hot," said Edward Cornish, president of the World Future Society, based in Bethesda, Md. "The field is developing because the technology is becoming available to do it." He added: "Its appeal will depend on what features

are offered and the price. I'm sure a large number
of people would want such products."[1]

Before we proceed in our investigation of how we are
going to move from the present to the world that Mark
and Chip live in, we would first like to state that the most
important aspect of the mark of the beast is neither economic nor an identification decision. To have the mark of
the beast will be a *spiritual* decision.

Over the years we have received letters asking if
someone could accidentally take the mark by using a debit
card or agreeing to be identified by their fingerprint at
their bank. The answer to these questions is a definite *no*.
Consider what happens to those people who agree to take
the mark during the tribulation period:

> The third angel followed them, saying with a loud
> voice, if any man worship the beast and his image,
> and receive his mark in his forehead, or in his
> hand, the same shall drink of the wine of the wrath
> of God, which is poured out without mixture into
> the cup of his indignation; and he shall be tor-
> mented with fire and brimstone in the presence
> of the holy angels, and in the presence of the
> Lamb:
>
> And the smoke of their torment ascendeth up for
> ever and ever; and they have no rest day nor night,
> who worship the beast and his image, and whoso-
> ever receiveth the mark of his name.[2]

God, by His very nature, would never dole out such
severe punishment to those who were completely ignorant of what they were doing. Choosing the mark is not
an economic decision like choosing Visa over MasterCard.
While God is very much interested in our daily lives, He
is not as concerned about our economic decisions as He

is about our spiritual decisions. You may have noticed from the above Scripture that this punishment is given to those who take the mark AND who "worship the beast and his image." When people accept this mark, they will be consciously and deliberately telling the Antichrist they are willing to worship him as a god. At the same time they are telling God that they, in a final act of human defiance, are choosing freely to reject Him and His Son.

National IDs

The history of identification cards goes back to the ancient Roman Empire. Slaves, soldiers, and citizens of the Roman Empire were required to carry identification tiles known as *tesserae*. As the Roman Empire is being revived in its new sophisticated form today, so too are new sophisticated forms of identification.

In the past few years, pressure for national ID's has been climbing in this developing empire. Thailand is probably the most advanced in its implementation of a national identification system for its citizens with its Thailand Central Population Database and ID Card System. Everyone in Thailand has been issued a national ID card, which holds an electronic image of their fingerprint and face. The ID card is linked to an electronic government database which is essentially controlled by the Interior Ministry, a de facto military and police agency.

Slowly, other nations, even democracies like Canada and the U.S., seem to be heading in the same direction. Canada's Ontario provincial government, for instance, has proposed a multi-purpose smart card to replace driver's licenses, health cards, and welfare cards. In the U.S., many feared that President Bill Clinton's proposed national health-care card would become a de facto national ID. Of course, the Clinton administration's health-care proposals died, and along with them, the health-care card. Nonetheless, U.S. citizens are still not out of the woods as far as national ID's are concerned. The INS, as well as many of those who are in favor of curbing illegal immigration, are pushing for identity cards for working purposes. Privacy advocate Janlori Goldman told us at *This Week in Bible Prophecy* that, although "this is a very popular issue right now ... in reality, this is a very, very tiny problem. Less than 1 percent of all people in this country are illegal and are getting jobs illegally."[3]

Furthermore, although proponents of the proposed identity card claim it would only be used as a work card, history has shown that once such ID cards are introduced, they eventually come to be used for a broad array of government purposes. One need only look at the history of such identification cards in the U.S. to see that. Goldman continued:

> Whenever there has been a call for a national ID card, the proponents always say, "We just want to use it in this limited context." ... There will always be an irresistible temptation to use a card or an identifier for other purposes. I think that the arguments in favor of using it for other purposes will overwhelm any concerns about privacy, any concerns about discrimination. ...
>
> In the early 1930s the government created the social security number, and it was with a great deal of trepidation that the number was issued to all working Americans. ... [O]n the original social security cards that were issued it said, "To be used for social security purposes only." That caveat does not exist any more because it is not used for social security purposes only. In fact, in a fairly short period of time, the social security number has become a de facto national identifier. ...

A number of years ago the government created the national crime information center. It is the centralized clearing house of criminal history record information. It was only to be used for criminal justice purposes. When it was created, it was created for that limited use and that limited use only.... Now, half of all inquiries into the FBI's national crime information center come in for law enforcement purposes. Employers [use it for] doing background checks. Licensing boards [use it for] background checks. It is only used in half of those instances for authorized law enforcement purposes.[4]

Of course, as unemployment rises, many will likely be willing to take their chances at privacy invasion if it will hinder jobs being given to illegal aliens. However, herein lies the real danger. A unique national identifier would make it a lot easier for the government to compile, consolidate and retrieve personal information about us. This is what makes networking work—the positive identification of citizens. Such an identity number would virtually give the government carte blanche over us, over our right to work, or our ability to access money. One key question we need to ask is, "How many innocent citizens will fall victim to errors in government files about their personal lives?" It is a well known fact that government files for many citizens contain incorrect information. About ten years after I [Patti] left the university, an official from the government's student loan program telephoned me. He wanted to discuss the house I owned while I was a student. I had never owned a house, and students who hold assets such as a house are not eligible for government assistance. Imagine the nightmare if, instead of having placed a phone call to straighten the matter out, the government just decided to revoke my right to work, or to drive, or to use my bank account and credit cards.

Another danger lies in the fact that the government could abuse its powers over national ID cards and personal information in the future. It could, for example, use such power to revoke the rights of those deemed to be social dissidents. It could never happen in a democracy like America, you say? Well, all one needs to do is look at history. *Government Technology* reprinted an article from the October 1995 edition of *REASON* magazine, which revealed:

> When the government stockpiles information, no matter how benign the intent, there is inevitably a malignant mutation somewhere along the way. Presidential misuse of the IRS is so routine that it's practically part of the job description....
>
> Even the supposedly apolitical head counters at the U.S. Census Bureau have been unable to keep their promises not to share their most intimate data with anyone else. During World War I, the Census Bureau provided the Justice Department with names and addresses of conscription-age young men to aid in the apprehension of draft dodgers.
>
> And in an even more infamous case, it helped carry out the internment of Japanese Americans after Pearl Harbor. Each time a roundup of Japanese was planned in a new city, Census Bureau statisticians joined the meeting. They "would lay out on a table various city blocks where the Japanese lived and they would tell me how many were living in each block," recounted Tom Clark, the Justice Department's coordinator of alien control at the time. (Clark, later a Supreme Court justice, gave his account in an oral history for the University of California.) From there it was a simple matter for the U.S. Army to conduct block-by-block sweeps until all the Japanese were safely penned up in barbed wire.[5]

Universal IDs

The next logical step from national identification numbers would seem to be universal identification numbers. As the world becomes borderless, people are going to roam around it more freely. The need for a universal ID, by which we could easily be identified anywhere on the globe, seems to make sense. We mentioned in the previous chapter that phone companies are now offering permanent phone numbers for cellular phone users. The step between a phone number for life and a universal identification number is a very small one. Furthermore, it would be one that many would readily accept without much concern over privacy or government abuse. As the digital mobile phone and wireless transmission industry is booming in North America, the European Union, and even in the Third World, a phone number for life may be the logical and ideal identification number that is selected in the future. In a report for *Business Week* on the information revolution in the Third World, Pete Engardio wrote:

> Places that until recently were incommunicado are rapidly acquiring state-of-the-art telecommunications that will let them foster both internal and foreign investment.... Russia is starting to install fiber optics and has a grand plan to pump $40 billion into various communications projects.... Over the next decade, [China] plans to pour some $100 billion into telecom equipment, adding 80 million phone lines by the year 2000.... Hungary has granted a license to Pannon, a Dutch-Scandinavian consortium, to build what it says will be one of the most advanced cellular digital communications systems in the world.
>
> In fact, cellular is one of the most popular ways to get a phone system up fast in developing countries. It's

cheaper to build radio towers than string lines across a country.... Look at Latin America, where cellular demand and usage have exploded in every country....

Thailand is also turning to cellular.... There are nearly 500,000 cellular subscribers in Thailand.... Vietnam is making one of the boldest leaps. Currently, it has one phone for every 435 people. But despite per capita income of just $220 a year, Hanoi wants the best. All of the 300,000 lines it plans to add annually will be optical fiber with digital switching, rather than cheaper analog systems. By going for next-generation technology now, Vietnamese telecom officials say they'll be able to keep pace with anyone in Asia for decades.[6]

As the world gets hooked on wireless telecommunications systems and phone numbers for life, there will be no such thing as being out of reach.

Computer Tracking

Many would scoff at the suggestion that we would let ourselves get to the point where our every move could be tracked. But when you think about it, we've already become a society which is accustomed to surveillance, and it doesn't seem to bother us because the surveillance is so discreet we don't even notice it. There are video cameras installed in obscure corners in banks and stores. There are often hidden cameras in elevators. Some ATMs are now equipped with hidden cameras. Surveillance technology is so sophisticated today it can be used from a distance with pinpoint accuracy. In 1988 the U.S. Department of Defense was instructed by Congress to begin development on UAVs, Unmanned Aerial Vehicles. The UAVs ran into problems during Operation Desert Storm, however, because of high winds. So, instead of wasting the technology, it was decided that the UAVs could be used for civilian purposes. In April 1995 *OMNI* magazine reported that California's Department of Transportation would be using them for inspection of bridges and overpasses. Other suggested uses were to inspect power lines, to televise sports events, or even to track forest fires. Some haven't forgotten, however, the original intent for UAVs: spies in the sky. *OMNI* noted that one UAV was "loaned by the Defense Evaluation Support Activity to Oregon's National Guard and State Police last February prior to their raid on a suspected drug compound. Where agents had expected one fence, a couple of dogs and cars and a few buildings, the [UAV's] spying revealed two fences, many dogs, and more of everything else. The raid was successful."[7]

We mentioned in the previous chapter that satellite technology combined with the Global Positioning System used during the Persian Gulf War has been used for spying purposes with pinpoint accuracy. Now add microchips to the mix, and the surveillance becomes even more accurate. Take the latest trend in intelligent highway systems, for instance. "Smart" cars equipped with microchips and computers can now direct us to our destination along the fastest route, or help us to skirt around traffic jams. They allow us to whiz through electronic toll collection booths without having to stop, or even to slow down, in order to toss a few coins down a chute. An electronic reading device records information from a smart card located on the vehicle's dashboard, and deducts the toll amount from the driver's prepaid account.

Microchips have even been used to thwart car thieves in systems like Lojack. If a car equipped with the microchip is stolen, authorities can easily locate and track it. The same technology can also be used for boats and snowmobiles.

What about tracking people? Surveillance cameras and satellites are not sufficient or accurate enough for tracking a specific individual. We recently watched the video *Clear and Present Danger*, in which the CIA is searching for a specific female terrorist. Spy satellites were able to observe members of the terrorist group which she belonged to at a military training camp. The spy satellite was even able to identify one of the group members as female because of the shape of her figure. However the spy satellite could not accurately identify whether the woman in the camp was the female terrorist the CIA was specifically looking for. They had to make a decision to destroy the camp without being one-hundred percent certain whether it was her or not. Just imagine if they were able to accurately identify her because of a microchip.

Now perhaps you are shaking your head and saying, "Cars and boats, sure. But people? No way. It will never happen." But think about it. There are already many examples in real life circumstances in which people are required to wear devices containing electronic microchips. Due to overcrowding in the prison system, some prisoners are now allowed to live in society. The hitch is, they have to wear an ankle bracelet containing a microchip so that authorities can monitor their whereabouts and ensure that they don't wander outside a pre-authorized perimeter. Stalkers are required to wear the same devices to ensure they obey restraining orders. Many senior citizen nursing homes have been monitoring residents who are prone to wandering off, especially those suffering from Alzheimer's disease. Employees working in high-security areas have been required to wear active badges—ID cards containing a microchip—so that they can be easily and accurately identified. Active badges are also used to locate employees within buildings. Some shopping malls have offered the use of similar devices to keep track of children. A few hospital nurseries have even been using ID bracelets containing microchips for newborns. Such systems have been adopted following media coverage of a couple of unfortunate abductions from hospital nurseries.

While microchips have been embedded only in badges or ankle and wrist bracelets for tracking people, they have been directly embedded in the flesh of animals for a number of years now. Several years ago pet shelters and veterinarians began injecting the rice-grain sized microchips under the skin of dogs and cats, for instance. If the pet were to become lost, any pet shelter across the nation would be able to read the microchip with a scanner and locate its owner. The three chip companies that have been involved in pet identification are *InfoPet*, which uses the Trovan system; *Identichip*, which uses the Avid system; and *Schering-Plough Animal Health*, which uses the Destron system. Interestingly, in the spring of 1996 Schering-Plough Animal Health announced that it would be distributing a "universal" scanner, capable of reading the microchips developed by all three chip manufacturers.

Microchips have also been used by ranchers for livestock in place of branding methods. They have been used by breeders of large birds, by tropical fish breeders, and even by Alaskan dog-sled racers. If the microchips have been so successful in animals, "Why stop with pets?," asked Simon Garfinkel in *Wired* magazine. "What about people? There would be no technical problem, says Barbara Masin, director of operations for Electronic Identification Devices, in implanting the chips in humans. But to avoid a public relations nightmare, the Trovan dealer agreement specifically prohibits putting chips under the skin."[8]

BUT, added Garfinkel:

That dictum hasn't slowed innovation one bit. In Australia, explains Masin, one nursing home gives each of its patients a bracelet equipped with a Trovan chip. . . .

The Trovan system is showing up inside identification tags as well. At least half a dozen European ski resorts are putting chips inside lift tickets. Electronic Identification Devices also recommends hiding them in parking passes, meal cards, amusement park passes, club identification cards . . . but what a pain carrying all those cards around. Wouldn't it be far simpler to implant a chip into your shoulder, and be done with it? Stay tuned.[9]

Indeed, the idea of a microchip implant in people was repugnant just a few short years ago. Now, however, a few are starting to bravely point out that it may have a useful place in our future. In the summer of 1994, Mark David, editor-in-chief of *Automatic ID News*, in an article about locating lost pets through microchip technology, wrote:

This happy tale got me thinking about the possible advantage of "chipping" children. . . .

Now, the idea of electronically tagging humans is not one that I could easily embrace. Numbering humans is tainted with the air of jails, concentration camps and people-as-numerals totalitarianism. . . .

I'm also well aware of the Big Brotherly potential for database abuse and invasion of privacy that grows with every scan of every item in our grocery carts.

But as a father of three small children, I can't help but feel there could be some legitimate arguments made for the voluntary "chipping" of kids.[10]

Likewise, in an article about smart cards and the cashless society, *Popular Science* quoted Ronald Kane, vice president of Cubic Corp.'s automatic revenue collection group as saying, "If we had our way, we'd implant a chip behind everyone's ear in the maternity ward."[11] In the meantime, however, added *Popular Science*, "The next best thing is giving everyone a card—a high-tech pass with a memory that may, sooner than we imagine, replace cash in our wallets."[12]

How Secure is Secure?

Until the day when microchip implants in humans possibly becomes a reality, our money and personal information are going to be nothing more than electronic bits of data, which either float around in cyberspace or are contained on microchips embedded in plastic cards. While this remains true, the issues of strong security and fool-proof methods of ID verification are going to be top-priority subjects. As Ben Miller, publisher of *Personal Identification News* and organizer of the annual CardTech/SecurTech conferences, noted:

> Identifying persons seems straightforward—people do it all the time in business and social encounters. But modern society has complicated things, most notoriously when a welfare recipient signs up for benefits under six identities, a child is released to a stranger from a day care center, a hacker accesses sensitive databases, a counterfeiter makes copies of bank cards, and the murderer switches places with the car thief leaving prison on a work release.
>
> At all levels, a sure-fire means of identification has never been more in demand.[13]

Indeed, these are real issues. Take the example of welfare fraud, for instance. Frank Abagnale, a former counterfeiter turned secure-document consultant, explained how easy it is to obtain false identification:

> A forger comes to Miami, goes to the Bureau of Vital Statistics and asks to see the death records for 1948. They'll let him view them in the office. He picks out an infant who died at birth and copies down all the information it's got there— the mother's name, the father's, the time of birth, all that stuff.
>
> Then he walks right down the hall to another office where he can apply for a certified copy of the birth certificate. All he has to do to get it is to pay $5.00. And once he has that, he goes across town to a Motor Vehicle Department office and gets a driver's license in the name of the baby on the birth certificate. And with a driver's license, he can apply for all kinds of documents. For just 50 bucks, you can create 10 different identities for yourself in just a couple of days.[14]

And with ten different identities, you can start collecting ten welfare checks. Mr. Abagnale also explained that despite all the security methods placed on plastic cards—holograms, special sealants, and so forth—high-tech thieves have managed to find their way around them. He helped develop the "secure" driver's licenses being used in California. A few months after the new licenses came out, the authorities arrested someone who had found a way to forge them.

In late 1995, Canadian authorities arrested thirteen Toronto-area residents who had been involved in a large credit-card fraud ring. Seized in the raid were a credit-card embosser, holograms, which are supposed to be a security device, and 2,000 existing credit-card numbers. Equipment for counterfeit driver's licenses and social insurance cards were seized as well. Credit-card fraud is so serious that in 1994 Visa and MasterCard combined lost $3 billion.

The other big challenge is database security. According to *Biometric Digest*:

> A survey on computer crime indicates U.S. businesses and institutions are aware of it, but they're not prepared to deal with it. That's according to the San Francisco-based Computer Security Institute.
>
> Of the 425 organizations responding to the survey, 41% said they'd experienced some form of intrusion or other unauthorized use of their computer systems in the last year.[15]

Such intruders into computer systems are known as hackers. In the winter of 1995, the most-wanted man in computer hacking was arrested by the FBI after two years of eluding authorities. Kevin Mitnick, known as the Condor, had allegedly used the Internet to work his way into personal computer systems and managed to steal billions of dollars worth of corporate data, personal cell phone codes, and over 20,000 credit-card numbers.

The Condor met his match, however, when he broke into the computer system of security expert Tsutomu Shimomura. A report in *The Toronto Star* explained:

> The intruder stole sensitive security files from Shimomura's machine at the San Diego Supercomputer Centre—files he feared could compromise security throughout the Internet.
>
> Since the Christmas attack, Shimomura has aggressively pursued the intruder. He painstakingly reconstructed the sequence of computer commands that were used to

hijack the Internet connection between the computer workstation at his house and the target computer at the research lab.

Shimomura was so angered that he made it his crusade to track Mitnick down and traveled to North Carolina to assist in the final stages of the investigation.

Using a portable computer and cellular technology, he pin-pointed Mitnick to within 100 metres of the Raleigh apartment where he was living.

The Federal Bureau of Investigation then moved in for the arrest.[16]

Mitnick's arrest followed closely on the heels of the arrest of six Russian computer hackers who had managed to break into Citibank's electronic funds transfer system and steal $10 million. In the fall of the same year, just as Internet users were getting ready to apply for the Capital One credit card designed to be used for shopping in cyberspace, the offer was withdrawn. According to an article which appeared in the *U.S. News & World Report*:

> Capital One was responding to news reports that two students at the University of California at Berkeley had discovered that *Netscape Navigator*, the popular Web-browsing software, had sprung a security leak. A sophisticated hacker could crack *Netscape's* encryption code and decipher messages on the Internet.
>
> The company moved quickly to plug the hole. "No thefts of actual customer information protected by our security have been reported," says Mike Homer, vice president of marketing for Netscape in Mountain View, California. More robust software should be available sometime this week. . . .

Until current users get the new software, just how risky is it to use the old version? Practically nil, says the company. Decrypting a single *Netscape* message would take several hours, and determined criminals can scoop up profitable data far more efficiently by other means. Still, says Homer, "You certainly wouldn't send your Swiss bank account number across the Internet at that level of risk."[17]

For the most part, the main method of security against unwanted intruders and users has been the use of computer passwords and personal identification numbers, known as PIN's. But it is obvious that sophisticated thieves like Mitnick are able to bypass such secret passwords if they are determined. Added to the mix of concerns is the fact that when the Condor was arrested, it was suspected he had already created damage, the repercussions of which may be felt far into the future. *Time* magazine reported:

One of the things Mitnick is believed to have stolen from Shimomura's computer is a set of utility programs—the electronic equivalent of a locksmith's toolbox—that would make, in the hands of a determined hacker, a potent set of burglar's tools. Given the speed with which such programs can be duplicated and transmitted, it must now be assumed that they have been distributed widely throughout the computer underground.

Even before Kevin Mitnick got his hands on these burglar's tools, says William Cheswick, a network-security specialist at AT&T Bell Labs, the average computer on the Internet was singularly vulnerable to attack. Security at most sites, says Cheswick, is so lax that passwords and other protective devices are almost a waste of time. "The Internet is like a vault with a screen door on the back," says Cheswick. "I don't need jackhammers and atom bombs to get in when I can walk in through the door."[18]

Time went on to explain some of the most common tools that hackers use. Among them are:

> **Password Sniffers:** These tiny programs are hidden on a network and instructed to record log-ons and passwords, which are then stored in a secret file.

> **Spoofing:** This is a technique for getting access to a remote computer by forging the Internet address of a trusted or "friendly" machine. It's much easier to exploit security holes from inside a system than from outside; the trick is to gain "root" status, the top-level access that the computer's administrator enjoys. With root status, a hacker could install a password sniffer or bogus software, like a "back door"—a secret return path into the machine. Mitnick was able to break into Shimomura's Fort Knox-like computer using a spoof.[19]

Sophisticated thieves are now using such snooping devices to intercept security codes for cellular phones as well. Personal identification numbers used for bank cards aren't one hundred percent secure, either. Many people write their PIN directly on their card, or on a piece of paper that they store in their wallet next to their card, because they're afraid they won't remember their number. Furthermore, in this day and age when security is a big issue, people are beginning to suffer from password overload. They have to have passwords or secret numbers for cell phones, or for access to databases at the office. They need PIN's for security systems at the office, maybe one for home, and another for the ATM. With so many PIN's and passwords, a lot of people are starting to forget which PIN is for the ATM and which is for turning off the security system at the office. According to security expert Winn

Schwartau of Seminole, Florida: "Computer managers he knows have as many as 48 passwords. But the epidemic extends beyond the domain of propeller-heads. Many poor souls can't even get into their cars—or the men's room—without the right password."[20]

Suffering from password overload, and just being plain sick and tired of fraud, many individuals, businesses, and financial institutions are searching for more secure and foolproof methods of identification. In this vein, many are looking to biometrics as the solution.

Raise Your Right Hand

Biometric identification is based on a unique physical characteristic such as your voice, signature, fingerprint, iris pattern, or hand geometry, which is a measurement of the size and shape of your hand. It is possible that, along with microchip technology, biometrics will play a role in identification for the mark of the beast system. God's Word specifically mentions that the mark of the beast will be taken in the right hand or in the forehead, the two places most accessible in cold-weather climates. Now, whether the mark will actually be a microchip, or whether hand geometry and facial image recognition will be part of the Antichrist's economic system, cannot be known for certain until the prophecy is fulfilled.

Nonetheless, there has been growing interest in biometric identification over the past few years. Several pilot projects using various biometric ID verification have been taking place around the world. One area in which biometric identification verification has gained wide acceptance and usage is in the welfare sector. As far back as 1986, Los Angeles County had started a manual fingerprinting system for welfare recipients to try to weed out double dippers. Within three years, the county found itself with 50,000 fingerprint records that were virtually useless. That's when Los Angeles County decided to investigate an automatic fingerprint verification system. The system, known as AFIRM, was used for the first time on June 3, 1991. Later, San Francisco County decided to adopt the AFIRM system as well.

While fingerprint ID seemed to be more popular than hand geometry verification in the earlier days of biometric technology, this may be changing. In the spring of 1995 it was announced that Sacramento County would be testing a biometric ID authentication system using hand geometry. Even though the hand geometry system would be incompatible with the systems used in Los Angeles and San Francisco counties, Sacramento decided to test it anyway, mainly because it was less expensive. Hand geometry verification is also a lot quicker than fingerprint identification. If the tests in Sacramento are successful, state officials said hand geometry would likely be chosen as the method of identification verification for the entire state.

Not Just Another Face in the Crowd

In the early days of biometric technology development, little was heard about facial image recognition. Again, this is beginning to change. As technologies for motion tracking continue to develop, facial recognition devices will likely be more useful in certain situations when, for example, it would be difficult or even impossible to obtain a fingerprint or hand geometry sample.

Alexander Pentland is the head of research into "perceptual computing" at MIT Media Lab. In an article on Pentland's research, *Discover* magazine wrote:

The marketplace may find even more applications for Pentland's face-recognition technology. Last year, for example, British Telecommunications—which provides partial funding for Pentland's work—began developing a security system based on Photobook (Pentland's face-recognition system). It would use video cameras to scan crowds of shoppers, and Pentland's software to match those faces against a database of mug shots of criminals who have repeatedly been caught shoplifting. If a match occurred, the system would alert security guards.

Recently the White House questioned Pentland about using face recognition to thwart terrorists and drug runners. "We know who the terrorists are," Pentland says. "There is a small set of bad guys." As was alleged in the Oklahoma bombing case, the suspects typically scope out a building or other target many times before doing a job. Face-recognition cameras around public locations could check whether certain known suspects were showing up frequently. In addition, cameras at customs checkpoints could spot the faces of known drug dealers who typically use disguises, fake passports, and phony visas.[21]

In speaking on the advantages of facial recognition systems, *Netscape* noted, "The process takes 20 to 25 seconds.... Successful impersonation (even by an identical twin) is totally ruled out."[22]

The Future Is Now Here

As such technology continues to be developed and perfected, the trend will likely lead us to a world like that of our friends Mark and Chip, whom we were introduced to at the beginning of the chapter. That world, however, is not as far in the future as many would think. The technology is already here. For example, Mark and Chip went to an amusement theme park known as *VR Land* in our original scenario. Such a place does not yet exist, but soon may be part of our future. Sega, the makers of computer games and software, has plans for a virtual-reality theme park that it says will leave Disneyland in the dust.

In the meantime, virtual reality "rides" already exist. We have taken part in the virtual reality experience offered by Universal Studio's "Back to the Future" ride, and sat in a machine designed to look like the DeLorean time machine of the movie. A massive screen enveloped the front view of the DeLorean, which was designed to move in sync with the images appearing on the screen. The effect made us feel as if we were actually zooming through the air and swerving to avoid hitting things. Then the time machine kicked in and we were floating through outer space or falling down caverns on other planets. During another time period we were swallowed by a dinosaur, and then spit out, zooming through the air backwards. Again, the coinciding movements and screen images made us feel as if we were actually experiencing all of these things. Disneyland has a similar ride based on the Star Wars film series.

So let's say that our friends Mark and Chip decided to go to Disneyland in our present world. When they arrived at the Magic Kingdom theme park, they decided to purchase a seasonal pass. They could use it to visit Disney MGM and Epcot while they were in Florida. They were required to have their photo taken for their visitor's seasonal pass, and they were required to give a sample of the geometry of their index and middle fingers. Actually, the Walt Disney theme parks in Florida had started a trial project using this method of biometric identification in 1996. According to *Netscape*, a spokesperson for Disneyland said, "Visitors are at first surprised to find a system in use which they might expect to see in the 'Innoventions' building rather than at the turnstile. When they find how easy it is to use—and what fun—they are delighted."[23]

Mark and Chip's American neighbors to the south have the same type of system known as INSPASS (Immigration and Naturalization Service Passenger Accelerated Service System). International travelers enrolled in INSPASS provide a sample of their hand geometry upon arrival at the JFK airport in New York City. Such automatic biometric identification systems for international travelers are beginning to crop up all over the world—Australia, Belgium, Germany, the Netherlands, Switzerland, Taiwan, France, Hong Kong, Slovakia, and Germany.

In our original scenario, all Mark and Chip had to do when they passed through the automated immigration line was hold up their arm and keep their hand outstretched. Even as we write, such technology is being developed. In a report by *Netscape* that we pulled off the Internet, we read:

> The latest advance in biometric technology will make it possible for individuals approaching a security area to have their identity verified without having to stop moving.

> This development by New Mexico State University in conjunction with Sandia National Laboratories is reported in the April issue of Biometric Technology Today....

> Anyone entering the area is required to approach with their arm raised and fingers spread, but can continue walking. Two cameras capture an image of the top and

side of their hand. If the images captured do not match the computer records of authorised personnel, the individual is denied access.[24]

We also mentioned in our original scenario that scanners were automatically reading radio-tags on items in Mark's cart, for which duty charges were applicable. Again, such technology already exists. The *Supertag* system, developed by the South African Council for Scientific and Industrial Research (CSIR), was being tested in South African supermarkets in early 1994. Three scanners and an "anti-clash" device were able to read, from distances of up to four meters, a maximum of fifty items equipped with radio-tags that were piled up in a grocery cart.

Arriving at the Pearson International Airport in Toronto, Mark and Chip are reflecting on the wonderful time they had on their vacation. After collecting their baggage, they head to an automatic electronic customs line. They're enrolled in the CANPASS program, and Mark has Chip go first. He helps his son insert his memory card into a terminal and tells him to place his index finger on a reader. The computer reads the fingerprint image stored on the card and compares it to Chip's finger resting on the terminal. The two are a match and Chip is allowed to pass. Now it's Mark's turn. The process takes a matter of moments, and all without the hassle of answering the questions of a customs official. Mark just drops a customs form, which he filled out on the plane, into a special slot. The appropriate duty charges will show up on his next credit-card statement.[25]

Indeed, we are Mark and Chip's generation, the first generation in which the mark of the beast prophecy of Revelation 13 can actually be fulfilled. The technology is here which will allow the Antichrist to control the entire global economy. The only piece to the puzzle now missing is the Antichrist, who will require that the peoples of the world take his mark as a sign of adoration for him.

17

The End

At the outset of the twentieth century, the global power structure was stable. There was widespread optimism that the world was about to enter an era of peace and prosperity. Technological breakthroughs and scientific discoveries offered hope for the betterment of mankind. The twentieth century, however, turned out to be far different than many had envisioned. In the opening pages to his book *Out of Control: Global Turmoil on the Eve of the 21st Century*, Zbigniew Brzezinski, former director of the National Security Council under President Jimmy Carter, wrote:

> Contrary to its promise, the twentieth century became mankind's most bloody and hateful century, a century of hallucinatory politics and of monstrous killings. Cruelty was institutionalized to an unprecedented degree, lethality was organized on a mass production basis. The contrast between the scientific potential for good and the political evil that was actually unleashed is shocking. Never before in history was killing so globally pervasive, never before did it consume so many lives, never before was human annihilation pursued with such concentration of sustained effort on behalf of such arrogantly irrational goals.[1]

Brzezinski refers to the twentieth century in his book as the century of "*megadeaths*, mega being a factor of 10^6."[2] He explains that while the figures of megadeaths he provides are estimates:

> ... what is important is the *scale* and not the exact numbers. It is the scale—so unprecedented that it becomes almost incomprehensible...

> In brief, this century's wars extinguished no less than approximately *87,000,000 lives*, with the numbers of wounded, maimed or otherwise afflicted being beyond estimate.[3]

Mr. Brzezinski then proceeds to give figures in the millions for the atrocious killings committed "in the name of doctrine" by despots like Hitler, Lenin, Stalin, and Mao. In conclusion to his chapter, he calculated that 170 million human beings had lost their lives as a result of war and genocide so far in the twentieth century, an estimate that, is in his own words, is "perhaps somewhat low."

As appalling as this figure is, somehow the world senses that if another war were to erupt on a global scale, the death toll would far surpass it. Indeed, Jesus said if He were not to return at the time of the end, "there should no flesh be saved" (Matthew 24:22). We are the first generation in which this prophecy rings true. And if we are the first generation in which this prophecy can be fulfilled, then it follows that we may truly be the last generation prior to Christ's return. What makes this generation different from any other are weapons of *mass* destruction. The weapons of yesteryear were swords and battle-axes, cannons and bayonets. Such weapons could not destroy ALL flesh. It was during World War II that things began to change. German tanks and missiles created great problems for the allies. But even these were not capable of destroying all flesh. What truly changed the shape of World War II and the path of history was the nuclear bomb.

The Birth of the Bomb

In 1942 General Leslie Groves and physicist Robert Oppenheimer began operations on Project Y, better known as the Manhattan Project, in Los Alamos, New Mexico. Three years later the aim of the Manhattan Project had been achieved. By harnessing the energy released by the splitting of an atom, the team members of the Manhattan Project created "Little Boy" and "Fat Man," the nuclear bombs responsible for devastating Hiroshima and Nagasaki. Stunned by the effect of these weapons, the likes of which the world had never known, the Japanese government surrendered. While indeed putting a stop to the atrocities of the second World War, Little Boy and Fat Man created a burgeoning nightmare over future wars in the years to come. The age of nuclear weapons had been born.

Sole knowledge for developing the nuclear bomb at first resided with the United States, where it was created. This was to be short-lived, however. Soon the Russians were filled in on the secret. One of the British team members of Project Y, German-born Klaus Fuchs, later admitted to passing design details along to the Soviets. Recent allegations have also been made against Robert Oppenheimer, the scientific director of the Project—known as a communist sympathizer—for passing along secret instructions to the Soviets as well. It is suspected, from comments made by Oppenheimer following the bombs creation, that he feared leaving the knowledge for creating a weapon of total death in the hands of one global power would make the world a dangerous place. By placing such knowledge in the hands of the Soviet Union, he apparently believed a balance of power would be created, making the world a safer place. Ironically, this is what gave birth to the Cold War and the nuclear arms race.

During the Cold War years the world lived in fear that a nuclear war would break out between the two superpowers. When the Cold War ended, many believed the chance of a nuclear war erupting had ended as well. It did not take long for many to recognize the irony of the situation. During the Cold War years the Soviets and Americans had both recognized that by triggering a nuclear war against the other, they would be destroying themselves as well. Thus, their programs of *Mutually Assured Destruction* may have actually been what prevented a nuclear war from breaking out.

When the Cold War came to an end, many began to realize that the U.S. and the Soviet Union were not the only two nations that possessed nuclear weapons. The first nuclear device following Little Boy and Fat Man was detonated by the Soviets in 1949. The U.K. exploded its first device in 1952. France followed in 1960, and China, with the help of the Soviets, detonated its first nuclear device in 1964. These were the first five nuclear powers: the U.S., the Soviet Union, Britain, France, and China. But knowledge for building a nuclear bomb did not end with these five. A chain reaction had begun.

France provided Israel with the knowledge to become a nuclear power. Then, along with the U.K., Canada, and the U.S., it helped India to become a nuclear power. The Chinese helped Pakistan. South Africa admitted it had built six nuclear devices, but now claims to have dismantled its nuclear weapons program before handing over power to black-majority leadership. With the dismantling of the former Soviet Union, three other nations were added to the list of nuclear powers: Belarus, Kazakhstan, and the

Ukraine. Argentina, Brazil, South Korea, and Taiwan are referred to as "advanced threshold nations," which means they have the technology to build a nuclear device if they so desire. And it is highly suspected that Iran, Libya, Algeria, and North Korea all have the potential to become nuclear powers within a few years if they haven't already. Iraq was suspected of being able to become a nuclear power by 1993 if the U.N. had not curtailed its nuclear program following the Persian Gulf War. Saddam Hussein has not been cooperative with U.N. inspectors concerning his weapons programs, however. Some suspect that Iraq may still be on the verge of becoming a nuclear power.

In addition to the existence of these nuclear and potential nuclear powers, thirty-two nations have civilian nuclear power programs that could easily be converted to produce weapons of mass destruction if the desire arose. David Shukman, former defense correspondent for the BBC, observed in his book *Tomorrow's War: The Threat of High-Technology Weapons*:

> The world is now caught in a dangerous paradox: the more the Bomb spreads, the more countries will feel the need to get it, the greater the danger of global annihilation. . . . Nuclear anarchy may be the result. One analyst has likened this prospect to the Wild West where "everyone thought they needed a six-gun" to defend themselves. "We may be moving into an era of the nuclear six-gun."[4]

Once it was revealed that the secret was out, it didn't take a rocket scientist to recognize there was no turning back. The nuclear bomb would become part of history, never to be erased. But if the bomb were to become a permanent part of world history, it would take rocket scientists to build bigger and better weapons to keep ahead of everyone else.

The Launching of the Missiles

The nuclear devices created during the Manhattan Project were only a foreshadow of what was to come in nuclear weaponry. Following on the heels of the nuclear bomb was the hydrogen bomb, a thermonuclear weapon far more devastating than the bomb that destroyed Hiroshima. Just to give you an idea of its power, take the following explanation given of the H-bomb by Shukman: "An initial fission explosion is used to trigger a vastly larger fusion reaction which can readily yield energy one million times greater than that achieved at Hiroshima."[5] In addition, Shukman noted:

> A further step has been to take this design and miniaturise it, scaling down each component so that the weapon as a whole became sufficiently small and light to fit inside the nose-cone of a missile. Thus the lightning speed of a rocket was harnessed to the staggering power of an H-bomb and, with flight-times of less than thirty minutes between the United States and the Soviet Union, the nuclear hair-trigger of the Cold War was established.[6]

According to statistics given by Shukman, between 1945 and 1992 the U.S. had produced 70,000 nuclear warheads that could be fitted to such rockets known as ballistic missiles, or other delivery systems such as torpedoes and artillery shells. The Soviets had manufactured 55,000. Other nations are also reported to have produced nuclear warheads, but in smaller numbers: the U.K., 834; France, 1,100; Israel, possibly 200; India, 20; Pakistan, 4-7; China, 600; North Korea, possibly 1 or 2. The latter two are also known to be the main sources of ballistic missiles for Islamic countries in the Middle East. (These missiles can also be used for conventional warheads.) According to a special Intelligence International report on weapons of mass destruction in relation to the Middle East peace process:

> Egypt, Iran, Syria, Yemen, Saudi Arabia, Iraq and Libya all have ballistic missiles. The Saudi Arabian DF-3A missile, 30 of which were supplied by China in 1987, has a range of 3,000 kilometres; Iraq's Tammus 1, which is under development, will have a range of 2,000 kilometres; and Iran is thought to be working on a variant of China's M-11 missile with a range of 1,000 kilometres. Beyond these three missiles, there is a myriad of lesser-range missiles in the hands of Israel's potential and actual enemies including many of the 300-kilometre-range Scud-Bs.[7]

The fear of the destabilizing effect created by the nuclear arms race and the spreading of ballistic missiles, both long and short range, have lead to the establishment of treaties like START 1 (1991), START 2 (1992), The Nuclear Non-Proliferation Treaty (1968, 1995), and the Missile Technology Control Regime (1987). As in the early days following the development of the nuclear bomb, most recognize that such weapons appear to be here to stay. Following the example of the Wild West six-gun, just about everyone will soon have them. Therefore, in what seems to be a never-ending treadmill ride, the need to produce weapons and establish defense systems that can outsmart the enemy has been created.

Smart Weapons

The first implication the world had that tomorrow's wars would be different came with the outbreak of the Persian Gulf War. On January 18, 1991 the first of Iraq's scud missiles was launched, and so was the first U.S.

Patriot, an anti-missile. In *Tomorrow's War: The Threat of High-Technology Weapons,* David Shukman wrote:

> The allied commander, General Norman Schwarzkopf, later wrote of his "delight" in the first attack in which Patriot "knocked the Scud from the sky." The British commander in the Gulf, General Sir Peter de la Billiere, noted that "as people saw the Patriot work, confidence gradually returned." Of the eighty-one Scuds fired in all during the course of the war, official figures said most had been engaged. The manufacturer of Patriot, Raytheon, saw its share price rise. One of the missiles was even given pride of place in the lobby of the main media hotel in Dhahran, "We Love You" scrawled on its side. The phrase "Scud-busters" appeared on T-shirts. American technology seemed to be working miracles.[8]

Later reports suggested that only about one-third of Iraq's Scuds had actually been defeated by the Patriots. Nonetheless, the world had its first taste of the role technology would play in future wars, not only in defensive, or anti-ballistic missile systems, but in offensive situations with "precision guided munitions." Again, Shukman noted:

> At a news briefing on 18 January 1991, the allied air commander, Lieutenant-General Chuck Horner showed video clips taken from his fighter-bombers as they attacked targets with laser-guided bombs the previous night. "Keep your eye on the entrance," he said as a gray image of a Scud storage bunker loomed into view on a television screen. "The pilot has released the bombs two miles away . . . lasing the target and you'll see two bombs fly into the door of the storage bunker. You'll be able to count each bomb—one, two." The screen erupted with

a flash of light. Another bomb was seen falling into the central air-conditioning shaft of the Iraqi air-defence headquarters; smoke billowed out of the sides of the building. It was a "technology war," according to General Horner, and it amazed a world unfamiliar with the revolution in military development brought about by the Cold War. Of the 88,500 tons of bombs dropped in the Gulf War, only some 6,250 were precision guided—around 7 per cent—yet it was those "smart" weapons which accounted for about half the Iraqi targets destroyed. It was a technical success rate which spawned the concept of "surgical bombing," attacks so accurate they could achieve their ends with minimum of harm to others.[9]

Indeed, the world had been introduced to intelligent munitions, most of which are essentially "fire-and-forget" weaponry that rely on the sophisticated computing power of microprocessors. In an article on fire-and-forget military technology, *Machine Design* reported:

One of the first of these weapons was the Strix from Bofors Weapons Systems of Sweden. . . . After launching . . . it acts more like a guided missile than a conventional mortar shell. Once over the target area, it stabilizes its fall and searches the area with a passive infra red sensor. Microprocessors suppress false targets while detecting tanks and other vehicles, moving or stationary, day or night. They also guide the projectile to a favorable angle above the target . . .

Bofors has also added smarts to an artillery round, the Bonus 155, a sensor-fused, antiarmor shell . . .

Each munition then scans the area beneath it in a helical pattern. Once it locates a vehicle and decides it's a valid target, the warhead fires an explosively formed penetrator (EFP), a very high-speed, dense projectile, down at the target.

A similar system called Damocles from Textron Defense Systems uses submunitions delivered by aircraft or possibly artillery. Once over the target area, each Damocles submunition deploys a parachute to control its descent while searching the area with passive infrared and active millimeter wave radar. With a steep look-down angle, it can 'see' through dense foliage while it scans 360^0 along the flight path. The parachute gives the system enough time to search the battlefield, analyze a target of interest, and acquire a new one if necessary.[10]

This is only the beginning of smart weapons, military strategists tell us. According to a report by Douglas Waller for *Time* magazine, "Future warfare, in fact, may look like today's science-fiction thrillers."[11] "By 2010," he continues:

the Army hopes to "digitize the battlefield" by linking every soldier and weapons system electronically. A research team led by Motorola and the Army R.-and-D. lab in Natick, Massachusetts, plans to unveil next year a prototype of the equipment that the "21st century land warrior" will have. His helmet will be fitted with microphones and earphones for communications, night-vision goggles and thermal-image sensors to see in the dark, along with a heads-up display in front of his eyes to show him where he is on the ground and give him constant intelligence updates.[12]

But that's not all. The military would also like to see "smart" technology being used to map out war strategies as well. Dick Lawrence of the British Defence Research Agency calls it "crystal-ball gazing." According to Shukman, Lawrence's goals are to:

"predict the target's behaviour and get the computer to work out what'll happen—that's the way we're going now." His idea is to develop programs that take account of all known intelligence about the performance and likely manoeuvres of particular planes and missiles. . . .

The next step is to teach the computer to guess the objective of the aircraft or missile. The scientists call this "Goal-Oriented Tracking," judging the attackers likely destination.[13]

Indeed, it seems that with the aid of high technology and smart weapons, there may be no limit to the scope and lethality of future wars created by man. However, in an age that has seen the births of the nuclear bomb, the hydrogen bomb, and the neutron bomb (designed to kill people but spare buildings), some see sophisticated weaponry designed to hit selected enemy targets with precision aim as a welcome change. In an age that has been dubbed the century of "megadeaths," such intelligent munitions can be seen as a way to reduce casualties of war, both within the military and civilian population. Military strategists can even envision the day when wars will be fought with non-lethal weapons—a day of information warfare befitting an age of peace and prosperity for the next millennium.

The Tech Wars

There is an unwritten expectation that military operations conducted by democracies—especially under the auspices of the United Nations—will involve as little bloodshed as possible. Although the Security Council's Resolution 687 authorized the use of "all necessary means" to eject Iraqi forces from Kuwait, the U.S. President, George Bush, felt obliged to halt the fighting when the first television pictures emerged of the route of the fleeing Iraqi army. He clearly had a sense of how violent allied forces could be seen to be. Television images, public opinion and politicians' nerves were combining to demand that if combat should take place at all, it should ideally be bloodless.[14]

Recognizing this, the U.S. has spent millions of dollars on researching non-lethal weapons. Military scientists have been working on everything from robots to perform dangerous tasks human soldiers were once required to do, to noise bombs designed to disorient and incapacitate humans, to laser "dazzling" weapons reminiscent of Star Trek phasers, which can be set on "stun" instead of "kill."

It was during the Persian Gulf War that the world got its first taste of non-lethal warfare. One of the first tasks carried out by Tomahawk cruise missiles was to wipe out Baghdad's electrical power grid—not with explosives—but with carbon fiber, which caused short circuits. Then the 193rd Special Operations Group, whose motto is "We fire electrons not bullets," got their sophisticated psychological operations—"psy-ops"—campaign under way. Psy-ops specialists, using the *Commando Solo*, a $70 million dollar plane equipped with computers, fax machines, VCRs and powerful transmitters, sent radio broadcasts to Iraqi soldiers wanting to hear a progress report on the war. As a result of *Commando Solo's* transmissions, as well as millions of propaganda leaflets that were dropped on them, many Iraqi soldiers deserted their posts. According to Douglas Waller, writing for *Time* magazine:

> Future broadcasts may be more unconventional. Specialists for the Army's 4th Psychological Operations Group, which prepares the taped messages that *Commando Solo* airs, have considered morphing the image of a foreign leader and putting words in his mouth to get him in trouble—for instance, Saddam Hussein appearing on Iraqi

TV before the Gulf War, sipping whiskey and carving a ham, both forbidden in Islam.... For now, ethics and strategy argue against such tactics. Says Colonel Jeffrey Jones, former commander of the psy-ops group: "The truth is our best weapon."[15]

Indeed, some of the top-secret cyber weapons being proposed are creating ethical questions. For instance, asks Waller, "Is it a war crime to crash another country's stock market?" This is just one of the ideas being dreamed up by military cyberstrategists. Waller continues:

The National Security Agency, along with top-secret intelligence units in the Army, Navy and Air Force, has been researching ways to infect enemy computer systems with particularly virulent strains of software viruses that already plague home and office computers. Another type of virus, the logic bomb, would remain dormant in an enemy system until a predetermined time, when it would come to life and begin eating data. Such bombs could attack, for example, computers that run a nation's air-defense system or central bank. The CIA has a clandestine program that would insert booby-trapped computer chips into weapons systems that a foreign arms manufacturer might ship to a potentially hostile country—a technique called "chipping." In another program, the agency is looking at how independent contractors hired by armsmakers to write software for weapons systems could be bribed to slip in viruses.

Infowar weapons may be even more exotic than computer viruses. Los Alamos National Laboratory in New Mexico has developed a suitcase-size device that generates a high-powered electromagnetic pulse. Commandos could sneak into a foreign capital, place the EMP suitcase next to a bank and set it off. The resulting pulse would burn out all electronic components in the building. Other proposals combine biology with electronics. For instance, Pentagon officials believe microbes can be bred to eat the electronics and insulating material inside computers just as microorganisms consume trash and oil slicks.[16]

While some see non-lethal weapons as a way to make war "bloodless," others see them as an additional tool with which to attack the enemy: a double whammy. Shukman noted that this type of thinking "is most apparent in the first draft of a U.S. Army training and doctrine booklet on so-called *Disabling Measures....* The document sees non-lethal weaponry 'augmenting' lethal force not replacing it."[17]

Furthermore, he added:

> War games involving non-lethal weapons shed further light on military attitudes. In one U.S. Army game, designed as a re-run of Operation Desert Storm, the team playing the allied side was given the option of using non-lethal weapons against the Iraqis....
>
> The allied team regarded this non-lethal act as a mere prelude to what was to follow: a full-scale attack by conventional weapons, more effective for being aimed at static targets. Sam Gardiner, the strategist who led the war-game, concluded that in this case the battlefield had been made "more lethal, not less."[18]

Whether or not the democracies of the future choose to fight virtual wars because of their conscience, the fact remains that in the real world there are despots, terrorists, and maverick nations that do not appear to have a conscience. And in the real world today, many of these pariah nations and terrorist organizations are accumulating deadly weapons for mass destruction of yet another kind.

Enemies Seen and Unseen

Reconnaissance—from the air or from space, using radar, satellites, cameras, or infra-red sensors—is an integral part of today's warfare. Spying on the enemy is the first step in determining his potential and intentions. Again, it was the event of the Persian Gulf War in which American surveillance technology was pushed to maximum use. Advanced as such technology is, however, a lesson learned is that it has its limits.

For instance, the U.S. was unable to keep track of one of Saddam's most potent weapons during the Gulf War: the mobile missile. According to Shukman:

> Because the Scuds were fired from the same vehicles that carried them—Transporter-Erector-Launchers (TEL) in the military jargon—they could be prepared for use within twenty minutes and moved off in less than six. Even if a take-off was spotted by satellite or a surveillance aircraft, the launcher could have left the scene by the time a fire-fighter-bomber arrived. During the day, the vehicles and their weapons remained hidden from view in civilian buildings or under bridges and, when they were deployed to their launch positions at night, they were barely distinguishable from ordinary articulated trucks; they looked especially similar to fuel tankers.[19]

One of the greatest fears that arose during the Persian Gulf War, however, was that Saddam Hussein would use a brand of weapons more deadly than Scuds—chemical weapons. There was no doubt that Hussein would not think twice about using such weapons. After all, he had used them to kill 50,000 Iranians during the Iran/Iraq war.

He had used them in the late 1980's against Kurdish rebels in northern Iraq.

According to a report by the *Islamic Affairs Analyst*, inspections of Iraqi weapons manufacture sites following the war revealed that:

> Amongst other weapons, U.N. inspectors found 50 chemical-filled ballistic missile warheads; 12,694 mustard gas-filled 155mm artillery shells; and over 10,000 sarin-filled 122mm artillery rocket warheads. Over 300 tonnes of bulk agent (mustard and sarin) were found. This material was ready for filling chemical munitions.[20]

It is suspected that besides Iraq, about two dozen nations possess a chemical warfare potential, including Iran, Syria, Ethiopia, Sudan, India, North Korea, Pakistan, Taiwan, Argentina, Chile, and Cuba. Libya is considered to be one of the most aggressive in obtaining chemical weapons. It is highly suspected, from the observation of tunnels bored into a remote hillside near Tarhuna, that Libya has constructed a production and storage facility for mustard gas.

While chemical weapons have been around for a long time, they had been used only in limited cases by national governments. Then something different occurred in March of 1995, giving the world something else to be fearful of. Members of a Japanese cult released a deadly chemical agent known as Sarin in Tokyo's busy subway system. Twelve people were killed and 5,500 were wounded. Shukman noted:

> A threshold had been crossed: for the first time a weapon with sarin's potency had been deployed by an organisation other than a national government.[21]

Several cult members of the group Aum Shinri Kyo and their leader Shoko Asahara were arrested for launching the chemical attack. In searching the premises of the Aum Shinri Kyo cult, Japanese officials made alarming discoveries. The cultists were also producing weapons of an even deadlier kind. Evidence of materials found on the premises suggest they were manufacturing biological weapons—weapons that kill by spreading deadly diseases.

While germ warfare has been around since the middle ages—attackers used to catapult the corpses of those who had been infected by plagues over the walls of towns they were attempting to besiege—today's biological weapons are even more terrifying and deadly. Shukman noted:

> Germ weapons are "the special weapon to be most concerned about in the future," according to Lisa Bronson, a senior official in the Pentagon's Counter-Proliferation Office, speaking in a BBC documentary on biological weapons in late 1994. General Colin Powell, Chairman of the U.S. Joint Chiefs of Staff at the time of the Gulf War, told a congressional enquiry that his "greatest concern" during Operation Desert Storm was "that the Iraqis had been working on such a capability." Biological weaponry, he said, was "the one that scares me to death, perhaps even more so than tactical nuclear weapons." In part this is because—pound for pound—germ weapons can kill more people than any other weapon.[22]

In the fall of 1995 one of Saddam Hussein's sons-in-law defected and threatened to reveal all about Iraq's biological weapons program. He had been the mastermind behind Iraq's weaponry. The Iraqis felt compelled at that point, after years of uncooperation with U.N. inspectors, to be open about their biological weapons program. According to an article in the *U.S. News and World Report*, Rolf Ekeus, head of the U.N. inspection team, learned that:

> More than 1,500 gallons of anthrax toxin was loaded into 50 bombs and 10 missile warheads. Nearly 3,000 gallons of Botulinum toxin, an agent that attacks the nerves and chokes its victims to death, was poured into 100 bombs and 15 missile warheads and sent to airfields. Riacin, another deadly nerve agent that can kill with one drop, had been tested in artillery shells. The Iraqis had even made 78 gallons of a toxin that produces gangrene.[23]

To give you an idea of the lethality of biological weapons, consider, for example, that all it takes is less than a millionth of a gram of anthrax to kill one person. What creates the gravest of situations is that biological and chemical weapons can be produced easily and inexpensively with commercially available ingredients commonly used in the manufacture of other products. Chlorine, for example, is commonly used for water purification and in the making of plastics. But it can also be used to produce mustard gas. Phosphorous oxychloride is used to produce plastics and hydraulic fluids, but it can be used to create Tabun as well. One hundred and sixty tons of peptone, along with clostridium botulinum, were unearthed on the premises of the Aum Shinri Kyo cult. The cultists claimed the ingredients were used to research diseases and medical cures, but they could also have been used to produce botulism poisoning as a biological weapon. Considering the cult had already poisoned innocent passengers on Tokyo's subway system, the latter was likely their intent.

Another example of easily available ingredients is the common agricultural fertilizer used in the construction of the bomb that destroyed the federal building in Oklahoma City in the spring of 1995. The problem is that such common ingredients, readily available to virtually anyone, can be used for good or evil. The sad truth is that it is essentially impossible to prevent the sale of such items. Even with the aid of advanced technology, it is extremely difficult to monitor the manufacture of chemical and biological weapons. For that matter, it is even difficult to monitor the manufacture of nuclear weapons.

As we approach the eve of the twenty-first century, we find ourselves in a position that is unique from any other generation before us. Sadly, this position of uniqueness could turn the twenty-first century into one that is even bloodier than the twentieth century has been. Many nations in the world now possess, or will soon possess, devastating nuclear weapons. Many nations are secretly manufacturing deadly chemical weapons or biological weapons which can be even more lethal. Again, noting the words of Shukman, "germ weapons can kill more people than any other weapon invented."

Can we not truly say that we are the first generation in which this prophecy can be fulfilled? Can we not say that we are the first generation which could truly be the last if Jesus does not return when He does? He warned in Matthew 24 that the final generation of the end times would be that generation in which no flesh would survive. This could truly happen if any of these weapons were to be unleashed on a global scale.

But remember, there is no need to fear. This was just one of the many prophecies given by God as a sign to where we are along the river, floating in this boat of life. Jesus said that when we see this sign, along with all the other signs we have documented in this book—the development of a world religion, the development of a world government, the creation of a mark of the beast system and global economy, Israel in her homeland, preparations for the Third Temple, the aligning of nations today which are prophesied to invade Israel, and so forth—we are to look up into the skies because our redemption is at hand. We are not to fear the turmoil coming upon the world.

It has been prophesied that this boat will go over the brink of the fall. Sadly, those who have placed their faith in this boat, and in the future Antichrist rather than Jesus Christ, will fall with it into a pit of eternal punishment.

"The Son of Man shall send forth his angels..."[24]

We have been promised as children of God, however, that our eternal future does not reside in this boat of life. If our faith is in Jesus Christ as our Savior, we will be lifted out of this boat before it goes over the fall.

"For the Lord himself shall descend..."[25]

These signs have been given as a warning to those who will not listen to God's Word. They are given as an encouragement to those who already have.

Notes

Chapter 1: A Way That Seems Right

1. Evangelical Fellowship of Canada; *Discerning the Times Seminar Workbook.*
2. *Harvest Time*; June, 1984; p. 2.
3. Revelation 1:3.
4. Luke 21:26.
5. Matthew 24:6; Mark 13:7; Luke 21:9.
6. 2 Peter 3:10-13.
7. *The Orlando Sentinel*; January 14, 1996; "Conflicts, Wars Cover Most of the Globe."
8. Matthew 24:6.
9. Luke 21:26.
10. Price, John Randolph; *The Planetary Commission*; Quartus Foundation: 1984.
11. Planetary Initiative brochure distributed by Planetary Citizens in Menlo Park, CA.
12. Peck, M. Scott; *The Different Drum*; Simon and Schuster; New York: 1987; p. 19.
13. Gorbachev, Mikhail; *Perestroika: New Thinking for Our Country and the World*; Harper and Row; New York: 1987.
14. *The New York Times*; June 5, 1990; "Gorbachev at Stanford: Excerpts From Address."
15. Gorbachev, Mikhail; *The Search For a New Beginning: Developing a New Civilization*; Harper/San Francisco: 1995; pp. 68-70.
16. Bush, George; excerpt from his address to the nation on September 16, 1990 while serving as U.S. president.
17. *Westchester Newspaper*; "World Council of Churches striving to tear down barriers among Christians"; Westchester County, New York; January 23, 1988.
18. As quoted in *This Week in Bible Prophecy Magazine*; February, 1995; "Leaders of World Faiths Call for World Council of Religions; p. 6.
19. *Time*; April 8, 1996; "The Undead Red" by Bruce W. Nelan; p. 38.

Chapter 2: The Promised Land and the Holy City

1. Deuteronomy 28:64.
2. Ezekiel 36:24.
3. Genesis 15:18.
4. Genesis 15: 8-12, 17-18.
5. Mark Twain, *Innocents Abroad*, pp. 384, 403, 414, 442, 480, 485-86; as cited in *A Place Among Nations*; Netanyahu, Benjamin; A Bantam Book; New York: 1993; pp. 39-40.
6. Deuteronomy 28:65-66.
7. Zechariah 12:2,3.
8. Netanyahu, Benjamin; op. cit.; p. 179.
9. Zechariah 12:6.
10. Netanyahu; op. cit.; p. 179-180.
11. Israeli Consul General to Canada, Dror Zeigerman, in an interview with the *This Week in Bible Prophecy* ministry.
12. *Islamic Affairs Analyst*; April 1996; "Peres's Plan to Divide Jerusalem."
13. *Islamic Affairs Analyst*; June 1996; "A Likud Government for Israel"; p. 10.
14. Ibid.; p. 11.

15. Palestinian Authority Chairman Yasser Arafat in a speech given on August 25, 1993, prior to the signing of the Declaration of Principles.
16. Hanan Ashrawi in a message given in September, 1993.
17. *The Jerusalem Post, International Edition*; January 8, 1994.

Chapter 3: The Third Temple

1. Al-Tabarai, *Annals of Kings and Prophets*, Arabic text, edited by De Goeje, Permia Series, Vol. V, p. 2408 (translation by Hava Lazarus-Yafeh in "The Sanctity of Jerusalem in Islam," in *Jerusalem: City of the Ages*, p. 324).
2. Ice, Thomas and Price, Randall; *Ready to Rebuild*; Harvest House Publishers; Eugene, OR; 1992; pp. 90-92.
3. *The Jerusalem Post, International Edition*; May 6, 1995; "PA furious at J'lem land seizures" by Bill Hutman.
4. *The Associated Press*; May 23, 1995.
5. Daniel 9:25.
6. Anderson, Sir Robert; *The Coming Prince*; Kregel Publications; Grand Rapids, MI; 1984; pp. 121-122.
7. Matthew 21:4-5.
8. Mark 11:9-10.
9. Luke 19:42-44.
10. Daniel 9:26.
11. Daniel 9:24.
12. I Thessalonians 4:16-17.
13. John 5:43.
14. Gershon Salomon, founder of the Temple Mount Faithful in an interview with the ministry *This Week in Bible Prophecy*.
15. Revelation 11:1-2.

Chapter 4: The Great Pretender

1. Zechariah 14:3,4,9; 12:9,10.
2. 2 Thessalonians 2:9
3. Fischer, Dietrich; "United Nations Reform: A Systems Approach"; *United Nations Reform: Looking Ahead After Fifty Years*; Science for Peace; 1995; p. 59.
4. Price, Randall; *In Search of Temple Treasures*; Harvest House Publishers; Eugene OR; 1994; pp. 208-209.
5. Ibid.; pp. 209-211.
6. Genesis 15:18.
7. Hebrews 8:8-12.
8. Beilin, Dr. Yossi, Israeli Deputy Minister of Foreign Affairs, during a speech given as head of the Israeli Delegation to the Steering Committee of the Multilateral Peace Talks; Tokyo, Japan; December 15, 1993.
9. *Islamic Affairs Analyst*; June 1996; "A Likud Government for Israel"; p. 10.
10. Daniel 8:25.
11. Daniel 2:39.
12. Pentecost, J. Dwight; *Things to Come*; Zondervan; Grand Rapids, MI; 1958; p. 325.
13. Daniel 7:8.
14. Daniel 7:24.
15. Canadian External Affairs Minister Joe Clark, May 1990.

16. Excerpts from a speech given by U.S. Secretary of State James Baker in Berlin Germany; as quoted in the *Financial Times*; December 13, 1989; "A new architecture for a new era . . . ."
17. *Intelligence Digest*; September 9, 1994; "Global Government: The Next Step"; The Stoneyhill Centre, Brimpsfield, Gloucester, GL4 8LF, UK.
18. *Europe*; February, 1996; "Reinvigorating the Transatlantic Alliance:; p. 21.
19. Cleveland, Harlan; *Birth of a New World Order*; Josse-Bass Publishers; San Francisco, CA; p. 217.
20. Revelation 13:7.
21. Daniel 2:41-42.
22. Pentecost, J. Dwight; op. cit.; p. 319.
23. Gibbon, Edward; *The Decline and Fall of the Roman Empire*; Dell Publishing Co. Inc.; New York, NY; 1963; p. 27.
24. Ibid., pp. 32-33.
25. Cleveland, Harlan; op cit.; pp. 150, 218-219.

Chapter 5: New Democracy in the Revived Roman Empire

1. Kissinger, Henry; *Diplomacy*; Simon & Schuster; New York, NY; 1994; p. 65.
2. A special report from Intelligence International Ltd.; The Stoneyhill Centre, Brimpsfield, Gloucester, GL4 8LF, UK.
3. Ibid.
4. Gorbachev, Mikhail; *The Search for a New Beginning: Developing a New Civilization*; Harper/San Francisco; 1995; pp. 21-22.
5. United Nations Fact Sheet for "The World Summit for Social Development"; May, 1994.
6. United Nations Fact Sheet; "Backgrounder 2: Attacking Poverty"; May, 1994.
7. United Nations Fact Sheet; "Backgrounder 4: Population and Social Development"; May, 1994.
8. United Nations Literature; "Why a Social Summit?."
9. James 4:1-3.
10. Peres, Shimon; *The New Middle East*; Henry Holt and Company, Inc.; New York, NY; 1993; pp. 33-35.
11. Ibid.; p. 34.
12. Ohmae, Kenichi in a speech given before the Council on Foreign Relations Corporate Service Program in Chicago, IL; Feb. 7, 1992; as quoted in *Vital Speeches*; June 1, 1992.
13. Intelligence International Ltd.; op. cit.
14. U.N. Secretary General Boutros Boutros-Ghali; as quoted in *The European*; October 19-25, 1995; "The elusive search for global peace in a world scarred by conflict"; p. 11.
15. Held, David; *Democracy and the Global Order*; Stanford University Press, Stanford, CA; 1995; pp. 16-17, 21.
16. Newcombe, Hanna; "Third-Generation World Organizations"; *United Nations Reform: Looking Ahead After Fifty Years*; Science for Peace; 1995; pp. 82-83.
17. Mikhail Gorbachev during a speech given in Tulsa, Oklahoma on October 2, 1995. He recruited retired national leaders such as George Bush, Margaret Thatcher and Brian Mulroney to join him in promoting his vision of a new world order.
18. Newcombe, Hanna; op. cit., p. 90
19. Ibid.

20. Oliver, Michael; "Commentary on Part II"; *United Nations Reform: Looking Ahead After Fifty Years*; Science for Peace; 1995; p. 27.
21. Revelation 17:12-13.
22. *International Herald Tribune*; June 16, 1990.
23. *The Toronto Star*; October 5, 1987.
24. Gorbachev, Mikhail; in his opening address at the State of the World Forum held in San Francisco, CA; September 27, 1995.
25. Naisbitt, John; in his Plenary Address at the State of the World Forum; September 28, 1995.
26. Gorbachev, Mikhail; State of the World Forum opening address.
27. Grenville-Wood, Geoffrey; "An Agenda for United Nations Reform"; *United Nations Reform: Looking Ahead After Fifty Years*"; Science for Peace; 1995; p. 10.

Chapter 6: Spirituality in the Revived Roman Empire

1. *Rome of the Caesars*; Bonechi-Edizioni (Il Turismo); Firenze, Italy; pp. 37-38.
2. Gibbon, Edward; *The Decline and Fall of the Roman Empire*; Dell Publishing Co.; New York, NY; 1963; pp. 218-219.
3. Held, David; *Democracy and the Global Order*; Stanford University Press; Stanford, CA; 1995; pp. 33-34.
4. Brzezinski, Zbigniew; *Out of Control: Global Turmoil on the Eve of the 21st Century*; Macmillan Publishing Company; New York, NY; 1993; pp. 26, 27.
5. Revelation 17:1-9.
6. Revelation 1:1-3.
7. Walvoord, John F.; *The Revelation of Jesus Christ*; Moody Bible Institute; Chicago, IL; 1966; p. 244.
8. *The Toronto Star*; July 3, 1985; "Let Christian faith unite Europe: Pope John Paul."
9. *The Washington Post*; December 1, 1989; "Gorbachev Receives Welcome in Rome Fit for a King" by Jennifer Parmelee; p. A39.
10. *World Press Review*; July 1990; "John Paul's New 'Crusade': He sees Christianity at the root of European culture"; by Martin Kettle; p. 32.
11. *The New Day Magazine*; September 1990; "Jacques Delors-man with a mission"; p. 16.
12. *The Sunday Telegraph*; February 28, 1993; "Faithful urged to lead Euro crusade: Hear the word of Delors: blessed is the Community spirit" by Boris Johnson.

Chapter 7: Ecumenism and a New Morality for Man

1. *The Pope Speaks*; Jan/Feb 1990; "A Primacy for the Bishop of Rome"; Address of Archbishop of Canterbury Runcie given after the Pope's homily during Vespers in the Church of St. Gregory; September 30, 1989.
2. Barrows, John Henry; *The World's Parliament of Religions: An Illustrated and Popular Story of the World's First Parliament of Religions Held in Chicago in Connection with The Columbian Exposition of 1893*; Vol. 1; Parliament Publishing Co.; Chicago, IL; 1983; p. 71.
3. Ibid.; p. 5.
4. Excerpts from the document "Towards A Global Ethic (An Initial Declaration)" signed by representatives of the world's religions at the second World Parliament of Religions; Chicago, IL; August 28 to September 5, 1993.
5. Gorbachev, Mikhail; *The Search for a New Beginning; Developing a New Civilization*; Harper/San Francisco; 1995; pp. 38, 60, 62.

6. Matthew 24:37.
7. Genesis 6:5.
8. Gorbachev, Mikhail; op. cit.; pp. 64-65.
9. Conroy, Donald B., President, NACRE; in a letter to NACRE supporters; October, 1991.
10. *Religious Herald*; January 25, 1990.
11. *St. Petersburg Times*; June 2, 1990; in a report on the Inter-Continental Conference on Caring for Creation in Washington, D.C. (May 16-19, 1990).
12. Gore, Al; *Earth in the Balance: Ecology and the Human Spirit*; Houghton Mifflin Co.; New York, NY; 1992; pp. 258-259.
13. State of the World Forum; *Action Plan 1996*; San Francisco, CA; May 23, 1996.
14. Held, David; *Democracy and the Global Order*; Stanford University Press; Stanford, CA; 1995; pp. 101-103.
15. *Towards a Global Ethic (An Initial Declaration)*; signed by representatives of the world's religions at the World Parliament of Religions held in Chicago, IL (August 28 to September 5, 1993).
16. Galatians 2:20-21.

Chapter 8: Fraud and Deceit

1. Kissinger, Henry; *Diplomacy*; Simon & Schuster; New York, NY; 1994; pp. 56-57.
2. Revelation 13:12.
3. II Thessalonians 2:11-12.
4. II Thessalonians 2:9.
5. Revelation 13:13.
6. Kissinger, Henry; op. cit.; p. 57.
7. Attali, Jacques; *Millennium: Winners and Losers in the Coming World Order*; translated version by Random House, Inc.; New York, NY; 1991; p. 5.
8. *Time Special Issue*: "Beyond the Year 2000: What to Expect in the New Millennium; Fall 1992; "A Cosmic Moment" by Lance Morrow; p. 6.
9. *Time* magazine's special Man of the Year issue; January 6, 1992;
10. Snyder, Alvin A.; *Warriors of Disinformation*; Arcade Publishing; New York, NY; 1995; p. 6.
11. Author's telephone interview with Victor Sheymov, 21 October 1993.
12. Snyder, Alvin A.; op. cit.; p. 23.
13. Ibid.; p. 47.
14. Snyder, Alvin A.; op. cit.; pp. 120, 122-123, 125.
15. *The Toronto Star*; December 21, 1992; "How Television Is Reshaping World's Culture" by John Lippman; p. A21.
16. *The Holocaust*; Yad Vashem, Jerusalem; Martyrs' and Heroes' Remembrance Authority; pp. 14-15.
17. Titus 3:1; see also Romans 13:1-7.
18. "Religious right preaches politics of hate, intolerance" by Marianne Means, Washington, DC columnist with Hearst Newspapers; as quoted in *This Week In Bible Prophecy Magazine*; October, 1994; pp. 25, 28.
19. Book review of *On the Psychology of Fundamentalism in America* by Charles B. Strozier; "The True Believers: Is the end at hand? A serious look at some people who think so."
20. *Cedar Rapids Gazette*; Cedar Rapids, IA; December 9, 1994.
21. The Algerian newspaper *Algerie Actualite*, March 13-19, 1985; feature article by Lofti Maherzi.

Chapter 9: Signs and Wonders

1. 2 Thessalonians 2:6-11.
2. *Time* magazine; April 10, 1995; "The Message of Miracles" by Nancy Gibbs; pp. 65-66.
3. Matthew 12:25-28.
4. Matthew 12:39-41.
5. Hebrews 3:18–4:2.
6. Hebrews 11:1, 6.
7. Hebrews 11: 4-5, 7-11.
8. Luke 18:8.
9. I Timothy 4:1.
10. II Corinthians 11:3.
11. II Corinthians 11:13-15.
12. MacLaine, Shirley; *Out on a Limb*; Bantam Books; 1983; p. 50.
13. Strieber, Whitley; *Communion: A True Story*; Avon Books; New York, NY; 1987; pp. 49-50.
14. Ibid.; pp. 4, 94.
15. *Parade Magazine*; March 7, 1993; as quoted in *This Week in Bible Prophecy Magazine*; May, 1993; p. 4.
16. *OMNI* magazine; January 1995; "AntiMatter: UFO Update." p. 79.
17. *New York Times*; September 4, 1994; "Angels Everywhere."
18. Harner, Michael; *The Way of the Shaman*; Bantam Books; New York, NY: 1982; pp. 10, 54.
19. Ibid.; p. 175.
20. *Press Telegram*; August 28, 1994.
21. Strieber; op. cit.; p. 26.
22. Strieber; op. cit.; pp. 3-4.
23. Vallee, Jaques; *Dimensions*; Contemporary Books; Chicago, IL; 1988; pp. 272, 278-279.
24. *TV Guide*; October 5, 1996; "Alien Invasion" by Andrew Ryan; pp. 18-19.
25. Genesis 3:1-5.
26. Montgomery, Ruth; *Strangers Among Us*; Fawcett Crest; New York, NY; 1979; pp. 11-12.
27. MacLaine, Shirley; op. cit.; pp. 181-183.
28. *OMNI* magazine; April 1994; as quoted in *This Week in Bible Prophecy Magazine*; June 1994; p. 12.
29. MacLaine, Shirley; op. cit.; pp. 202, 208-209.
30. Ibid.; p. 138.
31. Marx Hubbard, Barbara; *Happy Birthday Planet Earth*; Ocean Tree Books; Santa Fe, NM; 1986; pp. 9-10, 17, 19.
32. Matthew 24: 5, 23-27.

Chapter 10: Mystery Babylon and the Goddess Within

1. *Goddess Remembered*; part 1 of a 3-part video series on Women's Spirituality offered by the National Film Board of Canada.
2. *The Wall Street Journal*; June 7, 1990; "Is Goddess Worship Finally Going to Put Men in Their Place?" by Sonia L. Nazario.
3. Revelation 17:5.

4. Walvoord, Dr. John F.; *The Revelation of Jesus Christ: A Commentary by John F. Walvoord*; Moody Press; Chicago, IL; 1966; pp. 246-247.
5. *Goddess Remembered*; op. cit.
6. Genesis 3:16.
7. Starhawk; *Dreaming the Dark*; as quoted in *This Week in Bible Prophecy Magazine*; May, 1995; p. 17.
8. *The Winnipeg Free Press*; March 4, 1995; "Christianity Was New Once: Don't Discount New Age Stuff" by Karen Toole-Mitchell.
9. Woolger, Jennifer Barker and Roger J.; "The Wounded Goddesses Within; *New Realities*; March/April 1990; p. 11.
10. Kjos, Berit; *Under the Spell of Mother Earth*; Victor Books; Wheaton, IL; 1992. p. 97.
11. *Full Circle*; part 3 of a 3-part video series on Women's Spirituality offered by the National Film Board of Canada.
12. Kjos, Berit; op. cit.; p. 49.
13. Genesis 3:17-18.
14. Genesis 4:3-5.
15. *Newcastle News*; July 2, 1993; "Religious turn to check-out stand charms" by Leda Ciraolo; p. 7.
16. *The Toronto Star*; March 31, 1995; "Belief in the occult rules Saudi rulers" by Shyam Bhatia; p. A17.
17. *Washington Post* article, as cited in *The Cedar Rapids Gazette*; April 12, 1995.
18. *The European*; May 5-11, 1995; "Black Magic Holds Sway over a Paranoid Kremlin" by Miranda Anichkina.
19. *Full Circle*; op. cit.
20. Montgomery, Ruth; *Strangers Among Us*; Fawcett Crest; New York, NY; 1979; pp. 163-164.
21. Harner, Michael; *The Way of the Shaman*; Bantam Books; New York, NY: 1980; pp. 59-60.
22. Castaneda, Carlos; *A Separate Reality: Further Conversations with don Juan*; Simon & Schuster; New York, NY; 1971; pp. 5-6.
23. Genesis 11:4.
24. Genesis 11:6, 8-9.
25. Revelation 9:20-21.

Chapter 11: Who Is Able to Make War with Him?

1. As quoted in Morton Blum, John; *The Republican Roosevelt*; Harvard University Press; Cambridge, MA; 1954; pp. 824-825.
2. *Islamic Affairs Analyst*; June 1996; "U.S. Role in Middle East Weakened"; p. 4.
3. Ibid.
4. *Intelligence Digest*; September 6, 1996; "Wider Implications of U.S. Action Against Iraq"; p. 1.
5. *The Toronto Star*; December 9, 1994; "Russia taking centre stage in emerging New Europe" by Gordon Barthos.
6. *The European*; July 16-19, 1992; "Who can impose peace on Europe?"; by Ian Mather.
7. *The Washington Times*; November 7-13, 1994; "Talbott promotes new Africa policy" by Ben Barber.
8. Ibid.
9. *The Toronto Star*; August 14, 1994; "The Case for a World Cop" by Ron Lowman; p. E1.

10. *The Toronto Star*; May 29, 1995; p. A3.
11. *The Toronto Star*; June 15, 1995.
12. *The Toronto Star*; July 12, 1995.
13. Cleveland, Harlan; *Birth of a New World: An Open Moment for International Leadership*; Jossey-Bass Publishers; San Francisco, CA; 1993; pp. 56-57, 59.
14. Simoni, Arnold; *United Nations Reform: Looking Ahead After Fifty Years*; Science for Peace; Toronto, ON; 1995; "A United Nations Peace Force"; p. 155.
15. Ibid.; pp. 155-156.
16. Ibid.
17. Ibid.
18. *The Toronto Star*; August 14, 1994; "The Case for a World Cop" by Ron Lowman; p. E1.
19. Ibid.; p. 156.
20. Simkin, Jay: Zelman, Aaron: Rice. Alan M.; *Lethal Laws: "Gun Control" is the Key to Genocide; Documentary Proof: Enforcement of "Gun Control" Laws Clears the Way for Governments to Commit Genocides*; Jews for the Preservation of Firearms Ownership Inc., Publisher; 2872 South Wentworth Ave. Milwaukee, WI 53207; pp. 14-15.
21. *The Wall Street Journal*; April 26, 1995; "A Millennium of Paranoia" by Daniel Pipes.
22. Luke 21:28
23. Titus 3:1.
24. Ephesians 6:12.
25. Ephesians 6:14-17.

Chapter 12: The Russian Bear in Prophecy

1. *Intelligence Digest*; The Stoneyhill Centre, Brimpsfield, Gloucester, GL4 8LF, UK: June 14, 1996; "Russian Realities"; pp. 1-2.
2. *The Wall Street Journal*; August 25, 1995; "Russia Threat Beneath the Surface" by Robert J. Murray.
3. Ibid.
4. Ibid.
5. *Associated Press*; November 25, 1995.
6. Smith, Hedrick; *The New Russians*; Random House; New York, NY; 1990; pp. 131-132.
7. As quoted in *Policy Review*; Fall 1987; "Seventy Years of Evil: Soviet Crimes from Lenin to Gorbachev" by Michael Johns; p. 19.
8. *The Buffalo News*; August 16, 1992; "Russians Recall Better Days During Communism" by Michael Dobbs of the *Washington Post*; p. A6.
9. Smith, Hedrick; op. cit.; p. 121.
10. *The Toronto Star*; June 27, 1996; "Anti-Semitism Plays Role in Russian Vote" by Julia Rubin of the Associated Press; p. A22.
11. Ibid.
12. Smith, William, LL.D.; *Smith's Bible Dictionary*; A Spire Book; Old Tappan, NJ; 1970; p. 584.
13. Ezekiel 38:3-4.
14. *Policy Review*; op. cit.; pp. 11-12, 14.
15. Deuteronomy 28:64-66.
16. Ezekiel 36:24.
17. Jeremiah 16:15.
18. *Intelligence Digest*; February 17, 1995; The Stoneyhill Centre, Brimpsfield, Gloucester, GL4 8LF, UK; "Russia on the road to ruin"; p. 1.

19. *The European*; August 31, 1995–September 6, 1995; "Russian bank crisis 'may spark return to dictators'"; by Miranda Anichkina.
20. *Intelligence Digest*; March 3, 1995; "More Details on World Grain Fears" p. 3.
21. *Intelligence Digest*; April 21, 1995; p. 4.
22. *The Toronto Star*; October 26, 1995; "Russia Reported Short on Grain."
23. *The Wall Street Journal*; April 28, 1995; "Decrepit Oil Arteries Threaten Health of Russia" by Allanna Sullivan and Ann Reifenberg; p. A8.
24. *The Wall Street Journal*; April 28, 1995; "Spring Brings Fear as Last Year's Big Spill Thaws" by Steve Liesman.
25. Source: *Intelligence Digest*; July 5, 1996.
26. Peres, Shimon; *The New Middle East*; Henry Holt and Company; New York, NY; 1993; p. 120.
27. Ibid.; p. 118.
28. *The Jerusalem Report*; May 2, 1996; "If You Can Afford It, It Is No Dream" by Margo Lipschitz Sugarman and Hanan Sher; pp. 37, 41.
29. Ibid.; p. 37.
30. Interview with former Israeli Economic Minister, Pinhas Dror; as quoted in *This Week in Bible Prophecy* magazine; May, 1995; pp. 24, 30.
31. Isaiah 27:6.
32. Smith, Hedrick; op. cit.; pp. 199-200, 202, 243-44.
33. Ezekiel 38:12.
34. Ezekiel 38:17-18; 39:2-6, 11.
35. Yosef, Reuven, Ph.D.; *Wildbird*; February, 1995.
36. Ibid.
37. Ezekiel 38:11.
38. *Intelligence Digest*; October 14, 1994; address above; "Ominous signals from Russia"; p. 1.
39. Ibid.
40. *The Washington Times*; March 6-12, 1995; "Belarus Says It Won't Honor Treaty" by Martin Sieff.
41. Ezekiel 38:16.
42. Ezekiel 39:7.
43. Daniel 9:27.
44. Revelation 13:5.

Chapter 13: The Aligning of Nations Against Israel

1. *Foreign Affairs*; May/June 1996; "Dealing with a Russia in Turmoil" by Jack F. Matlock, Jr.; pp. 41-43.
2. Ibid.; p. 45.
3. *Intelligence Digest*; November 18, 1994; The Stoneyhill Centre, Brimpsfield, Gloucester, GL4 8LF, UK; "Russia Spells Out Mideast Policy"; p. 1.
4. *Intelligence Digest*; February 24, 1995; "Yeltsin Confirms Russian Mideast Policy"; p. 1.
5. *Intelligence Digest*; January 13, 1995; "More Evidence of Russia-Iran Strategic Link"; p. 1.
6. *Islamic Affairs Analyst*; October 1994; address same as for *Intelligence Digest*; "Reasons for War"; p. 7.
7. *Intelligence Digest*; April 12, 1996; "Israel's Nuclear Deterrent and the Lure of Martyrdom"; p. 1.

8. *Intelligence Digest*; April 19. 1996; "Russia Warns United States over Libya"; p. 3.

9. *Intelligence Digest*; October 28, 1994; "Turkey: From Ataturk to Islam"; pp. 3-4.

10. *Islamic Affairs Analyst*; July-August 1995; "Turkish Islamists Get Their Chance"; pp. 12-13.

11. "Jihad in America"; PBS special; September 21, 1994.

12. Ibid.

13. *The Toronto Star*; June 13, 1995; "Arab States to Pursue Nuclear Arms, Saudi Warns" by Gordon Barthos.

14. Ibid.

15. *Intelligence Digest*; June 9, 1995.

16. Excerpts from a speech given by Libyan leader Moammar Gaddafi; as quoted in *Islamic Affairs Analyst*; June 1995; "Authentic Voice of Arab Radicalism"; pp. 4-5.

17. *Islamic Affairs Analyst*; June 1994; "Arafat Gives the Game Away"; p. 11.

18. Excerpt from a speech given by Palestinian Authority Chairman Yasser Arafat; as quoted in *Intelligence Digest*; March 1, 1996.

19. Excerpt from a speech given by Nabil Shaath, adviser to PA Chairman Yasser Arafat; as quoted in *Intelligence Digest*; March 22, 1996.

Chapter 14: The Peacemakers

1. *Islamic Affairs Analyst*; January 1995; The Stoneyhill Centre; Brimpsfield, Gloucester, GL4 8LF; UK; "Agreeing Strategies on Israel"; p. 7.

2. *The Toronto Star*; July 18, 1996; "Egyptians Blast Netanyahu"; p. A19.

3. *The Toronto Star*; July 19, 1996; "Egyptian President Upbeat After Talks with Israeli PM"; by Norma Greenaway; p. A2.

4. Isaiah 19:1-10.

5. Isaiah 19:16-22.

6. Isaiah 19:23-25.

7. Lynn, Betty; *Pathways to Armageddon . . . And Beyond*; published by This Week in Bible Prophecy; Niagara Falls, NY/ON; pp. 186-187.

8. Ibid.; pp. 176-177.

Chapter 15: A New World Economy

1. *The Toronto Star*; July 25, 1995; "Movie Gives Computer Expert Identity Crisis" by Jamie Portman.

2. Revelation 13:16-17.

3. Koelsch, Frank; *The Infomedia Revolution*; McGraw-Hill Ryerson; Whitby, ON; 1995; p. 26.

4. Janlori Goldman, deputy director of the Center for Democracy and Technology; in an interview with *This Week in Bible Prophecy*; June 27, 1995.

5. *Los Angeles Times*; February 12, 1995; "On-Line IRS Checks Databases Against Returns" by Kathy M. Kirstof; p. D4.

6. *Time*; Spring 1995; "The Future Is Already Here" by Barrett Seaman; pp. 31-32.

7. *The Ottawa Citizen*; September 21, 1993; "Quick Search Finds Personal Data Easily."

8. Interview between *This Week in Bible Prophecy* and Bob Gellman; June 27, 1995.

9. *The Ottawa Citizen*; op. cit.

10. *The Globe and Mail*; August 14, 1993; "Farewell to the Private Life."

11. *The Globe and Mail*; August 20, 1993; "Nowhere to Hide in the Information Age."

12. Cleveland, Harlan; *Birth of a New World: An Open Moment for International Leadership*; Jossey-Bass Publishers; San Francisco, CA; 1993; pp. 137-138.
13. *The New York Times*; November 1, 1987; "Can Nations Set Aside Their Parochialism in Time?."
14. *Time*; November 9, 1987.
15. *The European*; August 24-30, 1995; "Plugging in to an Interconnected Future."
16. *The Chicago Tribune*; May 7, 1996; "In Future, Tiny Chip May Get Under Skin Critics Argue Device Invites Big Brother; p. 1.
17. *U.S. News & World Report*; July 25, 1994; "A 500 Number is Forever"; p. 63.
18. *The New York Times*; September 6, 1994.
19. *The Edmonton Journal*; January 23, 1995.
20. *The Toronto Star*; February 16, 1996; "Bank debit card use surges 111% in '95: Shoppers make 390 million direct payments."
21. *New Scientist*; April 8, 1995; "Banking on electronic money" by Kurt Kleiner; p. 26.
22. *Bell News, Ontario Edition*, Vol. 25 No. 23; November 13, 1995.
23. *Sunday Mail*; April 21, 1993.
24. *The European*; week ending July 30, 1992; "Spies in sky zero in on farm cheats."
25. *The Toronto Star*; August 19, 1994.

Chapter 16: The Mark of the Beast

1. *Chicago Tribune*; May 7, 1996; "In Future, Tiny Chip May Get Under Skin Critics Argue Device Invites Big Brother" by Jon Van; p. 1.
2. Revelation 14:9-11.
3. Janlori Goldman, deputy director of the Center for Democracy and Technology; in an interview with *This Week in Bible Prophecy*; June 27, 1995.
4. Ibid.
5. http:\ \www.govtech.net\1996\gt'may'guestcolmay'guestcolmay.htm
6. *Business Week / The Information Revolution*; 1994; "Third World Leapfrog" by Pete Engardio; pp. 47-49.
7. *OMNI* magazine; April 1995.
8. *Wired*; September 1995; "A Chip for Every Child?" by Simon Garfinkel.
9. Ibid.
10. *Automatic ID News*, August 1994, "If 'chips' are for pets, why not for kids?" by Mark David, editor-in-chief; p. 6.
11. *Popular Science*; July 1995; "e-money" by Phil Patton; p. 74.
12. Ibid.
13. *IEEE Spectrum*; February 1994; "Vital Signs of Identity" by Benjamin Miller; p. 22.
14. http:\ \www.govtech.net\1996\gt\may\guestcolmay\guestcolmay.htm
15. *Biometric Digest*; May 1996; http:\ \www.icon-stl.net\~jsweeney\biometric\biodigest.html; p. 6 of 13.
16. *The Toronto Star*; February 17, 1995; "Computer Ace Nabs 'Condor,' the Most Wanted Hacker" by Robert Brehl.
17. *U.S. News & World Report*; October 2, 1995; "Can hackers break into 'Netscape'?" by Margaret Mannix; p. 84.
18. *Time* magazine; February 27, 1995; "Cracks in the Net" by Joshua Quittner; p. 34.
19. Ibid.; p. 45.
20. *The Wall Street Journal*; April 19. 1995; "To Read This, Give Us the Password . . . Ooops! Try It Again"

21. by William M. Bulkeley.
22. *Discover*; December 1995; "A Face of One's Own" by Evan I. Schwartz; p. 86.
23. *Netscape* - [http:\\www.sjb.co.uk\pr\01059601].
24. *Netscape* - [http:\\www.sjb.co.uk\pr\18069603.txt].
25. *Netscape* - [http:\\www.sjb.co.uk\pr\01059601.txt].

Chapter 17: The End

1. Brzezinski, Zbigniew; *Out of Control: Global Turmoil on the Eve of the 21st Century*; Collier Books; New York, NY; 1994; pp. 4-5.
2. Ibid.; p. 7.
3. Ibid.; pp. 8-10.
4. Shukman, David; *Tomorrow's War: The Threat of High-Technology Weapons*; Harcourt Brace & Company; San Diego, CA; 1996.
5. Ibid.; p. 25.
6. Ibid.
7. *Islamic Affairs Analyst*; December 1994; The Stoneyhill Centre; Brimpsfield, Gloucester, GL4 8LF; UK; p. 5.
8. Shukman; op. cit.; p. 103.
9. Ibid.; p. 148.
10. *Machine Design*; October 26, 1995; "Smart Weapons Define Tomorrow's Battlefield"; pp. 20, 22.
11. *Time*; August 21, 1995; "Onward Cyber Soldiers" by Douglas Waller; p. 41.
12. Ibid.
13. Shukman; op. cit.; p. 159.
14. Ibid.; pp. 210-211.
15. *Time*; August 21, 1995; "America's Persuader in the Sky" by Douglas Waller; p. 43.
16. *Time*; August 21, 1995; "Onward Cyber Soldiers" by Douglas Waller; p. 41.
17. Shukman; op. cit.; pp. 226-227.
18. Ibid.; p. 228.
19. Ibid.; p. 124.
20. *Islamic Affairs Analyst*; December 1994; "Special Report: Weapons of Mass Destruction and the Madrid Peace Process"; The Stoneyhill Cenre, Brimpsfield, Gloucester, UK; GL4 8LF.
21. Shukman; op. cit.; p. 241.
22. Ibid.; p. 244.
23. *U.S. News & World Report*; September 11, 1995; "Baghdad's Dirty Secrets; New Iraqi Disclosures May Help Explain What Ails Gulf Veterans"; pp. 41-42.
24. Matthew 13:41,42.
25. 1 Thessalonians 4:16,17.